The German Way of War in the North Africa Campaign

The German Way of War in the North Africa Campaign

A Lesson in Tactical Management

Jaap Jan Brouwer

Pen & Sword
MILITARY

First published in Great Britain in 2025 by
Pen & Sword Military
An imprint of Pen & Sword Books Limited
Yorkshire – Philadelphia

ISBN 978 1 39903 284 1

A CIP catalogue record for this book is available from the British Library.

Typeset by Mac Style
Printed in the UK by CPI Group (UK) Ltd, Croydon, CR0 4YY.

MIX
Paper | Supporting responsible forestry
FSC® C013604

The Publisher's authorised representative in the EU for product safety is Authorised Rep Compliance Ltd., Ground Floor, 71 Lower Baggot Street, Dublin D02 P593, Ireland.
www.arccompliance.com

For a complete list of Pen & Sword titles please contact

PEN & SWORD BOOKS LIMITED
47 Church Street, Barnsley, South Yorkshire, S70 2AS, England
E-mail: enquiries@pen-and-sword.co.uk
Website: www.pen-and-sword.co.uk
or
PEN AND SWORD BOOKS
1950 Lawrence Road, Havertown, PA 19083, USA
E-mail: uspen-and-sword@casematepublishers.com
Website: www.penandswordbooks.com

Contents

Introduction

It is not easy to reconstruct my reason for writing this book. The foundation was probably laid during the lectures on Polemology (the study of human conflict) and International Relations during my legal studies in Groningen. It was the early eighties and the era of 'major issues' in the field of armaments and détente. Relations between East and West were threatening to acquire a completely new and uncontrollable dynamic due to the deployment of SS-20 and Cruise missiles. We did not yet know that the Berlin Wall would fall only nine years later, just as we did not know we would be experiencing comparable dynamics now. In this world, large military organizations played a major role, and my interest at that time was principally in their organizational dimensions. In the years since, I have been able to observe and analyse many organizations up close as a management consultant. This prompted me, a few years ago, to pick up the subject again based on the expertise I had gathered. I wanted to reconstruct the organizational dimensions of the German and British armies that had been lost due to the 'fog of war'. I chose North Africa because the number of troops involved and the geographical dimensions made this theatre less complex and easier to analyse; and because, as an enthusiastic model builder, I was intrigued in my youth by, amongst others, one of the Airfix kits, a Flak 88mm gun behind a tractor.

The result of this quest is now before you, somewhat larger in scope than I had intended: like many others before me, I became gripped by the subject.

In line with my professional background, I have focused principally on the organizational dimensions of the conflict, along lines that are customary in the practice of consultancy. In other words, I try to answer the question 'How did they do it?' I first sketch both armies as they appear on paper and then examine how this played out in the harsh reality of the battlefield. This combination of the dynamics of the confrontation in North Africa with an analysis of both organizations gives, I hope, a new dimension to this period of history.

Finding the right photos was not always easy. Thanks to the mediation of Mr S. Pallad, I was able to access 400 photos by Mr S. Klein. Herr Klein went through the entire campaign in North Africa with the 1st Abteilung of the 33rd Flak Regiment, riding on precisely the equipment represented by that Airfix model. His photos provide a superb view of a combat unit in wartime. Since I do not have a comparable British collection, photos of German units are somewhat overrepresented, but I have been able to use photos from the British Tank Museum in Bovington and from various other collections. I hope that they provide an image of the reality of battle in North Africa.

J. J. Brouwer
The Hague, November 2025

References in brackets in the text are to the Bibliography. The first figure denotes the source number, the second the page number(s).

Glossary

German/Italian/abbreviation, etc.	**English**
Abteilung	Battalion
AP grenades	Armour-piercing grenades
Artillérie portée	Guns on trucks
Auftragstaktik	Decentralized command concept that defines clearly what the goal is, but gives freedom in how to reach it
Ausf. (Ausführung)	Mark
Befehlstaktik	Centralized command concept that gives no room for own initiative; a unit has to follow strict orders and act according to the plan
Beweglichkeit	Manoeuvrability
Bewegungskrieg	War of manoeuvre
Breitkeil	(Tank formation) a triangle with the base of the triangle forward
C-in-C	Commander-in-Chief
Corpo d'Armata di Manovra	Mobile Corps
COS	Chief of Staff
DAK	German Africa Corps
Einheit	Unit, also unity
Erfahrungsberichte	Feedback report
Ersatzabteilung	Replacement battalion
Ersatzheer	Reserve Army
Fähnrichsexamen	Ensign exam
Fallschirmjäger	Paratrooper
Feldersatz Battalion	Replacement battalion at the front
Flak (Flieger Abwehr Kanon)	Anti-aircraft gun
Flivo (Fliegerverbindungsoffiziere)	Liaison officer between Army and Luftwaffe
Führen durch Aufträge	*See* Auftragstaktik

Führung und Gefecht der Verbundenen Waffen	Leading and fighting with combined arms
Führen unter der Hand	Leading behind a superior's back
General Stab	General Staff
Grundlagen der Erziehung des Heeres	Ground rules for education of the Army
HE grenades	High explosive grenades
Heer	German Army
Innere Führung	Internalized discipline, self-discipline
Instandsetzungsabteilung	Logistics battalion
Jock column	British combat group named after Lieutenant Colonel J. C. (Jock) Campbell, who deployed these for the first time
Kaiserliches Heer	Army of the German Kaiserreich 1871-1919
Kampfgemeinschaft	Unity in fighting
Kampfgruppe	Combat Group
Kampfstaffel	Mobile combat unit protecting the divisional commander
Keil	(Tank formation) a triangle with the tip of the triangle forward
Kriegsakademie	Military Academy
Kriegsspiel	Wargame
Krisenfest	Stress-resistant
Kriegsschule	Military school
Landser	Private
Leichter Panzerzug	Light tank platoon for conducting reconnaissance
Nachrichtenzug	Communications Unit
NCO	Non-Commissioned Officer
Oberkommando des Heeres (OKH)	Supreme Command of the Army
Oberkommando der Wehrmacht (OKW)	Supreme Command of the Armed Forces
PAK (Panzer Abwehr Kanon)	Anti-tank gun
Panzerjäger	Anti-tank units
Panzer Kampfwagen (PzKpfw)	Tank
RECAM (Raggruppamento Esplorante)	Reconnaissance unit
Reichswehr	Army of the German Republic 1919-35
Sonder Kraftfahrzeug (SdKfz)	Special vehicle, often a half-track
Schwerpunkt	Focal point of the attack

Stosstrupp	Shock troop
StuG (Sturmgeschütz)	Assault gun
Trigh	Track
Truppe	Troops, units
Truppenamt	Troop office
Verbundene Waffen	Combined arms
Wadi	River valley, usually dry except when it has rained
Wehrkreis	Military district
Wehrmacht	German Army, Air Force and Navy
Werkstatt Kompagnie	Maintenance company

Preface

In the evening of 15 February 1941 the lights came on in the port of Tripoli. The city had been packed out in the previous weeks by exhausted and demoralized Italian soldiers chased out of Egypt and Cyrenaica by the British. The inhabitants waited with bated breath for what would happen next, as British troops were reportedly advancing further and further west. The entire city was darkened for fear of air raids. That evening, the lights in the harbour came on, and Italian and Arab residents rushed to the port to see what was happening. There, lit by many spotlights, newly arrived ships were being unloaded rapidly and with the utmost precision by confident German soldiers speaking in hushed voices. The cargo consisted of military vehicles, guns, ammunition and other military stores. The Italian army doctor Tobino described the event as follows:

> We had been awaiting the British fatalistically – almost gladly. At least the whole business would be over. But the Germans came instead …Until then, our troops had always disembarked amid great chaos, their faces grim. It took us at least three days to disembark one division. Then everything would get mixed up, so that it took at least ten days to find it all again and reorganize the troops. But the Germans were parading about the streets in white gloves by the next morning. The people who had fled from Cyrenaica and the war-weary population of Tripoli just stood there and stared. (29: 24)

Among the first troops to be landed was the 3rd *Aufklärungsabteilung*, a reconnaissance unit equipped with eight-wheeled armoured vehicles. This unit was chosen to parade the next morning for the people of Tripoli. To make the newly arrived force appear larger, after passing the dignitaries' stands, units quickly drove around the block and rejoined the rear of the parade.

> 24-year-old Warrant Officer Claus Wernicke crouched on his heavy BMW and did his best to keep a deadpan expression on his face, although he had the definite impression that he had been recognized and greeted with extra applause the second time round. Like most of his comrades in the unit and throughout the German Army, he had a feeling of boundless superiority. (29: 25)

Wernicke had every reason to feel that way at that moment: the German Army had been astonishingly successful in the past two years. Poland and much of Western Europe had been brought within the Greater German Empire in two rapid campaigns with relatively minor losses; only Great Britain still resisted. The German Army had shown itself to be a particularly effective organization, and it would maintain that effectiveness throughout the war.

Analyses of Second World War battles show that, on all fronts throughout the entire period of the conflict, the Germans consistently outperformed the armies that ultimately defeated them. Even in the period 1943–44, German combat effectiveness on the battlefield was 20–30 per cent higher than that of the Americans and British. At the level of the individual soldier, this meant that the Allied armies suffered 50–80 per cent more casualties than their German opponents under all circumstances. In other words, it did not matter whether the Germans were attacking or defending, whether they had air superiority or not, whether they had local superiority or were outnumbered, whether they ultimately won or lost: the German Army always demonstrated a much better '*battlefield performance*'. (*See* Appendix for more information on this point.) This situation was not new; in the First World War, too, the performance of the German Army had far exceeded that of its opponents.

Before we describe the struggle in North Africa we will discuss the two great powers involved and their armies. We will describe and analyse the German and British Armies in the context of their mission, doctrine, tactics, hierarchy, leadership style, men, officers, non-commissioned officers, recruitment, training, etc., before in the following chapters looking at how the campaign played out in the harsh reality of the North African battlefields.

Chapter 1
The Two Armies

1.1 The German Army

We will first analyse the German Army in more detail. We will look at its mission, command concept, tactics and structure, the men and the way in which they and their non-commissioned officers and officers were trained, and its leadership principles. We are going to try to discover why the German Army was such a formidable adversary. A few quotes from prominent authors will indicate the areas for discussion.

Trevor Dupuy, a US Army Colonel was surprised to find that:

> [The] record shows that the Germans consistently outfought the far more numerous Allied armies that eventually defeated them …On a man for man basis the German ground soldiers consistently inflicted casualties at about a 50 per cent higher rate than they incurred from the opposing British and American troops under all circumstances. This was true when they were attacking and when they were defending, when they had a local numerical superiority and when, as was usually the case, they were outnumbered, when they had air superiority and when they did not, when they won and when they lost.

In 1962 Dupuy formed the first of his research companies dedicated to the study and analysis of armed conflict, the Historical Evaluation and Research Organization (HERO), which analysed many battles in terms of the relative battlefield performance of the armies and units involved.

The relative battlefield performance he mentions above concerns the front in the west after the Normandy landings, where only a small number of German units fought and were not equipped with the best materiel available. The superior battlefield performance of 150 per cent that Dupuy outlines here would have been much higher in earlier years; on the Eastern Front it could rise to more than 500 per cent. Ultimately, however, as history shows, it is still possible to lose a war with such superb battlefield performance if your opponent can only bring enough men into the field.

Another interesting analysis is contained in Martin Creveld's book *Fighting Power*, in which he describes how people have been misled:

> Contrary to the widely held clichés about 'blind obedience' (*Kadavergehorsamkeit*) and Prussian discipline, the German Army had, from the time of Moltke the Elder at the latest, always emphasized the crucial importance of individual initiative and responsibility, even at the lowest levels.

How did the German Army acquire such high battlefield performance? After the First World War, the Army – the *Reichswehr* as it was then called – faced major challenges.

The Peace Treaty of Versailles limited its size to 100,000 men, including 4,000 officers, and seven infantry and three cavalry divisions, and its armaments were restricted to light weapons and field guns; heavy field guns, tanks and aircraft were prohibited. In addition, the General Staff, seen by the Allies as one of the most important elements of the German Army, had to be disbanded. This forced von Seeckt (1866–1936), the new German commander-in-chief, to thoroughly reorient and re-evaluate the functioning of the organization. During the First World War all belligerents had faced the dilemmas of trench warfare and considered possible solutions. The Germans were the only ones who went a step further and subjected this war to a thorough analysis, Von Seeckt setting up a total of seventy-five committees to look at all fronts. These committees were headed by staff officers and staffed by experts in the various fields. More than 400 officers (10 per cent of the officer corps) were ultimately involved in these evaluations.

This resulted in the key report, *Führung und Gefecht der Verbundenen Waffen*, one of the twentieth century's most important but least known documents in the field of military organization and doctrine. In this chapter we describe how the *Reichswehr* used this and other documents to develop in the period 1918–1941 into the military force that the world would come to know from 1939.

Mission: a continental army

The mission of the *Reichswehr* was and remained related to Germany's geopolitical position within Europe. Surrounded by seven to nine (depending on the date) other countries, Germany's primay need was for a strong land army. A fleet was of much less importance to Germany, since she possessed no colonies. Great Britain, on the other hand, had a large overseas empire to which a fleet was vital; also, the British Army was spread all over the empire to deal with local political, military and economic circumstances. Diplomacy might serve to prevent wars with neighbouring countries, but in the case of war Germany needed to be able to deliver a decisive blow quickly against a single enemy; after all, there was always the danger of coalition formation and a two-front war. Should such a war break out, rapid troop movements between the various fronts would be necessary. Based on this mission, a vision of the organization and its further development was formulated.

The vision of the organization

In the course of the hundred years before the Second World War the Germans had formulated a number of important command principles for their military organization. Perhaps the most important of these was the principle of *Auftragstaktik*, formulated by von Moltke at the beginning of the nineteenth century. (34: 57)

Evaluation of the German Army after the Battle of Jena in 1806 had shown that it was of little use in war to go into battle with plans worked out in detail: gunpowder fumes above the battlefield made central control impossible, and only the commanders in the field could assess the local situation. In 1860, von Moltke (1800–1891) introduced the command concept of *Auftragstaktik*: *Führen durch Aufträge*, as opposed to *Befehlstaktik*, in which central control was predominant, the concept used by other armies (*See* Glossary). The starting point of this new command concept was that planning of combat actions should only take place in outline; local commanders in the field then had the responsibility and authority to act according to circumstances. In other words, the objectives and context were clearly formulated in advance ('*what* should we have achieved by *when* and *why*'), but the paths towards them could largely be defined according to local commanders' judgement ('*how* are we going to achieve these goals'). This separation of 'what'/'why' on the one hand and 'how' on the other resulted in a flexible organization with decision-making power at a low level and a high degree of self-regulation. In other words, within *Auftragstaktik* the emphasis was on mission-orientation, not order-orientation. As an extension of this, units were given a very high degree of independence instead of having to operate within written plans and having to fall back on their commander when making important decisions. A high degree of flexibility was expected from the commanders in the field, so that they could respond quickly to actual developments on the battlefield.

This concept, with its blitzkrieg-like characteristics, was demonstrated in the Prussian-Austrian War of 1866 and the Franco-Prussian War of 1870. Both were relatively short conflicts settled within three months. Its success also explains the enthusiasm with which the various armies marched into the First World War, believing it would not be long before a clear victor emerged. However, *Auftragstaktik* did not fully come into its own during the First World War due to the extremely static nature of trench warfare, which offered no room for the type of flexible operation that the Germans had in mind. One of the biggest problems in trench warfare was how to force and successfully follow up a breakthrough. If a breakthrough was achieved at all, the infantry and artillery were unable to keep up with the rapidly advancing vanguard units; due to the difficult terrain, they simply got bogged down in the mud. The advance units thus became isolated and could then easily be neutralized by the enemy. To cope with the problem of breaking through the front, the Germans developed *Hutiertaktik* in the last phase of the war, whereby heavily armed units (*Stosstruppen*, or storm troopers) infiltrated through the front line at certain places (*Schwerpunkte*) and then quickly advanced into the hinterland to disrupt lines of communication and destroy artillery positions. The problem remained, however, that the regular infantry could not support the *Stosstruppen*: the horse-drawn waggons of the infantry and the supply columns could not keep up with the fast pace of the attack because of the muddy and shell-pocked terrain. This allowed the enemy to regroup and close the gap in the front. The weakness of *Hutiertactik* was overcome in the Second World War by the use of tanks and tracked armoured vehicles for the transport of infantry, which could move easily over difficult terrain. (2: 191)

Hutiertactik

The tactic is named after the Supreme Commander of the German Eighth Army in Russia in 1917, General Oskar von Hutier. The High Command of the German Army ordered him to apply the new tactics developed by the General Staff to the fortifications of Riga, which had withstood a two-year siege by the Germans. Optimal application of the concept meant that the fortifications were taken within two days. From that moment on, the tactic was known as *Hutiertaktik*. (8: 172–3 and 41: 2 5)

This new doctrine of *Angriff im Stellungskrieg* (attack in trench warfare) fitted in well with the existing concept of *Auftragstaktik*: within a general framework, the various commanders and men themselves at the front had to act as they saw fit, without awaiting orders from above. This suited the reality of the front in the First World War, where communications – in reality, telephone lines – were almost immediately blown to pieces by the artillery during combat. This forced small groups of soldiers to fight independently of each other and to take advantage of opportunities on their own initiative. The German Army was the only organization that recognized and acknowledged the limitations and challenges of the First World War battlefield and responded to them by developing a new doctrine, training their men and promoting the key leadership abilities that made it possible to delegate decision-making to the lowest levels. (31: 205–6)

The new tactics led to local successes in 1918, but could do nothing about the growing preponderance of power on the Allied side, which eventually led to the surrender of the German Army later that year.

After the First World War the Germans analysed their combat performance very thoroughly at all levels and in all kinds of situations. Their experiences were laid down by von Seeckt as a supplement to the doctrine of *Auftragstaktik* in a number of guiding documents, including *Führung und Gefecht der verbundenen Waffen* (Leading and Fighting with Combined Arms). Part I was published in 1921 and Part II in 1923. As the title suggests, a central theme was cooperation between the various branches of the Army in integrated units. These documents formed the theoretical framework for the further development of the *Reichswehr*'s vision in the interwar period.

Parallel to this was the development of ideas about the deployment of tanks. We have already seen that one of the problems after successfully breaking through the front was how to follow up with a second-wave attack and regular infantry. Horse traction and the available vehicles proved not good enough to follow up quickly and consolidate a breakthrough. So the combination of *Auftragstaktik*, *Verbundene Waffen* and new ideas about the deployment of tanks and motorized infantry laid the basis for the tactical doctrine and organization of the *Reichswehr*.

The connection in the field of mobility between the two world wars was personified by, among others, General Heinz Guderian: he was one of those who linked the aforementioned tactical offensive doctrine to the flexibility and firepower of tanks. This resulted in a new, powerful offensive doctrine, in which tanks were supported by motorized infantry in armoured vehicles. An important difference with the First World War was that the offensive no longer focused on eliminating artillery, but on destroying the opponent's C3I (Command, Control, Communications and Intelligence) capability – the enemy's brain and nervous system. If this could be damaged or destroyed, the enemy's front generally collapsed quickly.

Key to the success of this concept was cooperation between the various branches (infantry, cavalry, artillery, engineers, etc.) in the mobile and hectic situation during an attack and after a breakthrough. The principles of *Verbundene Waffen* and *Einheit* (unity) played an important role in this: the various arms had to be able to operate as integrated multifunctional combat units. In other words, cooperation between these different branches always had to run smoothly, ignoring the traditional divisions between them. Great emphasis was therefore placed on creating *Einheit* in joint training and exercises, to ensure that there would always be intensive and optimal cooperation in combat situations.

The combination of *Auftragstaktik*, *Verbundene Waffen*, *Schwerpunkt* and the tank offensive was the basis for the success of the German Army, especially in the early period of the Second World War. If all the above elements fell into place, this was blitzkrieg, as seen in the Polish campaign of 1939 and in May 1940, when the evolution of the concept was complete. (39: 51–2)

The tank offensive in reality

The German philosophy is best exemplified by their tank offensives, which represented blitzkrieg in its truest form. The Germans realized that no opponent could have the upper hand all along the front; therefore, as a result of the lessons learnt in the First World War, they concentrated their forces at the *Schwerpunkt* (the weakest point) of the enemy's defensive line, the ideal attack route which also offered a good opportunity for artillery support. (2: 37) A tank offensive (in fact, any type of offensive operation) would be concentrated on this part of the front. The ultimate goal of the tank offensive was not the front itself but far beyond the front line, in the enemy's hinterland. Following the principles of *Auftragstaktik*, the tanks were tasked to penetrate as far and fast as they could, and individual commanders were given considerable discretion to manoeuvre and act according to their own insight, as long as the set goals were reached. (7: 139)

Reconnaissance in force

One of the features of these tank offensives was reconnaissance in force. The Germans attached a much higher value to information collection by exploration than their opponents. At the outset, separate reconnaissance units were established and trained; and as the Germans believed in fighting if necessary to gain information, these units were not only very mobile and well equipped, they were also heavily armed. Each division had such a reconnaissance battalion, the *Aufklärungsabteilung*, whose task it was not only to collect information but also to respond to any opportunities that arose during an armed reconnaissance.

The *Aufklärungsabteilung* was also the strategic reserve for the less motorized divisions. (7: 137) Reconnaissance units were therefore a serious factor that had to be taken into account at all times. In tank offensives, as in everything the Germans undertook, the formula I = S × M occupied a central place. Impact = Speed × Mass often proved that even units of small size could have a major impact on the course of a battle, provided they were able to act quickly. For that reason, the Germans wanted to keep the time lag between observing enemy movements and responding to them as short as possible.

Kampfgruppen

For tactical operations, the German Army frequently and effectively used ad hoc and locally organized units, the Kampfgruppen. The underlying philosophy was this: although the German Army might be formally described in organizational charts and diagrams, in more practical terms the Germans regarded it as a 'pool' of men and materiel from which, depending on the situation, different units could be extracted in the form of Kampfgruppen. These were composed of the various parts of one or more divisions. Tank, infantry and artillery units were combined as building blocks into a larger whole according to the needs of the operation in question. In other words, they were an example of *Verbundene Waffen* at its best: all units were able to work together in any situation in an integrated multifunctional force. (2: 29)

A temporary commander was appointed to head each Kampfgruppe, usually the man who held the highest rank within the units concerned. In this way unity in leadership/command was guaranteed. This unity of command was so deeply entrenched in the thinking of the German Army that Kampfgruppen were named after their commander.

It also made them recognizable, created *Einheit* (unity) and made it possible for the troops to identify with their leader.

The size of a Kampfgruppe could vary from that of a division (8,000–12,000 men) to that of a company (100 to 200 men), depending on requirements and the availability of men and materiel. The most common size was that of a regiment (1,500–2,000 men) or a battalion (300–800 men).

The Kampfgruppe concept made very high demands on the flexibility and organizational capacity of all those involved, but it turned out to be very effective in practice due to the high training level of (staff) officers and men in the German Army. (11: 78)

A 'School of Thought': the German General Staff

Crucial to the organization of the German Army was the General Staff. This, together with the Staff Officer Corps, was of great importance in maintaining a high level of professionalism; indeed, the Allies had recognized it as the basis of the German Army's effectiveness and promptly banned the institution at the end of the First World War. The Germans took counter-measures, and a General Staff was recreated in a secret cover organization, the *Truppenamt*, from 1918, enabling them to start planning and building a new army. The Allies were particularly apprehensive about the General Staff because they saw it as the brains of the German Army. It played an important role in the development and monitoring of the Army's command concept and tactical doctrines, because it:

- updated doctrine and tactics, and the methods and techniques derived from them, in the form of Standard Operating Procedures for all kinds of combat situations
- trained the officer corps in the application of doctrine and tactics, in both theory and practice
- embedded them throughout the command structure in such a way that officers and units actually used the whole system
- selected for key positions officers who met high standards, while rejecting those who did not. (28: 331–6)

The German General Staff can thus be seen as the 'academy' of the German Army: free exchange of ideas was central to its functioning and considered of great importance for the further development of doctrine and tactics. This approach was initiated by von Schlieffen, the Prussian commander of the General Staff before the First World War. He regularly commissioned junior staff officers to work out complex strategic problems, on the premise that in wartime these men would need to have the knowledge and skills to be able to lead large combat units. Von Seeckt, a pupil of von Schlieffen, embedded this culture of openness in the General Staff of the *Reichswehr* after the First World War. (41: 109)

The Staff Officer Corps of the General Staff was an important factor in ensuring cohesion within the German Army. Officers of the Corps, recognizable by the red piping on their trousers, belonged to the elite of the Army, and every intelligent and promising officer was transferred to the Corps for training; here they became, in effect, guardians of the doctrine developed by the General Staff.

Staff officers rotated between the front and the General Staff, so that optimal use could be made of their experience. In addition, the knowledge of the General Staff was constantly supplemented by evaluation and analysis of important combat actions (*Erfahrungsberichte* –

see below). This knowledge was used to adapt the standard methods and techniques and to improve their application in combat situations. (28: 127)

In this way there was a constant exchange between theory and practice, and concepts and doctrine could constantly be adapted to match the reality of the front. The officers of the Staff Officer Corps functioned almost literally as 'repositories of knowledge' for the German Army.

This way of working led to a high degree of exchangeability of officers and men between the different units and fronts. It was not the personal vision and approach of the individual officer or the army unit that was decisive, but the approach developed by the General Staff and the Staff Officer Corps and tested in practice. By choosing similar approaches and frameworks to evaluate combat actions, structured and unambiguous feedback was guaranteed.

Erfahrungsberichte: the learning organization

Many modern students of management will be aware that the origins of what we now know as a 'Quality Cycle' can be traced back to the work in the 1950s of an American professor and management consultant, W. Edwards Deming. However, in practice, the German Army had been operating such a cycle since the beginning of the nineteenth century. It was this approach that led to the evaluation of the Battle of Jena in 1806 and to evaluations of every significant combat action thereafter. It took the form not of a limited amount of feedback with a focus on what went wrong, but of feedback explicitly focused on what could be learned from it. What became known as *Erfahrungsberichte* (evaluation reports) were extremely powerful elements of a quality management system. All combat actions were evaluated, and this could lead to adjustments in command concept, doctrine and tactics. It made the German Army an unprecedentedly powerful learning organization. *Erfahrungsberichte* were concise and quickly shared.

Men, teams and training

The concepts and structures described in the preceding paragraphs are meaningless without the men and leaders to fulfil them. In this regard, the Peace Treaty of Versailles can be seen to have been a blessing in disguise, since it forced the new *Reichswehr* to reduce its size considerably. Consequently, they had the opportunity to select the very best officers and non-commissioned officers for the new organization. This created a pool of men of unprecedentedly high quality, who provided an excellent basis for the further development and later expansion of the *Reichswehr* in the 1930s.

The limitations of the Versailles Treaty

The Treaty limited the size of the German Army to 100,000 men, including 4,000 officers. However, as a result of the high educational and training level of the troops and officers of the *Reichswehr*, growth from ten divisions and 100,000 men in 1934 to thirty-one divisions by the end of 1935 was easily achieved. The main goal of this 'new' army was to train recruits. After 1935 the *Reichswehr* was renamed the *Wehrmacht* (7: 112), and in order to strengthen the cadre, many First World War officers were recalled to active service. Qualified conscripts were promoted to officer, and a substantial training programme for new officers was set up, leading to an almost exponential growth of the Army thereafter.

In the early 1920s, von Seeckt formulated in the document *Grundlagen der Erziehung des Heeres* clear principles for the officers and men of the demoralized *Reichswehr*. These principles would be further elaborated and implemented in the years that followed.

Recruitment, selection and the psychological dimensions of warfare

The Germans were aware early on of the importance of psychology in getting the right man in the right place, boosting morale and hardening troops against the strains and stresses of modern technological warfare.

The First World War, in which troop units were quickly dispersed, had shown the need for a new type of soldier, no longer one who could only function under the all-seeing eye of his officer, but one who could operate independently in the no-man's-land of the front. Efforts in the field of psychology focused on creating this new type of independent-thinking soldier, in line with *Auftragstaktik*'s views on preferred leadership styles. In addition, it was realized that the psychological aspects of new weapons such as tanks and planes demanded more than just knowledge and skills. They also made demands on the personal qualities of the men. In contrast to the British or American Army, men were not only tested for intelligence, but also for social, emotional and character traits. The high command placed more value on mental qualities and the emotional attitude of recruits than on formal knowledge or physical strength. Much effort was put into developing methods to analyse the willpower, stamina and mental resilience of officers and men.

The Germans also realized that the next war would be mainly technological in nature and would demand nerves of steel from soldiers, especially men in special units such as paratroopers, tank crews and the crews of anti-tank guns. It did not take long for psychologists to conclude that truck drivers do not necessarily make good tank drivers, any more than commercial airline pilots make good fighter pilots. (20: 163) Technical knowledge and skills had to be combined with the qualities of a soldier.

Profiles were developed for the different types of soldier, and tank crews in particular were carefully selected. They had to be highly individualistic and able to act independently, have a good sense of technique and be willing to sacrifice themselves for the homeland. Strict selection and subsequent intensive training contributed greatly to the later success of the German tank divisions. Other elite units, such as anti-tank gun crews, required nerves of steel, willpower and perseverance. These units were not called *Panzerjäger* (tank hunters) for nothing, reflecting the combative attitude the role required.

All these efforts served to prepare officers and men for the battlefield of the future. Despite initial scepticism and opposition, psychological knowledge was widely applied within the *Reichswehr* and later the *Wehrmacht*.

Training

On the surface, training in the German Army differed little from that of other countries. But appearances are deceptive. In the first place, *Auftragstaktik* as a doctrine provided clear starting points for training all army units throughout the country. These were laid down in the aforementioned document *Grundlagen der Erziehung des Heeres*, and this prevented the various army units and branches from setting up separate training programmes based on their own experience and insight, without taking the bigger picture into account. While responsibility for the training of recruits was delegated to the divisions, there was a very high degree of consistency in approach. (28: 125)

The training programmes were extremely practical and aimed at developing the capabilities of the individual soldier first, then those of units. The only limitation in western Germany was the lack of sufficient military training grounds to practise in larger groups. Only after the conquest of Poland and France did larger training grounds became available. (2: 82) The overall programme was detailed, methodical and carefully monitored. (31: 237) In addition to learning how to deal with the technical aspects of military life, the training also served to ensure an offensive attitude in individuals and in the cadre. Drill, seen in other countries as one of the most important instruments for instilling discipline, had largely been abolished well before the First World War. The Germans recognized that this way of treating troops was not in line with their views on modern warfare.

Team building (*Kampfgemeinschaft*)

The German Army placed great emphasis on team building from the lowest level. Everything within the German training and personnel planning system – from the recruitment and selection of men within a defined geographical area (*Wehrkreis*) and the division rotation system, to the reception of rehabilitated men within their own units – was aimed at achieving and maintaining a high degree of social cohesion. In the military context this meant that every man in a unit knew his comrades well, and all had worked together in combat situations. It was believed that this cohesion allowed units to function more smoothly and to hold together better in combat. (2: 80)

In addition, units in the German Army had a remarkably democratic character. In the context of *Auftragstaktik*, the emphasis was on achieving objectives together as a team and thus on horizontal communication. This was in contrast to other armies, where all too often vertical, hierarchical communication between officers and men was predominant. By being involved in working out the objectives of the mission, troops were better able to see its overall scope ('why') and place their efforts ('what' and 'how') in a larger context. In this way they were also able to continue with a mission independently, even if their officers were killed.

The Germans had also learned lessons from the gap that had opened up between officers and men at the end of the First World War. They wanted to avoid this at all times, which is why they attached great importance to the development of relationships between officers and their men while preserving the outward appearances of discipline. This relationship should not be based, they believed, on power, but on mutual respect and authority. Future officers were urged from the outset of training to gain the confidence of their men without compromising their authority. (40: 215) The Germans therefore did not have separate mess rooms for officers and men, or other privileges for officers.

***Wehrkreis* and the rotation system**

Each German division recruited its men from a well-defined geographical area, the *Wehrkreis*. As a result, many recruits had known each other for years before they were collectively called up for service. Divisions trained their recruits themselves, within the framework of the overall training programme, so that recruits – including those called in to replace losses – could immediately be fully integrated into the division.

The Army itself was made up of the field army (*Feldheer*) and the reserve army (*Ersatzheer*). The *Feldheer* was commanded by the commander-in-chief; all other units came under the command of the *Ersatzheer*. (4: 43) Once the division was on active service, a training battalion (*Ersatz Bataillon*) remained stationed at home base as part of the *Ersatzheer*. This battalion was responsible for training and supplying men to the division at the front. There was a rotation system in which (non-commissioned) officers with combat experience (often convalescing after injury) were deployed to the 'mother' units of the *Ersatzheer* at the home base. This system ensured that the recruits:

- quickly got a feel for the *esprit de corps* of the division
- were trained in the most up-to-date combat tactics (2: 81–2)

This prevented officers left behind on the home front feeling alienated from the active combat. The officers of the active division at the front and their counterparts in barracks were expected to maintain close, often personal relationships, in order to achieve optimal coordination of training and practice. To ensure a smooth transition between theory and practice, each division of the *Feldheer* had a so-called *Feldersatz Bataillon*. This provided additional training and acclimatization to newly arrived troops and officers from the *Ersatzheer* during breaks in combat. (4: 72) The three companies of the Feldersatz Bataillon each had a close relationship with the three regiments of the division. Officers and non-commissioned officers of these regiments, who would later become the commanders of the newly arrived recruits, were attached to the companies as instructors, with the aim of encouraging team-building between officers and their men at an early stage.

Leadership style

The leadership style linked to *Auftragstaktik* was elaborated in the early 1920s in many documents, including Regulations Number 5 and 6 of *Führung und Gefecht der verbundenen Waffen*. Great value was attached to fast, unambiguous and agile thought and action, and to being prepared for the unexpected. In addition, the independence and sense of responsibility of officers and men was constantly emphasized. Officer training did not rely on standard solutions but emphasized personal qualities such as responsibility, imagination and initiative.

Due to its mission orientation, communication in the German Army was relatively informal; a word or two was often enough. Much more than in other armies, the Germans relied on global verbal orders; other armies, especially the American and British, generally worked with detailed plans, which were quickly overtaken by the realities of the battlefield. Consultations in the German Army during combat often took place on an ad hoc basis, leaving much to the further elaboration and initiative of subordinates. (36: 48)

In all, this resulted in the following situation:

> *Bei nähere Betrachtung entwickelte sich das Bild einer Armee, die einander offensichtlich widersprechende Eigenschaften wie Gehorsamkeit und Initiative, Drill und Kreativität, Autorität und Selbständigkeit erfolgreich auf einen Nenner zu bringen vermochte.* (33: 176)
>
> (On closer inspection, the picture developed of an army that was able to successfully bring together apparently contradictory characteristics such as obedience and initiative, drill and creativity, authority and independence.)

Non-commissioned officers

Special attention should be paid to the position of the non-commissioned officers, since the Germans considered this level of management to be extremely important. (31: 206) While the Treaty of Versailles limited the size of the *Reichswehr*, it also had the effect of enabling it to select only the very best non-commissioned officers. The Treaty also extended the service period to twelve years, as a result of which the training of NCOs had to be intensified. This in turn made it possible to ensure that non-commissioned officers were able to lead units two levels above that of their normal command. Moreover, attention was explicitly paid to the training skills of the candidates, so that numbers of fully qualified NCOs enriched the overall quality of the officer corps; this assisted the rapid expansion of the *Reichswehr* in the 1930s.

The quality of recruitment, selection and training in the interwar period made it possible, within the framework of *Auftragstaktik*, to delegate many operational responsibilities to non-commissioned officers. As a result, officers were able to concentrate more fully on organizational tasks. This considerably improved efficiency, flexibility and cohesion within the German Army.

Officers

Officers' careers began with enlistment with the regimental commander of the regiment of choice. Candidate officers were expected to have received an education which gave access to university. Until 1926, the regimental commander determined whether someone was admitted to officer training, the personal qualities of the candidate being among the most important criteria. In 1926, with growing interest in the psychological aspects of warfare, a central psychological testing centre was established. Candidate officers were given a two-day assessment, in which the candidate's social functioning within a group was assessed in particular.

In the period up to the outbreak of war in 1939, officer training lasted two years and three months. After a first six months of service in the *Reichsarbeitsdienst* (labour service), the candidate received a one-year training as a non-commissioned officer. During this period he was guided by a coach/sponsor, an older officer whose job it was to 'iron out the wrinkles' and teach the recruit the behaviour and attitudes expected in his future military role. It was then decided whether the recruit could attend officer training. This lasted five months, followed by four months at a specific weapons training course. Finally, after a minimum of two years and three months in the Army, the candidate was awarded his first rank, that of second lieutenant. (20: 161)

As the war progressed it became increasingly difficult to maintain the existing system of training and promotion, with the result that both commissioned and non-commissioned officers were sometimes promoted in the field on the basis of their proven qualities. Increasingly, seniority and the competence of the person involved played a role in promotion, and a new criterion, whether an officer was *Krisenfest* (stress-resistant), made its appearance. The advantage of the system was that proven courage and competence were rewarded; the drawback was that the homogeneity of the officer corps and its *esprit de corps* were diluted. (4: 141)

An important requirement for officers was that they should be present on the front line in order to personally evaluate the battlefield and enemy positions. This had a beneficial effect on their soldiers' morale, but led to relatively heavy losses of officers in combat. This relationship between officers, NCOs and their men was noted and recorded by the Allies during interviews with German prisoners of war:

> Almost all non-commissioned officers and officers at the level of the company during the campaign in Western Europe were considered brave, efficient and compassionate by the German soldier. (4: 129)

A better compliment is scarcely conceivable

Openness in the vertical hierarchy

The German Army placed great importance on good personal relationships and an atmosphere of openness and trust within the hierarchy. An important reason for this was that open communication meant it was possible to keep an eye on the functioning of units and their commanders. By creating a sense of security within the vertical hierarchy, commanders were able to critically examine their own efforts and those of their troops through the *Erfahrungsberichte.* (17: 22) The commanders, in turn, expected to hear from their superiors if there were weaknesses in their performance. There was, however, no question of not complying with this system: the Army Supreme Command, the *Oberkommando des Heeres* (OKH), demanded honest and accurate reports on the quality and combat power of the various units. If a unit underperformed, its commander was expected to report this and take measures to attend to the weaknesses identified. If he did not report a weakness, the commander was held responsible. (31: 22)

This generally critical attitude towards its own functioning, which found its origins in the *Reichswehr*'s focus on efficiency, when combined with the necessary sense of security and trust within and between all levels of the organization, meant that the German Army in the Second World War was constantly able to learn and adapt to changing circumstances.

Authority and trust

Establishing authority and winning the trust of their men were central themes in the training, evaluation and promotion of all officers. They were expected, on the one hand, to show clear leadership and initiative and to promote an aggressive *esprit de corps*, and on the other, to have a watchful care for their subordinates and to supervise and coach them. Officers and NCOs needed to create a sense of trust and security within the unit that they led and to stimulate socialization within the group; good personal relations were all-important. (31: 11) The bond between officers and men was reinforced by the use of the term 'soldier' for both. As a result, troops had to salute not only their officers but also each other. Because officers and men received their training in the same units, contacts between them outside the service were frequent and encouraged from above. (4: 129) We have already seen that that the mission-orientated nature of *Auftragstaktik* demanded trust and a sense of equality: the idea was to work together on every assignment. However, both subordinates and superiors were sufficiently realistic to know that such trust was not a given; as with authority, it had to grow over the course of time as a result of attitudes shown in clearly defined roles before, during and after combat. To promote this process, units were kept together as much as possible along the principle of *Einheit.* (33: 270)

1.2 The British Army

Having examined the history and organization of the German Army, we will now examine the British Army, starting with its mission.

An imperial army

In 1939 Britain was an island nation with an empire spread across the world. The mission of the British armed forces was to project the power of the empire over great distances, to protect the ocean trade routes and to supply men, weapons and materiel. The wars fought had mostly been (small) colonial conflicts, far from home and rarely requiring large numbers of soldiers. A regiment or a few battalions was often sufficient, partly due to their superior armament, to put down a local uprising or subdue a colony. These were 'low intensity conflicts'.

In the colonies, a high proportion of the troops were locally recruited men, trained and led by British officers. The British were adept at training and organizing such troops. In both world wars, significant contingents of colonial troops (Sikhs, Gurkhas, Africans, etc.) served on the European fronts, as did Dominion troops (Australians, New Zealanders, Canadians, South Africans). This was, of course, at the expense of a certain degree of cohesion; differing dietary requirements (sometimes for religious reasons) were just one example of the logistical problems involved.

Another aspect that determined the post-1918 mission of the British Army, given the enormous losses suffered in the First World War, was that it was essentially no longer prepared to fight a war on the European mainland. Little attention was paid to the possibilities of a continental expeditionary force; it was assumed that the sea and the Royal Navy would provide sufficient protection against enemy powers.

The vision of the organization

The mission of the British Army and the experiences gained in 'low intensity conflicts' and 'small wars' meant that at the beginning of the Second World War it lacked an overall, unambiguous organizational and command concept. Rather, local solutions were sought for local problems. Given the type of war the British were used to fighting, a single concept was only relevant to a certain extent. They regarded the First World War as an extremely costly excursion on the European mainland and, protected by a strong navy, did not intend to be tempted to participate in a European war again. The First World War confirmed the mission of the British Army and kept Britain's focus on the empire, where the concepts and tactics developed over the centuries still proved to be extremely effective.

The experience of the First World War did not lead to in-depth evaluation or a fundamental reconsideration of doctrine, tactics, structure, recruitment, selection, training or management. The fact that the British emerged victorious from the First World War strengthened their belief that their military doctrine and organization were adequate, including for a war on the continent. They attributed the successes of *Hutiertaktik* and the *Stosstruppen* to the existence of elite troops, just as they later saw the successes of the Germans in the Second World War as being the achievement of elite armoured units. (41: 3) They did not realize that *Hutiertaktik*, combined with new views on management and organization, would be deeply embedded in the *Reichswehr* in the period between the two world wars, and that the quality and professionalism of the German soldier was based on a broad and well thought-out philosophy – a philosophy that the British would pay little attention to even after the Second World War. (16: 7) The geographically dispersed deployment of the British Army meant that units had to fend for themselves far from the mother country and, on a case-by-case basis, had to find pragmatic solutions to the military problems they faced. The conflicts facing the British Army in the colonies had little in common; it was difficult for units to learn from each other, develop ideas together and place lessons in a broader context. (16: 32 & 34) A central body such as a strong German General Staff could have combined these experiences and taken the development of a vision to a higher level, but the British Army had no such institution. The experiences gained in the colonies simply led to the concept of 'small wars' as described in the book of the same name by C.E. Callwell (1896), whose ideas were embedded in British military culture and methods of approaching an opponent. (16: 31)

British command concepts were based on very diverse experiences from the various colonial conflicts, and their interpretation was often left to individual regiments and commanders. Common principles or a common assessment framework were lacking, and may indeed not have been necessary, given the diversity of the conflicts faced. Analysis of the fighting in North Africa will show that the personality of the commander, for example Auchinleck or Montgomery, had a major effect on the organization and command structure, the culture of leadership, and so on. This is in contrast to the German Army, where institutions such as the General Staff carried out evaluations, introduced new methodologies and developed and implemented new organizational structures.

To understand the way in which the British Army was organized and managed at the beginning of the Second World War, we will often have to fall back on material relating to the First. In the description and analysis of battles in the following chapters, case studies also play an important role, in which ideas, views and innovations linked to individuals will often prove to be decisive.

Influence of the regimental system

Regiments played an important role in the British Army; hence this organizational structure will be discussed in more detail. Regiments were divided into two parts on the basis of the Cardwell Reforms of 1873, namely one part stationed in Great Britain and another sent to the colonies. This system, which continued after the First World War, was in contrast to Germany, where, as we have seen, under von Seeckt a strong centralized control of divisions was introduced, while at the same time the maintenance of units' strong individual identity was stressed. Because there was a greater focus on regional recruitment during the First World War, the British regimental system became increasingly linked to a specific regional identity. For example, the proportion of Scots in the Scots Guards grew from 42 per cent in 1914 to 63 per cent by 1918. This strengthened the regiment's position within the British Army and also increased cohesion within the regiments themselves. (43: 208–9)

Although recruitment, selection, training, etc. was centralized and standardized, a very strong regimental subculture ran through it. After a relatively short preparatory training of officers at Sandhurst, their actual training took place within the regiment. The role of the regiment was therefore decisive in an officer's further career. Since each regiment was a social system with its own values and norms, the officer in question also made a choice for life within a certain, clearly defined social group. Due to this structure of the British Army around regiments, officers identified primarily with their own regiment, with its values, norms and traditions, and within it the microcosm of the officers' mess, rather than with the British Army as a whole. In addition, regiments had clear ties with certain regions (infantry) or parts of the aristocracy (cavalry). (43: 195–8)

Over-identification with the regiment

Major General D.N. Wemberley of the 51st Highland Division emphasized that its *esprit de corps* was closely linked to the regiments' Scottish identity. He urged his men that 'if wounded and separated from your units, do not allow yourself to be drafted to other battalions, but see that you can come back to us.' In 1943 1,200 men from two divisions, one of them the 51st Highland, were ordered to join the 46th Division inland from Salerno. Three hundred men refused, of whom 191 stood their ground even after their commanders announced that they were no longer instructed to remain with their own units at all times. These men were accused of mutiny. In their defence it was argued that 'to ask a soldier of the Highland Division to fight with another division is, in my mind [i.e. that of their lawyer], akin to asking a Hindu to worship Mohammed.'

By 1944, however, manpower shortages had become so great that the barriers between regiments and even other units fell away. For example, the 2nd Battalion of the Scots Guards, regrouping in Harwick, received 400 men as reinforcements from an RAF regiment. The latter arrived dressed in RAF blue while defiantly singing, 'We are the RAF, RAF, RAF!'

During the course of the war, the Scots Guards became part of the Guards Armoured Division and were combined with parts of the Welsh Guards, so that slowly but surely the distinction between the different regiments disappeared in practice. (31: 212–13)

In another example, at El Alamein a cavalry general refused to accept a regiment of the Royal Artillery under his command, because 'We only accept support from the Royal Horse Artillery.' (28: 111)

After Dunkirk there was a need for larger units such as divisions and corps, which meant that the regimental system became subordinate to the new organizational structure of the British Army. In line with this, Alan Brooke, Chief of the Imperial General Staff (CIGS), did much during the war to give the British Army a more 'corporate' identity. The result was that although the animosity between different regiments remained, the regiment was no longer the dominant structure. (43: 214)

All in all, the institution of the regiment, combined with the lack of a clear vision and the organizational and managerial views derived from it, led to fragmentation in thinking and action within the British Army in many areas well into the Second World War. (43: 195–8)

Tactical doctrine

To get an idea of British tactical doctrine in the Second World War, we will first look back on experiences before and during the First World War. Before 1914, British doctrine was, as we have seen, mainly based on experiences in relatively small-scale colonial wars. Operating in larger contexts was largely neglected. Morale was seen as an important condition for success – or as stated in 'Infantry Training' (1914), 'to close with the enemy, cost what it may.' W.R. Robertson stated in January 1914 that what should be avoided at all times was to 'interfere with the desire of the troops to push into fighting at all costs.'

The idea behind these principles was that a future war would be short and decisive victory would be achieved quickly. (43: 15) As the war progressed and the size of the British Army on the Continent increased, the top ranks of the organization increasingly turned to past solutions, in other words 'applying old principles to new conditions'. As a result, the predominant tactic was a massed infantry charge with the bayonet after a preliminary artillery bombardment. The attack had to be pressed home at all costs. In this view, the key to success lay in the deployment of increasingly large numbers of men and ordnance. (43: 16)

After the First World War, neither the British nor the French felt the need, as victors, for a fundamental analysis of the experiences and dilemmas of the recent conflict. Existing concepts were not further developed, nor were new ones advanced to address identified problems. It was not until fifteen years later that a British report was drawn up analysing operational methods: 'Notes on certain lessons of the Great War'. The report concluded that surprise was an important element and that the British had reacted too stereotypically in all kinds of situation. In future, commanders had to be better able to take the initiative, and the usefulness of prolonged artillery bombardments was questioned: they gave away the element of surprise and destroyed the infrastructure too severely to enable an attack to be successfully followed up. The solution was sought in far-reaching decentralization of artillery command. Although this seemed a logical solution, the ultimate consequence was that the British in North Africa were no longer able to concentrate the deployment of artillery – their best weapon – on specific points of the front. Montgomery would reverse this development and emphasize the importance of artillery in forcing a breakthrough at critical points. (16: 21–2)

There was lively discussion between the two world wars about the use of tanks in a future conflict. Publications by people such as Fuller and Liddell Hart did stimulate thinking about this, but it did not lead to a generally accepted, widely supported doctrine. (16: 13) We will return to this later.

At the beginning of the Second World War there was no clear concept of how to break the enemy's lines. The approved modus operandi most closely resembled the tactics of the First World War: after an artillery bombardment, to attack on a broad front in the hope that the artillery had sufficiently undermined the enemy positions – despite the fact that by 1918 the British were already experimenting with tactics comparable to German methods of infiltration and could therefore have gained experience of a different approach.

Due to the lack of a generally accepted vision, command concept and doctrine, case studies are an important way to reconstruct the British method of operating in different situations. A good example of a creative and effective use of various weapon systems from the period 1941–2 can be found in North Africa. The problem there was that the German artillery had a greater range than the British, but British tanks and 25-pounder howitzers worked together to halt a German tank attack. Part of the artillery positioned itself in front of the British tanks and bombarded the German tanks from a great distance. When the German tanks approached to within 1,000 metres, the guns were quickly coupled to trucks and driven to the rear. Another section of the artillery, positioned behind the tanks, covered the retreat of the artillery and in turn fired at the German tanks. When the German tanks got close enough, the British tanks fired on them from the flank and thus, together with the artillery, halted the German attack (43: 102).

Since this method of operation is not described elsewhere, it is impossible to determine whether it was the personal initiative of the local commander or part of a more widely supported tactical doctrine. Such relatively well-described examples are rare: in addition to the 'fog of war', the British 'fog of organization' also plays a role here.

It was Montgomery who first put a number of principles in the field of command and tactical doctrine on the agenda. During the Tripoli Tactical Talks (15–17 February 1943) he tried to formulate a joint framework. The purpose of these discussions was:

- to see how we stand
- to create a solid framework or base which will serve as a background to everything we do,
- to check on things that really matter when we go into battle fighting
- to examine the technique of certain more important types of operations
- to disseminate knowledge among ourselves

Montgomery understood that his generally poorly trained officers and men only functioned well under central direction and coordination and with clear and detailed planning. He made this the starting point for his method of command and control at strategic and tactical levels. He ignored the views of different factions and appointed protégés to key positions to ensure that his views were disseminated. In this way he was able to elevate his personal doctrine to the doctrine of the 21st Army Group, the most powerful British combat unit of the period 1939–45.

Montgomery's management views

- Clear principles must be formulated that must be elaborated in detail in the form of a Master Plan.
- The Master Plan should be prepared by the Army Group Commander based on what he wants to achieve, and not by his staff.
- The Master Plan must align resources with goals (the 'what' and the 'how'). The Master Plan details successive troop movements.
- Air superiority must first be obtained before sea and land actions can take place.
- The high command must be able to group and regroup units depending on the situation.
- Forces must be deployed in a concentrated manner under the central leadership of the Commander of the Army Group.
- Firepower takes precedence over the use of men and tanks. Artillery fire must be centralized and concentrated depending on the needs of the Army Group Commander. (16: 26–7)

The above is not so much a detailed and balanced doctrine, but rather a framework for Montgomery's management views. In practice, it functioned as a non-binding assessment of the actions that took place under Montgomery as commander.

It is unclear whether and to what extent Montgomery's ideas were further developed into a more balanced concept or took root in units other than those under his command.

The British also struggled to find an organizational concept that exploited the possibilities of motorization, mechanization (tanks) and cooperation with the Air Force. The effect was that they often fell back on old tactics from the First World War.

Theoretical development of tank warfare

The development of a British theory on the use of tanks between the two world wars was highly dependent on the involvement of a limited number of people.

After the First World War, F. C. Fuller was the first to discuss the role of the tank in a future conflict. As a staff officer, Fuller had drawn up 'Plan 1919' in 1918 which contained the core of his later ideas in the field of mobile warfare. He envisaged a frontal attack with 1,592 (!) heavy and 390 medium tanks, with the aim of forcing breakthroughs in different places. These were then to be followed by a second wave of 790 medium tanks aimed at destroying the German command centres, and a further 1,220 medium tanks to clear the last pockets of resistance. The plan never got further than the paper it was written on, as neither the types nor numbers of tanks were available. In the 1920s Fuller further developed his concept, of which the basic themes were:

- The introduction of the internal combustion engine will lead to a revolution in warfare
- The tank is the basic building block of any army
- The tactical doctrine of a rapid breakthrough and subsequent encirclement should replace the doctrine of the frontal attack.

Fuller's ideas were supplemented by those of a young infantry officer, Captain B.H. Liddell Hart. Based on his experiences in the First World War, he promoted the idea of concentrating forces on a limited part of the front with the aim of forcing a breakthrough there (the German *Schwerpunkt*). Once the breakthrough had been achieved, assault units were to advance through the gap without losing contact with the reserve units behind them. This introduced another problem: that reserve units advancing too quickly could easily be cut off; on the other hand, waiting too long before deploying reserve units would lead to the momentum of the attack being lost.

When combined, these ideas produced a new concept in the late 1920s, with the tank instead of infantry as the central element of the offensive and based on the speed and firepower of tanks, supported by infantry in armoured personnel carriers. This was very similar to ideas being aired in the *Reichswehr*. Experiments were carried out with this concept, but after initial successes no follow-up was undertaken, and an impasse arose in discussion about the deployment of armoured formations. There was no consensus within the Army's leadership about the future role of tanks, and the proponents of armoured formations were unable to jointly develop ideas about how these units should be organized and deployed.

A combination of the mechanized 7th Infantry Brigade and the 1st Tank Brigade, the two most modern units of the British Army combined into the so-called Mobile Force, proved to be no match for a conventional infantry division during exercises in 1933. The reasons for this were poor planning and execution and poor mutual coordination, problems that would continue to haunt the British in North Africa. This disappointing experience did nothing to further the cause of mobile warfare.

In 1935 it was finally decided to equip one cavalry division with tanks and rename it the Mobile Division, but in the years that followed, neither a vision nor a doctrine was developed by successive commanders regarding its role. There were two opinions regarding its deployment: either as a 'cavalry' screen up front, or as a unit to force breakthroughs. When the British Army started mechanizing on a large scale in 1938, it was not clear what the purpose of newly formed tank units was or how they would be deployed. The result was that Britain entered the war in 1939 without an effective tank division and without a coherent vision of mechanized warfare – nor had any thought been given to coordination between infantry and tanks or coordination between the Army and Air Force in the form of ground support by the latter. (49: 57–64)

Until the mid-1930s there was also an impasse with regard to the types of tank required. Lieutenant General Sir Hugh Elles, Master-General of the Ordnance, responsible for the procurement of weapon systems, did not share Fuller's and Liddell Hart's views on the shape of a possible future war and the role of tanks. He saw them only as support for the infantry or, in the case of light tanks, for reconnaissance. He was not interested in heavier tanks with sufficient speed and firepower to act as a relatively independently fighting force.

In line with this, all attention was focused on the production of infantry tanks, the ultimate result being the Infantry Tank Mark II, or Matilda, from Vickers, heavily armoured, equipped with a 2-pounder (20mm) gun and a crew of four. The Matilda only had a top speed of 22.5 kph, because it had to operate together with infantry. Vickers also supplied the Vickers Medium Tank for light reconnaissance duties.

In addition, impressed by the performance of the Soviet BT-26 tank, various so-called 'Cruiser' tanks were developed in the mid-1930s. This type was faster than the Infantry Tank and better armoured than the reconnaissance tanks.

In 1939, therefore, the British Army had three types of tank at its disposal:

- Light tanks for reconnaissance purposes
- Infantry tanks for support of the infantry
- Cruiser tanks for use in tank formations in a more independent role

These tanks were housed in two Mobile Divisions, one for deployment on the continent and in Great Britain itself, and one in Egypt. (32: 108–10)

The further development of the doctrine of mechanized and mobile warfare was left to the cavalry regiments. These were not interested enough or sufficiently intellectually

The place of the tank

In the 1920s, the British Army tried to reduce the number of its regiments. For this reason, the tank was assigned to existing cavalry regiments, rather than the Royal Tank Corps. During the 1920s and 1930s a battle raged between the British Army and the cavalry regiments over whether they should exchange their horses for tanks. When the cavalry regiments were eventually equipped with tanks, they continued to view tank tactics from a cavalryman's perspective, completely ignoring the fact that this was an entirely new weapon system. (43: 211) This can be seen in one of the first confrontations of British tank units with German armoured units in Cyrenaica, when a German officer saw 'the Hussars charging into Jerry tanks, sitting on top of their turrets more or less with their whips out.' The commentator dryly noted that 'they had incredible dash and enthusiasm, and sheer exciting courage which was only curbed by the rapidly decreasing stock of dashing officers and tanks.' (28: 111) It is also remarkable that the British had apparently learned nothing from the experiences of May 1940. After all, it was not the first time that these opponents had met.

equipped to explore such topics in greater depth in theory or develop them further through training and combat simulations. (28: 112)

However, the blame for the lack of a clear tank doctrine should certainly not be placed solely on the cavalry regiments; it also affected the very top of the British Army. General Paget, Commander-in-Chief Home Forces, expressed the views of the CIGS as follows: 'Anyone can handle armoured forces. No special knowledge is needed.' (28: 126) And in the field of cooperation between armoured and infantry divisions, it was noted in November 1942 that 'operations between an armoured division and one or more infantry divisions had not been studied and had certainly not been practised' – despite the fact that in the previous years it must have become clear that the success of the German Army could be explained to a significant extent by the joint deployment of infantry and tank units. Such lessons seem to have passed by the leadership of the British Army.

German defensive positions

The British clearly had difficulty evaluating their combat experiences and embedding them in training and education. As late as 1944, the Royal Scots Fusiliers found it 'most disconcerting to come over the top of hills to discover the Germans dug in on the reverse slope, something we had never envisaged'. This is all the more surprising since digging in on the other side of the hill had been one of the basic tenets of German defensive tactics since 1917. (28: 127)

As a result, the use of tanks and the integration of the various units and weapon systems remained some of the biggest operational problems for the British Army during the Second World War (28: 110).

The Germans, for their part, recognized the problems of the British and considered them among their most fundamental weakness. Combat assessments after *Crusader*, one of the major tank battles in North Africa, showed that the British were unable to concentrate on a single point in the front line (the famous *Schwerpunkt*), but instead dispersed their forces. Even in the breakthrough phase, in the eyes of the Germans the phase in which the opponent had to be dealt a final blow by destroying his C3I capacity, the British were not decisive enough. For example, after El Alamein the Afrika Korps was able to withdraw and reposition itself without notable losses.

This situation had not yet improved in 1944, as can be seen from the *Erfahrungsberichte* of the Panzer Lehr Division* about the performance of the British Second Army: successful breakthroughs were almost never followed up. (See also 16: 50) If the Germans could deploy sufficient men and materiel, lost territory was almost immediately recaptured. The flanks and close combat also appeared still to be weak points for the British. (28: 127)

Of course, the chaos and confusion of combat also made it difficult for the British to observe exactly how the German units were operating. When they were finally able to unravel the German system later in the war, it proved difficult in practice to develop effective counter-measures or to introduce a comparable command concept (28: 117–18).

* The Panzer Lehr Division was an armoured division in which new units were trained by experienced instructors and could be considered an elite formation. The division was commanded by Sepp Dietrich.

After all, mobile warfare places high demands on the flexibility of command and execution, the delegation of responsibilities and decision-making power, training, leadership style, communication, etc. Only when all these elements were optimally coordinated could units operate as independent combat formations in rapidly changing mobile warfare. British capacity in this area improved gradually during the war, but it remained one of the weak points in the eyes of the Germans. (28: 113)

Coordination between the various arms also improved during the course of the war (particularly between artillery and infantry), but it never reached the level of the Germans. The British sought it in a massive preponderance of men and materiel, a solution that had also worked during the First World War.

One would have thought that these problems should have required the continued attention of the CIGS. However, it seems that he was not very interested in tactical problems on the battlefield. (28: 124) Although there was a continuous flow of information from the Middle East theatre, it is questionable how much attention the Home Forces paid to it. The CIGS did not seem prepared to develop an overall tactical doctrine.

Structure

In the absence of an overall command concept and doctrine, structures within the British Army were largely determined by the regiment and the experience of 'small wars'.

Jock Columns

In September 1940, the British in North Africa concluded that their armoured cars were vulnerable to Italian artillery and aircraft. These units were therefore reinforced with artillery and anti-aircraft guns. The guns were mounted on the back of trucks, and the infantry also became motorized. The father of this concept was Lieutenant Colonel J.C. (Jock) Campbell of the Royal Horse Artillery. To the great shock of the Italians, these units appeared in all kinds of unexpected places to sow death and destruction.

Due to the success of these units, more independent formations, such as the Support Group, consisting of two infantry battalions and an artillery battalion, and the Selby Force, consisting of infantry companies with artillery and tanks, were deployed against the Italians later that year. (47: 119)

The success of these units against the Italians confirmed the experience of the various 'small wars'. Against German troops, the masters of mobile warfare with independent units such as Kampfgruppen, this tactic did not last long.

At the beginning of the war, and especially in North Africa, this led to experimenting with a large number of organizational concepts. A dominant theme was that British officers, in line with experiences in the colonies, constantly wanted to command their own 'group' or 'unit'. The idea was that this would allow them to manoeuvre across the battlefield with élan, without having to think about coordination with other units. In North Africa, these small units also fitted the romantic image of 'Lawrence of Arabia', moving through the desert to attack the enemy unexpectedly and destructively. Sometimes it was a good idea to deploy such units, but often they led to a fragmentation of scarce resources. We will encounter them again in the form of Jock Columns, the Long Range Desert Group and the Selby Force.

When circumstances called for larger units, smaller ones were relatively randomly combined and given distinctive names, such as the Western Desert Force, 'W' Force, East Africa Force, Creforce or Habforce. None of these formations was very effective, and these poorly thought-out methods of organization led to heavy losses of experienced officers and men. (43: 38)

In early 1942, after Operation *Crusader*, one of the major battles in North Africa, it was decided for unclear reasons that the division, as an autonomous combat unit, was too large to operate in the desert. (16: 24) The solution, following the success of the German Kampfgruppen, was sought in so-called 'Brigade Groups'. The problem was that the organizational background, doctrine and resulting preconditions of the Kampfgruppen were not understood by the British. The effect was that mutual cooperation came under even more pressure and the artillery, the British forces' most effective arm, was divided among these new units. The Brigade Groups were therefore not a success.

Later in the same year, another organizational variant was tried: infantry units were housed in static fortifications, so-called 'boxes', with a mobile tank reserve behind the front. In practice, these 'boxes' were bypassed by the Germans and cleared one by one, whereupon the frontally attacking British tanks, deployed in small units, were repulsed by a concentration of tanks, artillery and anti-tank guns. (3: 205–6)

Montgomery definitively put an end to discussions about structure by adhering to those basic laws of tactics and organization which the British Army mastered well. He attached great value to established organizational and hierarchical structures and saw little benefit in the less than transparent ad hoc structures of the preceding period. He also realized that the British Army in many respects did not have the qualities of the German forces. He refused to play Rommel's game with his mobile way of waging war: broad outflanking manoeuvres with independent units and objectives located deep behind the front. He concentrated instead on building a solid, static defence line, followed by relatively static battles and frontal attacks. Units had to be deployed under central leadership and direction and, in his view, a preponderance of people and materiel was necessary to guarantee victory. This was a way of fighting that best suited British capabilities. (35: 209, 28: 119, 43: 24 & 39, 47: 129)

Other structural elements

As we have seen, the General Staff played a prominent role in the German Army as a centre of knowledge. If the various units tried to develop their own doctrines or Standard Operating Procedures, the General Staff and the staff officer corps ensured that they still adhered to the general standard.

Such a structure was lacking in the British Army. It did not develop an overall doctrine or philosophy, and officers remained 'trapped' in the regimental system, lacking a common frame of reference in the field of command. There was also no in-house staff training for officers. This contributed to the frequently observed low level of training and understanding among British officers (16: 31).

During the Second World War a structure of staff officers emerged within larger units, headed by a Chief of Staff (COS). This officer was responsible for the administrative dimensions of his unit and could represent his commander at meetings. The commander himself could then focus on the main tasks, no longer bothered with administrative detail. This structure, which was often created on personal initiative, was not common and was not present throughout the organization. Montgomery, for example, introduced the COS structure to the 21st Army Group. In Montgomery's view, the COS had an administrative and supportive role: he, as commander, made all the plans and made the decisions, and the COS would then work things out in more detail. (16: 34)

Montgomery further divided his headquarters into a Main Headquarters and a Tactical Headquarters, from which he led the fighting. His position close to the front differed from that of his predecessors, who were often hundreds of kilometres behind it. He also positioned his headquarters next to that of the RAF in order to optimize cooperation with Air Marshal Tedder.

Another not unimportant element of the British Army was the lack of unity in leadership. Instead, command at strategic level was often conducted by a committee in which the three commanders-in-chief of land, sea and air forces each had an equal input, and the Army Commander-in-Chief had no decisive vote. Orders from this level were often seen at the tactical or lower level as suggestions about which everyone could have their own opinion. The resulting differences in interpretation led to a lack of coordination and concentration within and between units. Battle reports also show that, especially in the period we examine in the following chapters, at operational level the various arms (infantry, artillery and cavalry) were under their own command and operated side by side without any coordination once battle started.

Montgomery put an end to the free interpretation of orders and forced his commanders to operate within the hierarchy. Later in the war, the Americans imposed a Supreme Commander on the British Army. This at least guaranteed unity of leadership within the high command. (16: 34) Lower in the organization, however, coordination between the various units remained a matter of personal initiative, and unity in leadership was sometimes hard to find.

Another result of British forces being spread over large parts of the world was the linking of command structures to geographical areas rather than to military units. There were Commanders-in-Chief for the Mediterranean, India and South-East Asia. In addition to a military function, these men also had a political and administrative role. These political and administrative tasks were often very time-consuming and meant that military substructures were created in each region or country to manage military affairs. This resulted in a cumbersome and less than dynamic method of command. In addition, the deployment of troops was assessed against the 'grand strategy' of the region, which had much broader political and strategic implications. For example, at the end of 1940 the successful advance of British troops to Tripoli was aborted by Wavell, C-in-C Mediterranean, because they were needed for an intervention in Greece, which was threatened by the Axis powers. Making these types of strategic decision was part of the already overloaded brief of the C-in-C. (16: 38)

Men, teams and training

One of the important recurring themes in descriptions of the British Army in both world wars is the low level of training and education of both men and officers. The lack of a clear command concept and doctrine meant that training programmes were developed in practice by the regiments themselves, based on their own insight and experience. Some regiments developed excellent training programmes, others took unrealistic approaches. This resulted in a regimental and personal approach and therefore a high degree of inconsistency in training systems and the level of final qualifications. Common principles and assessment framework were lacking. (28: 112)

The fundamental weakness in the training of officers and men identified in the First World War was not addressed in the interwar period, as is evident from the complaints of various commanders in this period. For example, Major General Hobart, Commander of the Mobile Division stationed in Egypt in 1938, described the officers of the cavalry regiment which would eventually become the 7th Armoured Division as exceptionally nice people, full of the regimental tradition of swords and spurs, but too easily satisfied with results achieved, and when things went wrong inclined to blamed the technology or the tanks. They spent a lot of time playing sport, polo at the Gezirah Club or tennis. At five o'clock they called it a day, dressed for dinner and enjoyed their social life. (28: 111)

Sport

British officers had a fascination with sport. Officers before the First World War said things like:

> 'I should say [riding] is one of the things that matters most to an officer …Men will always follow an officer who has got the sporting spirit.'

> '[The army before 1914 was] a paradise for men, in which a subaltern thought very little, but kept fit, hunted for two days a week during the season'

An officer who had also served in the German Army complained that German officers had to work mornings and afternoons and had no time for 'the sports, so central to a British officer's life'. The same officer also felt that relations between officers and men in the German Army must have been bad, because 'everybody is being kept so busy that there was no time for sporting activities, which would bring them together.' The emphasis on sport in the British Army is evident, but it should be noted that officers and men often played different sports. German officers and men got to know each other during their intensive training. (41: 166)

Montgomery, regarded as an excellent trainer, confirmed this image when describing the state of the Eighth Army upon taking command: 'The condition of the Eight Army … was almost unbelievable …Gross mismanagement, faulty command and bad staff work.' Divisions were split into small parties across the desert, tanks were not concentrated, the riflemen had forgotten how to fire in a concentrated manner.

And after the Second World War, Liddell Hart noted how a divisional commander had been shocked by the results of two years training of the 44th, 51st and 56th Divisions in England. Another division, the 50th, had, he said, learned nothing at all during two years in North Africa: 'If I told you what I had seen myself among these divisions, you would not believe it. It was nothing to leave the tanks to hold a position at night and retire the infantry – for a rest? Too dangerous? – and let the enemy infiltrate back and take the position.' (28: 126)

The low level of training and education was clearly one of the fundamental and most persistent weaknesses of the British Army.

Recruitment and selection

We have previously seen that the recruitment and selection of recruits was mainly a matter for the regiments, with a regional focus. This system changed during the Second World War due to shortages of men. As a result, the boundaries between regiments became increasingly blurred, and the recruitment and selection system was forced to be reorganized by the Adjutant General of CIGS, Sir Ronald Adam, much against the wishes of the regiments. Recruits were first received in the General Service Corps, where their knowledge and skills were tested to gain an idea of which part of the armed forces they would be best suited to. They were then assigned to the different regiments. Only functional requirements played a role, no longer regional origin. In this way, a general assessment framework was created, to better guarantee that the right man was in the right place and the available manpower was optimally distributed among the various units. (43: 213)

Training

The Germans attached great importance to good and realistic training. Before the First World War, a German professional soldier received more training in two years than a British professional soldier did in four. (41: 162) One reason for this may have been that the battalions of a German regiment remained in the same place, while British battalions rotated, one (training) battalion stationed at home and the other overseas. There was a high turnover in these latter units, due to tropical diseases, and this led to a constant coming and going of troops, which disrupted training. (41: 99) British training was characterized by an emphasis on keeping uniforms and weapons in order, marching with the regiment's band, serving officers in the mess, keeping the barracks clean and other such 'housekeeping' activities. These things were important in the (often tropical) climate where battalions were deployed, which placed high demands on maintenance and cleanliness. In addition, marching with the band and outward military display clearly fitted the mission of an imperial army, to 'show the flag'. However, all these activities took a lot of time and meant that troops were rarely able to practise together at full strength. (41: 163)

In addition, British units were continually asked to provide personnel for household tasks in the regiment or at headquarters and bases. The Germans tried to limit these types of activity as much as possible in order to focus fully on training. British reservists, who would later form the bulk of the British Expeditionary Force in 1914, also received relatively little training after their discharge from service compared to their German counterparts. This lack of training meant that the British soldiers had to be constantly told what to do; in other words, they had to be led in a very directive manner.

As the British Army grew in size in the early months of the First World War, the quality of training correspondingly deteriorated, due to shortages of equipment and the

Confrontation at Landrecies

On 25 August 1914 the Germans attacked at Landrecies. The commander of a company of the 3rd Coldstream Guards ordered his men to fire in volleys. 'The fire-commander whistled and then gave the word of command, on which the men emptied their magazines into the darkness ahead. The Germans quickly got into the way of this. At the sound of the whistle they rushed to cover and as soon as the burst of fire was over they began to work forward again.' (43: 165)

lack of sufficiently experienced officers and non-commissioned officers. The emphasis in training was mainly on drill and marching, much less on learning to operate in combat situations or taking the initiative on the battlefield. (16: 16)

The British and French had their own perception of German training before the First World War. They imagined it to be rigid and often inhumane, while in reality the emphasis was on self-motivation (*Innere Führung*); the German soldier was regarded as a thinking person with his own feelings. (41: 56 & 99) German training of recruits was functional, focused on what the soldier would actually need in combat.

Officers and non-commissioned officers

What applied to the men also applied to non-commissioned officers and officers. For example, a British captain was expected to command a company, whereas we have seen that German officers were expected to be able to lead at one level above their usual command. A major, who usually commanded a battalion, was expected to be able to command a regiment consisting of three battalions. These differences only really came into play when officer losses mounted during the First World War; the Germans were able to fall back on their well-trained officer corps, most officers taking on higher positions than their rank suggested. For instance, it was common for a captain to lead a battalion. The British, however, were at a disadvantage from the start and encountered increasing problems during the course of the war. (41: 108)

With regard to the British non-commissioned officers, it was stated that only after approximately five years did they reach a level comparable to that of German non-

Loss of officers

According to the British Official History of the Great War, the loss of officers had major consequences for the fighting capacity of units. 'When British troops lost their officers, they were … apt to fall back, not because they were beaten but because they did not know what to do and expected to receive fresh orders. Perhaps the large numbers of officers commissioned and the fact that a sergeant rarely held command of a platoon for more than a few days lessened the prestige of the commissioned officer.' (41: 158) The Germans made similar observations during the Second World War. Due to the strict command structure, the great dependence on officers and the lack of training in using their own initiative, British attacks quickly faltered after officers were wounded or killed.

The Germans clearly recognized this weakness in their opponents. Their evaluations were illuminating, such as those of the German IV Corps in the first month of the Somme Offensive of July 1916: 'The frontal attacks over open ground against a portion of our unshaken infantry, carried out by several English cavalry regiments, which had to retire with heavy losses, give some indication of the tactical know-how of the (British) Higher Command.'

In June 1917, the 44th Regiment, fresh from the Eastern Front, classified the tactical operations of the British infantry as inferior to those of the Russian infantry.

In general, the efforts of the British rank and file were praised, but they were not used intelligently and failed to capitalize on successes – and these observations were repeated in the Second World War. (41: 168)

commissioned officers after two years of training (41: 102). Here, too, the rotation system outlined earlier will undoubtedly have played a role, as did the lack of clear and ambitious job requirements or a good training programme.

Due to the lack of a solid cadre of non-commissioned officers, officers were forced, for example, to lead platoons and carry out the work that was done in the German Army by corporals and sergeants. The result of this was even greater losses among officers, resulting in the disappearance of valuable experience and the officer corps being unable to take the necessary next step towards professionalization.

The ultimate result of all this was that many British officers functioned at the level of the German non-commissioned officer. This led to higher commanders sometimes having to intervene at four levels below them ('four down') due to officers being insufficiently qualified.

The rapid growth of the British Army after 1914 also meant that knowledge and experience at higher levels in the organization were greatly diluted. The number of officers with a degree from the Staff Colleges of Camberley and Quetta before the First World War was 447, too few to fill all staff positions since many of them were in leadership roles. By 1918 the number of staff positions had grown to approximately 10,000, now largely filled by officers without staff training. Most of these had been recruited from the wounded, or men who were no longer suitable for front-line service, and they were not trained in complex staff work such as planning logistics, preparing combat actions, and so on.

The lack of adequate training meant that the British Army was unable to operate with sufficient flexibility, and it led to a lack of initiative at the operational level. The British were forced to fall back on rigid, linear formations, which attacked enemy positions head-on in successive waves. Needless to say, these were particularly vulnerable to machine-gun fire, resulting in high casualties. (41: 160) We will see that this mode of operation remained the dominant tactic of the British Army in the Second World War.

The weaknesses outlined above were not recognized and acknowledged after the First World War, and thus there was no adjustment in the education and training of enlisted men, non-commissioned officers and officers.

Moreover, during both the First and Second World Wars, there appeared to be misconceptions about the German Army, which was regarded as a rigid fighting machine with little room for personal initiative and no ability to learn. The British assumed that at some point this system would reach its limits and be shown up as insufficient.

Misconceptions about the German system

A British officer wrote in mid-1915: 'When the war began we were all prepared for the Germans to be successful at first due to their study of war and scientific preparation, but we argued that very soon we should become better than they, not being hidebound by a system. The exact opposite was the case. The Germans with their foundation of solid study and experience have been far quicker to adapt themselves to the changed conditions of war and the emergencies of the situation than either we or the Russians have been – possibly even more so than the French.' (41: 110)

While the German system was regarded by the British as a rigid framework from which no deviation could be permitted, in practice it was a way of thinking and working aimed at learning and adapting. There were similar misconceptions about the supposed limits of the German system in the Second World War.

Due to the lack of a coherent British system of doctrine, tactics and training, great emphasis was placed on the courage and commitment of the ordinary soldier during the Second World War. British soldiers had this in abundance but, as Air Marshall Tedder noted of the period, and as we will see later, there was an 'excess of courage and a deficiency of brains'.

(Non-commissioned) officers and leadership style

To gain insight into British leadership style, we must also fall back on the experience of the First World War. The British used a strictly hierarchical command structure: command was centralized, orders were detailed and the various levels within the organization merely served to transmit orders down the chain. The reason for this was the previously discussed low level of training and education of officers and men. (16: 17) Central control by the Army and Corps command led to a high degree of inflexibility and rigidity at the level of the combat units. Deployment of units was determined 'three down', three levels below one's own, which meant in practice, for example, that within a division the location and deployment of companies was determined by the divisional commander. In comparison, German officers were urged to limit themselves to 'one down' and only as a last resort to interfere with a level lower in the organization. British corps and division commanders were thus saddled with a great deal of information, and units were sometimes literally not allowed to move a step without approval from central command. Units were given limited goals in the form of written orders, which they had to follow at all costs. (41: 140–2) Due to the amount of administrative work it faced, the Army's leadership was unable to evaluate combat experiences or develop new tactics. No ideas were developed about the role of innovations such as the tank and the fighter plane, or the cooperation between these new weapons and infantry and artillery, which was simply organized on an ad hoc basis lower in the hierarchy. (16: 17)

This centralized method of management also related to the deployment of reserve units. Here the rule was 'two down', which meant that, for example, a corps commander could have a brigade from each division under his command. As a result, the divisional commander could only deploy two of the three brigades at his disposal. Since these brigades were deployed on the front line, he could not deploy the reserve brigade in the event of a sudden opportunity or crisis without first obtaining permission from the corps commander. His only deployable reserve was the reserve battalion, which he had direct access to on the basis of the 'two down' reserve system. This system greatly limited the flexibility of the British Army. As long as operations ran smoothly there were no problems, but when decisions had to be made quickly, the long lines of communication to and from corps headquarters prevented a timely and adequate response (if these long lines of communication were functioning at all during combat actions and the corps headquarters could still distinguish between main and secondary issues).

In the German system, responsibility for the deployment of reserve units was decentralized, and commanders were able to respond quickly to unexpected situations. There were no long lines of communication, much was left to individual initiative and officers were expected to respond to situations as they arose.

There were many examples in the First World War of the British command and communication system losing the initiative or causing major losses because all actions that deviated from the agreed pattern had to be submitted to the corps commander. In one case, a brigade commander was unable to stop an attack by his own battalions, even though it was based on outdated orders from corps headquarters. Corps commanders ensured that absolute obedience was one of the central themes of command and that deviating from orders did not occur to officers' minds. In other words, 'obedience is far more important than initiative.' (16: 52) Considering that for a significant part of the First World War British doctrine was limited to 'attack at any cost', the effect of this on troop morale can only be imagined.

In addition, it has also been suggested that British commanders believed only strict orders could drive what they saw as a culturally degenerate working class, the soldiers in the trenches, forward towards the enemy. (41: 148)

A class-bound society

From descriptions of officers, men, their relationships and the chain of command, it is clear that the British class system was reflected faithfully in the British Army. The division between officers on the one hand and non-commissioned officers and men on the other reflected the gulf in British society. This is expressed succinctly in the comment of an officer: 'In England the salute is intended to mark the fact that the officer is acknowledged to belong to that class whose hereditary function it is to command.' A German who served in Great Britain with the British Home Army complained to Liddell Hart in 1942 about 'the tremendous gulf between officers and men ...Our C.O. – and we have quite a few already – never says a personal word to us, nor does even a subaltern.' (28: 124)

It is questionable whether leadership style changed much in the period between the two world wars. There are no indications of this in the literature, so we can assume that no fundamental changes occurred. Analyses of actions in the Second World War mention problems in the chain of command and control as well as lack of initiative on the part of officers in combat situations. The reasons given are the rapid growth of the British Army after 1939 and its level of training and education – German officers were trained to use their initiative in unexpected situations, British officers much less so. The question of whether there was a different command concept on the German side, with an emphasis on decentralization versus the British centralization of command, is not addressed in the literature. The problems identified in the command structure indicate that the British Army was still committed to this centralized and hierarchical style of management – and, in Rommel's words, 'any delay in one's own actions can lead to an acceleration of the enemy's.' (16: 52)

This hierarchy was also reflected in the relationship between officers and non-commissioned officers and between all officers and men. Training, as we have seen, took place at regimental level and while it stimulated *esprit de corps* and team building, it also reflected the class distinctions within British society. Unlike the German system, it also hindered the promotion of competent non-commissioned officers with combat experience to the rank of officer. It was also unclear whether and to what extent non-commissioned officers were involved in the preparation of combat actions.

No use was made of the valuable experience of many non-commissioned officers to raise the level of the officer corps, despite the fact that the British Army had an

The position of the non-commissioned officer
German evaluation of fighting in Italy in 1944 clearly illustrates a number of weak points in British organization and provides guidance for their own units: 'British attack formations were split into many small units, led by officers. NCOs were rarely well versed in the plan of attack, so that if an officer was wounded or killed, the NCOs were unable to act in line with the original plan. The result was that in rapidly changing situations, the junior officers showed too little flexibility and initiative. For example, when an objective was achieved, the enemy failed to exploit it and generally dug in defensively. The conclusion is: try to eliminate the opponent's officers and take over the initiative.' (28: 127)

excellent cadre of non-commissioned officers throughout the Second World War, as the Germans confirmed. They noted after Operation *Crusader*: 'British troops generally fought excellently ...Officers were brave and self-sacrificing, but developed little of their own initiative. NCOs were good across the board.' The lack of initiative repeatedly led to breakthroughs not being exploited. Such observations fit seamlessly with the experiences of the First World War and show that the British command concept still experienced the same fundamental weaknesses.

There was rarely a personal note in conversation between British officers and their men, while in the German Army, as we have seen, building a personal relationship with subordinates was of great importance. (28: 124) Senior officers also seemed not really interested in, had no knowledge of or were unwilling to use their own experiences to determine where the fundamental weaknesses in command or tactical operations lay. (28: 124) As we have seen, they were not encouraged by the High Command to exchange ideas about this, probably because the High Command itself simply did not see the problem. This led to personal views on leadership style and the interpretation of one's own place in the hierarchy being decisive for the way in which orders were handled.

As we have seen, Montgomery put such idiosyncrasies to bed. Although he allowed everyone to contribute their own ideas to preparatory discussions, once he had made a decision it had to be strictly implemented. The days of non-binding meetings involving everyone, differences in command and differing views on the meaning of orders were over. In his view, only through a directive style of leadership and hard training could the Eighth Army rid itself of its weaknesses and become the fighting force that he had in mind. (34: 209)

In the later phases of the Second World War, the development of personal initiative was completely subordinated to the deployment of equipment: the Allied predominance in all areas made initiative and flexibility, the essential prerequisites for seizing opportunities after breaking through the enemy line, largely redundant. Few officers and non-commissioned officers showed the required initiative and perseverance, and the available capabilities were not sufficiently appreciated and used during the later campaigns of the Second World War. (28: 129)

Morale

What applied to the German Army must have equally applied to the British, so it can only have been personal courage and high morale which compensated for all the weaknesses described above, especially in the first half of the Second World War. This is indeed what emerges from all descriptions of combat. No matter how badly things went wrong, for whatever reason, the British managed time and time again to avoid worse results by showing courage and commitment. The phlegmatic way with which setbacks and hardships were faced was characteristic. The limited space allocated to the subject here is therefore inversely proportional to its importance.

All in all, the British Army in 1941 did not have a clear and coherent vision of the organization in terms of its mission. This can be explained by the fact that the mission of an imperial army translated into different visions depending on place and time, expressed as 'Think global, act local'. And the British Army was particularly successful at this. Only in situations in which the German and British met in a larger context, such as the First and Second World Wars, did the lack of an overarching vision on the use of weapons, training of men, style of leadership, etc., become clear. As the victors of the First World War, there was no need for the British to indulge in critical reflection, and it was implicitly assumed that the methods and techniques of this war formed a good basis for future conflicts. On closer inspection, this appears not to have been the case; the British persisted in a number of mistakes made during the First World War and thus in 1941 they were looking at all levels for an answer to how to respond to current events. As we will see, this search took place in an unstructured manner, which meant that the British Army was constantly in danger of lagging behind in vision and command concept during this period.

Having looked at both combatants, we will now focus on the confrontation between these two fundamentally different armies in North Africa.

Chapter 2

Rommel and the First Confrontation

2.1 The strategic importance of North Africa

Why North Africa? To understand the strategic importance of the region, we must go back several hundred years. Britain had been a great power in the Mediterranean for centuries, with the aim of controlling its adversaries Spain and France and keeping the routes open to and from the British empire in Asia. Blockade of enemy ports was generally the weapon of choice, and the Royal Navy had a substantial Mediterranean fleet and bases in Gibraltar and Malta.

With the opening of the Suez Canal in the late nineteenth century the position changed: the Mediterranean now had an eastern entrance in addition to its western one. Gibraltar guarded the western entrance, and treaties with Egypt, which allowed Britain to establish military and naval bases, ensured the eastern entrance was secure. During the First World War, the offensive against Turkey's Middle Eastern possessions was launched from these bases, eventually leading to the collapse of the Ottoman Empire. As a result, British influence then extended from Egypt further north into Palestine and Transjordan.

The other important player in the North African conflict, Italy, also had a number of African colonies: Somalia, Eritrea and Libya. In the period between the two world wars, geographers of the Royal Engineers mapped the entire later North African battlefield, and troops in Egypt trained in desert warfare, so the British were at least partly prepared. The geographers did a good job, and captured British maps were later much appreciated by the Germans. British military expeditions were also sent out during these years to examine terrain and test equipment.

If war broke out, supply routes would be a problem for both sides. The British could try to ship material to Egypt via Gibraltar – a supply line easily threatened by the Italians and by U-Boats – or choose the longer but safer route round the Cape of Good Hope and through the Suez Canal. The Italians had relatively short supply lines between Sicily and Tripoli and they possessed a strong navy. However, they had to face the threat of equally strong British naval forces in the Mediterranean.

In 1941 a new player emerged in North Africa in the form of Germany. The German Afrika Korps arrived after the Italians failed to drive the British out of Egypt and realize the ambition of adding it to their empire. The Italians' campaign ended in fiasco at the end of 1940, and a final defeat could only be prevented by the deployment of German troops in early 1941. This was not part of a German 'grand strategy', just a short-term measure to prevent a rapid defeat of their Italian allies. However, when Rommel successfully took advantage of the opportunities presented to him and time and again cornered the British, the *Oberkommando der Wehrmacht* (OKW) began to see further possibilities, the most ambitious one being to advance from the Middle East through Persia to the Caucasus to make contact with Army Group Süd in southern Russia. The aim of the British was to maintain the age-old balance of power in the Mediterranean and eventually to invade Europe from North Africa. At the start of hostilities in North Africa, General Wavell was the Commander-in-Chief Middle East, responsible for a large area consisting of Egypt, Sudan, Palestine, Cyprus, Transjordan, Aden, British Somalia and the Persian Gulf. The British could thus launch an offensive in every direction: in the north to the Soviet Union via Iraq and Persia, in the north-west to Turkey, in the south to Arabia.

2.2 The geography of North Africa

Although the war in North Africa is often described as a desert war, giving Rommel his nickname of the 'Desert Fox', much of the area was actually not desert in the true sense of the word. The battles in the years to come would take place mainly in a strip of land about 60km wide and 2,000km long, sandwiched between the sea and the barren interior. The latter was true desert, the ground consisting of firm, fine gravel covered by sand or a mixture of gravel and sand, interspersed with patches of deep sand and salt marshes. It is an undulating, steppe-like terrain with ridges between 4 and 20 metres high. These sometimes rise gradually, but can also be very steep. Then there are valleys in which rivers once flowed, the *wadis*. The bottom of these consists of dry clay, and the tops of the hills are bare and rocky.

Vehicles used wide tracks, called *trighs* or pistes, which connected the various settlements in the area. The coast is marked by dunes, with salt marshes beyond which are usually dry. Only at Tobruk, Bardia, and Sollum is the coast rocky, with *wadis* which were sometimes impassable. The coastal region, however, was a favourite place for troops to camp, since it was easy to dig in and reach water. Further inland the desert began, an area without vegetation in which it was possible to move relatively quickly across the hard, sandy subsoil, although there are also dry riverbeds, ridges and sand-filled *wadis* that are very difficult to traverse. Further south still, the real desert begins, in which large troop movements were virtually impossible.

Military activities were thus limited to a relatively narrow strip along the coast and the northern part of the desert. The desert section permitted faster troop movements than the coastal strip, except where the Via Balbia, an asphalt road, connected some settlements. (45: 17) Along this road there was an overhead telephone line to Barcia, as well as various water points.

The climate is very warm, with temperatures in June, July and August occasionally reaching 60°C during the day, and cold nights with temperatures well below freezing. In the months of November, December and January the temperature is more moderate, 30° during the day, but still well below freezing at night. In winter there are also rare rain showers, which can start suddenly and be very heavy. Troop movements were virtually impossible during rain. There are also sandstorms, a regular phenomenon at all seasons. They usually last three days and they halted all activities on the ground and in the air, since it is often impossible to see more than three metres ahead. The climate, though relatively healthy on the coast, nevertheless took its toll on the troops, with conditions such as jaundice and dysentery. The area was, of course, very thinly inhabited, and consequently there were very few civilian casualties.

2.3 Rommel

It sometimes seems that the war in North Africa was mainly concerned with the campaigns of Rommel. He left his mark on the actions of both Germans and British from start to finish. But who was this great general?

Erwin Rommel was born in 1891 in Heidelheim, Württemberg, the son of a teacher. He was an easygoing, unremarkable child with, like his father, an interest in maths and science. He took more after his mother, Helene von Lutz, daughter of a local dignitary, than his formal and distant father. In addition to Erwin, the family consisted of two other sons and a daughter. As he grew older, Erwin became more interested in sport and developed into an intelligent, hard-working student. He also possessed unbridled energy, as we shall see in his actions in North Africa.

As he matured, typical Swabian characteristics such as stability, cleverness and common sense became increasingly apparent in him. These, combined with his quick reactions, flair and problem-solving ability, were the ingredients that would make him such a successful commander. After an attempt to build a career in the fledgling aviation industry at the Zeppelinwerke in Friedrichshafen, he chose the Army. The new requirements for officers, namely intelligence and a good education, fitted Rommel well, and he applied to the Army in 1910. Because there was no place with the artillery and engineers – his first choices due to his technical qualifications – he was posted to the 124th Württemberger Infantry Regiment. After first serving as a non-commissioned officer, he made the transition to the officer corps – the normal course of events in the German Army, as we have seen – successfully completing his training as an officer in March 1911. He was then admitted to the Kriegschule (War Academy) in Danzig for a further eight months of training, which he completed successfully and then returned to his regiment as a promising young officer. In Danzig he met Lucie Maria Mollin, to whom he became unofficially engaged and married in 1918. In all the years that he was away from home he wrote almost every day about what he experienced and what moved him.

For the next two years Rommel trained hard with his regiment, but just before the outbreak of the First World War he was transferred to the 4th Battery of the 49th Feldartillerie Regiment. This posting was short-lived, however, and to his delight he returned to his own regiment on his birthday and marched with his men to war. In the First World War, Rommel distinguished himself by his energy, his original approach and his constant presence in those places where fighting was fiercest. After leading several companies of the 124th Regiment and being promoted to Oberleutnant, he was transferred at the end of 1915 to the newly established Königliche Württemberg Gebirgs- und Schneeschuhbattalion (mountain and snow-shoe battalion). This elite unit made up of young veterans was specially created to meet the demands of fighting in the Vosges Mountains. Rommel was given command of the 3rd Company, consisting of 200 men. After being deployed to the Western Front in early 1916, the Gebirgsbataillon rotated between Romania and France in the following years. Rommel, having proved himself a capable and brave officer, was given command of three rifle and two machine-gun companies in 1917. Finally, the Gebirgsbataillon was deployed to the Italian front in Austrian Carinthia. There Rommel would receive the Pour la Merite – the highest German military award for personal bravery – for the capture of Monte Majur, a key position on the Italian front. Rommel's detachment had managed to infiltrate the Italian lines undetected and take the position in three days of fighting, capturing 9,000 men along with eighty-one pieces of artillery. To top it all, he and six men managed to persuade the entire garrison of the city of Longarone to surrender. After this stunning victory, Rommel became an assistant staff officer to one of the headquarters, although his heart remained with his men of the Gebirgsbataillon.

Between the two world wars

After the First World War, Rommel was an excellent candidate for one of the 4,000 officer positions in the new *Reichswehr*. Von Seeckt had had the foresight to determine that in addition to leadership capabilities, every officer also had to be a good instructor, with a view to the day when the *Reichswehr* was able to expand again. In 1921 Rommel was given command of a company of the 13th Infantry Regiment of the *Reichsheer* in Stuttgart. For the following nine years, now a captain, he was attached to this regiment, the last four years as an instructor. In these latter years he wrote *Infanterie greift an* (The Infantry Attack), which was finally published in 1937. The book contained a number of case studies based on his experiences of the First World War, together with analysis and recommendations for each.

In October 1933 Rommel was promoted to Oberstleutnant (Lieutenant Colonel) and was given command of the 3rd Jägerbataillon of the 17th Infantry Regiment at Goslar in the Harz Mountains. For the next two years he forged his battalion into a unit that could survive in all weather conditions and was at home in the mountains. This happy period ended in 1935 with a posting for three years as an instructor at the Kriegsschule in Potsdam, where the new officers of the rapidly growing army were trained – a force which at the end of 1937 already had 550,000 men under arms. Rommel, with his experience and ideas, was much admired by his students.

His first meeting with Hitler followed in the summer of 1936, when Rommel was responsible for Hitler's security during the party gathering in Nuremberg. Hitler complimented Rommel on his efforts, especially in dealing with an incident involving a number of party bosses. His reputation with Hitler was undoubtedly enhanced by the publication of *Infanterie greift an*: the Führer, with his own experience of the First World War, must have recognized much of what Rommel described. And there was more, of course: both men were self-made and both disliked the aristocratic elite which had thwarted the careers of many lower-ranking officers. In addition, it was Hitler who had made the expansion of the *Reichswehr* possible, the organization with which Rommel identified, and had put Germany back on the world stage. All this resulted in a bond of mutual recognition between the two men in the following years, which gave Rommel a much greater freedom of movement than other leading figures in the military. Hitler then appointed Rommel as liaison officer between the *Kriegsministerium* (Ministry of War) and the Hitler Youth.

Irreconcilable differences between Rommel and the Reichsjugendsführer Baldur von Schirach about the education and training of the Hitler Youth led Rommel to return to the Kriegschule in Potsdam in 1938. Just before the end of his three years there, Rommel became the commander of the *Führerbegleitungsbataillon* (battalion accompanying the Führer) during the occupation of the Sudetenland in March 1938, a prestigious appointment. After successfully completing this tour, he became head of the Kriegschule of Wiener Neustadt, and would twice more lead the *Führerbegleitungsbataillon* in 1939.

The outbreak of the Second World War

Rommel.

Now promoted to Generalmajor, Rommel and his battalion were tasked with protection of the *Führerzug*, the train that served as Hitler's headquarters during the campaign in Poland. The personal relationship between Rommel and Hitler blossomed in this campaign; they often had lunch together, at which they discussed all kinds of things. Rommel suggested that he would like to have an operational command, preferably a tank division. There was considerable resistance to this request within the Army's high command, given Rommel's infantry background, but Hitler personally decided otherwise. On 6 February 1940 Rommel was give command of the 7th Panzer Division in Bad Godesberg in succession to Lieutenant General Stumme, whom we will encounter again in North Africa. He immediately started a thorough training programme, with an emphasis on practice with live ammunition, fast manoeuvring, discipline during road movements and rapid and efficient two-way communication. It was with this division that Rommel would make his mark on the Western Front in the summer to come.

The 7th Panzer Division, together with the 15th under Hartlieb, formed the XVth Panzer Corps led by Hoth. This corps was assigned to advance through the northern part of the Ardennes to the Meuse between Givet and Namur during May 1940. After the start of the offensive on 9 May, Rommel successfully led his troops through the Ardennes to reach the Meuse on 12 May. Since all the bridges had been blown, the Germans had to cross the river in rubber boats to build a bridgehead on the other bank. The crossing, with Rommel in one of the leading boats, was successful, and soon the Germans were able to build a temporary bridge. They later crossed the river in two other places as well, forcing the commander of the French Ninth Army to fall back to a defensive line further south.

Events then followed in quick succession: the German armoured troops broke through all French and British defences and surged south, with the 7th Division often in the lead. Rommel himself was almost always found in the vanguard and often took personal charge of operations. His troops were advancing so quickly that they became known as the Geister (ghost) Division. During the following month the Geister Division crossed France rapidly, an advance that ended on 25 June in Cherbourg. In six extraordinarily successful weeks of combat the 7th Division had taken many prisoners of war and captured an impressive amount of materiel,* while losing 682 officers and men killed, 1,646 wounded and 296 missing. The division also lost forty-two tanks.

Rommel had established his reputation as a fearless general, both with his soldiers, who adored him, and with the public. He was a commander who stayed close to his men and was often to be found where the battle was fiercest. The OKW, however, saw him differently: he was considered to be a headstrong officer who often disregarded orders from above when he spotted opportunities on the battlefield. Later, in North Africa, this

* 98,000 French and English prisoners of war, 277 pieces of field artillery, 64 anti-tank guns, 458 tank, 116 armoured cars, 4,000 trucks and more than 300 buses.

reputation would be confirmed, leading to ongoing tension between him and the Italian and German High Command. For the rest of 1940 Rommel remained commander of the 7th Division, now stationed in Bordeaux, from where he was summoned to Hitler's headquarters in early February 1941 to be given a new assignment: Operation *Sonnenblume*, to support the demoralized Italian forces in North Africa.

2.4 The Italian prelude

After Italy's declaration of war in June 1940, skirmishes promptly broke out on the Libyan-Egyptian border. The Italian attacks were however, parried successfully, and the area remained quiet in the following months. The Italians now turned their attention to British Somaliland, which was captured after a short campaign. Enthused by this feat of arms, Mussolini ordered Marshal Graziani to launch an offensive from Libya against the British in Egypt, with Alexandria as its ultimate goal. Despite strong protests from Graziani, the offensive got underway on 23 September. After advancing 100km into Egypt, the advance came to a standstill, and the Italians started to dig in around Sidi Barrani. This was it for the time being, and the Italians remained stationary for the next three months. Churchill, meanwhile, was annoyed by the inaction of Wavell, C-in-C Middle East, but Wavell had built up his own forces during this period and waited for the right moment to strike. On 6 December he launched an offensive with his 'Thirty Thousand' – XIX Corps – against the much larger Italian force and drove them out of Egypt and almost out of Tripolitania, the eastern part of Libya. In nearly ten weeks, the Italians were pushed back 800km, and at the beginning of 1941 the British were at the gates of Tripoli. O'Connor was the successful commander of XIX Corps, which consisted of Australian, British and Indian troops. His small force had defeated the entire Italian Tenth Army, consisting of four corps. Against British losses of 500 killed, 1,373 wounded and 55 missing, 130,000 Italians had been taken prisoner, along with 400 tanks and 1,300 pieces of artillery.

The British gained experience during this campaign of a number of tactics which they would later use in their confrontation with the Germans. For instance, they learned to how use a frontal attack with tanks and infantry to achieve a breakthrough, followed by a pursuit in Cruiser tanks to cut off the retreating enemy.* In the next chapter we will examine this tactic further.

In addition, they frequently deployed so-called Jock Columns, mobile units made up of armoured cars, guns on trucks and infantry in trucks. These columns made rapid actions possible along the flanks and in the hinterland of the Italians. The conflict in North Africa would not have the place in history it has today if Wavell had been given more time. However, for the British there was a much greater strategic threat emerging in the north: Greece was threatened with conquest by the Germans, and Wavell had to redeploy his experienced troops to that front. Churchill sent Wavell the following telegram on 10 February: 'Extent of Italian defeat at Benghazi makes it seem possible that Tripoli might yield to a small force if dispatched without delay.' This interrupted the British advance, giving an opening to the newcomer: Rommel.

* Even then, some tank squadron commanders had the unstoppable tendency to engage the enemy immediately instead of waiting for artillery support. This will be discussed in more detail in the following chapters.

In early February, Rommel was called to Berlin, to learn that he had been selected to lead two divisions that would be deployed to North Africa as part of Operation *Sonnenblum*. This was intended to keep the Italians within the Axis despite their previous defeats. The German armed forces would serve as a *Sperrverband* (blocking formation) to prevent the British from taking Tripoli. Strategically, North Africa was of minor importance to the Germans. The divisions Rommel was given command of were the 5th Leichte (later the 21st Panzer) and the 15th Panzer. He was titled *Befehlhaber der Deutsche Truppen in Libyan* (Commander of German troops in Libya) and was technically subordinate to the Italian General Italo Gariboldi, but he had stipulated that in case of disagreement he could communicate directly with the OKW in Berlin. Rommel's orders were clear: prevent the British from advancing further west and conquering Tripoli, and recapture Cyrenaica from the British after the arrival of all units began in May.

2.5 The position of the British

The German plan to come to the aid of their Axis allies had not escaped the notice of the British. They were, thanks to Ultra, able to decipher the German Enigma codes – even if not completely – and managed to retrieve details of Operation *Sonnenblum*. Churchill's attention, however, was focussed on the situation in Greece, which on political grounds had to be supported at any costs. As a result, the 6th Australian Division was redeployed from the Middle East to Greece and replaced by the 9th Australian Division under General Morshead. One of the three brigades of this division became stuck in Tobruk on its way to the front through lack of transport; this brigade would later play an important role in the siege of the city. The other two brigades were stationed east of Benghazi.

The 7th Armoured Division was transferred to Egypt to rest and receive new equipment. It was replaced by one half of the 2nd Armoured Division, the other half being sent directly from Britain to Greece. The Support Group of this 2nd Armoured Division, however, was stationed in Mersa Brega, while the 3rd Armoured Brigade, the only armoured element of this division, was north-east of Mersa Brega. This Brigade consisted of one regiment with light reconnaissance tanks, one with captured Italian Carro Armato M-13 tanks and one with Cruiser tanks. This regiment only arrived in mid-March, with their Cruiser tanks in poor mechanical condition after they had been forced to travel by road from El Adem to the front on their own tracks, instead of on special transporters. This 2nd Armoured Division was led by Major General Gambie-Parry, who had previously been head of the military mission in Greece and had no recent combat experience.

This was the 'Western Desert Force'. All in all, O'Connor commanded a relatively small, dispersed fighting force, a part of which had poor equipment and no experience in desert warfare. The troops had little transport at their disposal, as a result of which rapid manoeuvres were out of the question and they had to stay close to their depots. The ability to manoeuvre was crucial, given the distances in North Africa: from Tripoli it is 810km to Mersa Brega, 1,000km to Benghazi, 1,250km to Tobruk and 1,785km to El Alamein.

*Command structure Western Desert Force, January 1941**

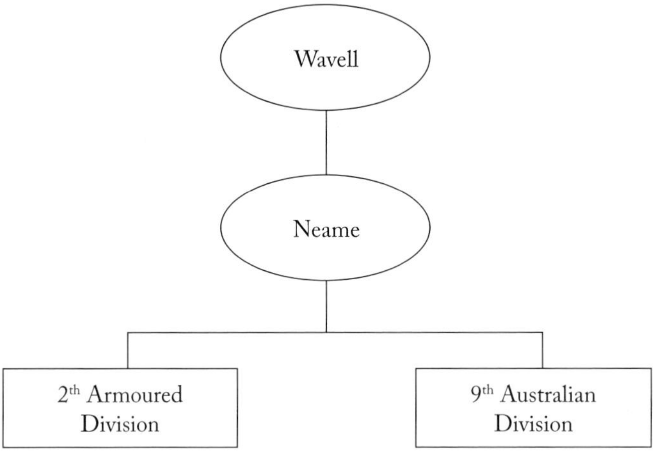

It is clear from this reshuffling of units that Churchill's and Wavell's interest in Libya was waning. When a representative of O'Connor reported at Wavell's headquarters on 10 February he was surprised to see that the maps of Libya had been replaced by maps of Greece. The British assumed that their relatively small remaining force would be able to conquer Tripoli, and the arrival of Rommel in Tripoli a day later did not change that. General O'Connor himself was recalled to Egypt, and General Neame, who had no experience of mechanized warfare, took command of the greatly reduced number of troops. Neame was instructed that in the event of a German attack on Mersa Brega he should save his units and fall back on Benghazi, 225km to the east. He was even permitted to surrender Benghazi, but was told he should keep control of the higher ground east of the city as long as possible. He had to manoeuvre prudently, although reinforcements were expected in late May. But things would not work out as expected.

Campaigns in East Africa

While the conflict in North Africa threatened to take on a new dimension, British troops were also active in Italian East Africa, Somalia and Eritrea. On 4 January General Platt advanced from Sudan with the 4th and 5th Indian Divisions into Eritrea. Five days later, General Cunningham with his African and South African units began to advance from Kenya. Platt had to fight hard at Keren, which was captured at the end of March. Cunningham captured Mogadishu on 25 February, Harrar on 25 March and Addis Ababa on 5 April. The two forces then advanced from the north and south to Bamba Alagi, where the Italian commander Aosta surrendered on 16 May.

By making good use of the available men and resources, the British were able once again to defeat a numerically superior adversary, at least on paper. An Italian force of 220,000 men with their materiel was neutralized and a very large area came under

* The 2nd Armoured Division consisted of the 3rd, 4th and 7th Armoured Brigades; only the 3rd was present in North Africa.

The standard Italian medium tank Carro Armato M- 13/40: relatively slow, lightly armed with a 47mm gun and mechanically unreliable. (*Model S. Tsang*)

British control. The success of this East African campaign increased Wavell's authority, but what no one realized was that warfare against the German Army would be a whole new ballgame. (44: 51)

2.6 The arrival of Rommel

On 11 February Rommel landed at Tripoli airport, followed two days later by his first troops. On the afternoon of his arrival Rommel flew in his Fieseler Storch to get a sense of the future battleground – a round trip of 1,000 km (!). In the days that followed he carried out several additional reconnaissance flights. The first German troops were mainly support elements, such as medics, supply units and the battalion responsible for field workshops. Rommel ordered this last battalion to build dummy tanks based on *Kübelwagen* (jeep-like field cars) to make his force appear more powerful.

The first real combat units arrived on 14 February in the form of the reconnaissance battalion and one of the two of anti-tank battalions of the 5th Leichte Division.[*] After a short parade to encourage their Italian allies and the civilian population, these troops were sent to Sirte to serve as a mobile reserve for the Italian units stationed there. Their assignments were:

- Covering the right flank of the Pavia Division, which occupied the heights east of Sirte
- Conducting reconnaissance towards Nofilia and El Agheila together with Italian units

[1] This concerned the 3rd *Aufklärungsabteilung* and the 39th *Panzerjäger Abteilung*

Over the next few days, Italian and German units operated together, and Nofilia was taken without resistance. As we have seen, the Germans attached great importance to obtaining information about the enemy, often by means of 'reconnaissance in force', and during the subsequent days heavily armed reconnaissance units moved deeper into the hinterland. In this way they could test their equipment and gain experience of operating in desert areas.

> Corporal Harry Short of the King's Dragoon Guards was patrolling with his unit of light Marmon-Harrington armoured cars between the fortress of El Agheila and the Marada Oasis, a stretch of 110 kilometres, when he encountered the first German reconnaissance units. Short looked uncertainly westward, where behind the hills a trail of dust was rising – and it was coming nearer …He gave a start and ducked a little, although the clear morning sun was behind his back, when a weird thing hove into distant view: an eight-wheeled armoured reconnaissance vehicle, with an awesome gun. Like a caterpillar in great haste, the elongated vehicle crawled to the top of the hill opposite. There was the soft rumbling of a powerful engine: from under a frame, hefty men wearing peak caps were looking eastward, only to reverse as quickly as they had come. It was an impressive sight, suggesting power and perfection, and it filled Short with apprehension. The whole performance, silent and decisive, had made as un-Italian an impression as possible. (14: 4–5)

The desert was an excellent arena for such mobile and heavily armed reconnaissance units, built around light and heavy *Panzerspähwagen* (armoured scout vehicles). These eight-

The SdKfz 232s were popular reconnaissance vehicles due to their speed, firepower and armour. This example near Agedabia has only been in North Africa for a short time and does not have the characteristic desert camouflage colour. (*Photo LKK*)

wheelers were most impressive, both in appearance and in armour and armament. The reconnaissance units were the ultimate example of *Verbundene Waffen* and could deploy mechanized infantry equipped with mortars, heavy machine guns and artillery. The infantry rode in a mix of *Sonderkraftfahrzeuge* ('special purpose vehicles') such as the SdKfz 251 and 250 armoured personnel carriers. This combination of weapon systems made the reconnaissance units in the desert very mobile and formidable opponents.

Sonderkraftfahrzeuge

The SdKfz 250 and 251 were half-tracks which allowed the infantry and artillery to accompany tanks over difficult terrain and to take full advantage of a breach in the enemy line. It was this innovation that made static war a spectre of the past and opened the door to a more mobile mode of warfare. The most famous of the family was probably the SdKfz 251, specifically developed for the transport of infantry over difficult and hostile terrain. Other SdKfzs served to tow guns and to transport their crews and ammunition.

The first three types of SdKfz, with a tensile load of 5, 8 and 12 tons respectively, were developed in 1932, supplemented in 1936 with a light type of 3 tons and a heavier one of 18.

On different chassis, all kinds of variants of SdKfz were developed, from simple crew vehicles to others with 88mm Flak and other anti-aircraft guns. Their role during this first phase of the conflict is clearly reflected in the actions of the 3rd *Aufklärungsabteilung*, the reconnaissance battalion of the Leichte Division: with their firepower and speed they were always there when a breakthrough had to be forced. We will encounter the 3rd *Aufklärungsabteilung* of the 5th Leichte and later the 33rd *Aufklärungsabteilung* of the 15th Panzer Division in this role many times over the coming months. For these reconnaissance operations, hundreds of miles from the main force, they needed strong communication equipment and powerful aerials, which can be seen on many of the *Panzerspähwagen* in the form of large tubular frames on top. These special conversions were a product of their own field workshops.

It was one of these reconnaissance units which the patrol of the King's Dragoon Guards met on 24 February on the edge of the Nofilia area. Apart from this encounter, the front remained calm for the time being – to Rommel's advantage, since he still lacked tanks. Only between 8–10 March, three weeks after Rommel had set foot ashore, did the first panzer troops of the 5th Leichte Division, the 5th Panzer Regiment,* arrive.

Rommel now discussed his plans to capture El Agheila with Streich, commander of the 5th Leichte Division, who had arrived on 21 February. To that end, from 15 March a German-Italian Kampfgruppe conducted a reconnaissance in force towards Muzuk. The vanguards of this Kampfgruppe covered more than 3,000km (!) deep into the enemy hinterland in a few days.

* This regiment included a total of 25 PzKpfw Is, 45 PzKpfw IIs, 61 PzKpfw IIIs, 25 PzKpfw IVs and additional command tanks, a total force of some 155 tanks.

The 5th Leichte Division (unmotorized)
This division was originally composed mainly of elements of the 3rd Panzer Division. Many vehicles still carried the insignia of this division, a reversed Y with two dashes. The division held a total of 9,300 men. Due to the lack of sufficient production capacity, the Germans were unable to fully motorize and mechanize all divisions and thus created so-called Leichte Divisions: formations that were not (yet) fully equipped with armoured personnel carriers and vehicles such as the SdKfz 251. In addition to a tank regiment, the division had an *Aufklärungsabteilung* (reconnaissance battalion) and two *Panzerjäger Abteilungen* (anti-tank units). The latter had 37mm and 50mm anti-tank guns. The *Flieger Abwehr Abteilung*, however, had the most effective anti-tank guns, in the form of a number of 88mm Flak guns. On 21 October 1941 the 5th Leichte Division was renamed the 21st Panzer Division.

Meanwhile, the Germans also conducted aerial reconnaissance. Henschel 129s operated in their own persistent way, which could even excite admiration from the British:

> First a Henschel 129 reconnaissance aircraft came buzzing about their [the King's Dragoon Guards'] heads – a particularly noisome type, whose pilots had earned grudging admiration by the way they could lurk between dunes to avoid the pom-poms and would suddenly come swooping over the ridges, even having the cheek to chuck hand grenades at the British armoured cars. (14: 31)

On 23 March Streich ordered his *Aufklärungsabteilung* to conduct a definitive reconnaissance towards El Agheila, followed by an order to take the place in a surprise attack. The next day, 24 March, the *Aufklärungsabteilung* attacked the fortress of El Agheila and captured it and the airfield in the early morning hours. Churchill, alarmed by these developments, immediately telegraphed Wavell:

> We are naturally concerned at the rapid German advance to Agheila. It is their habit to push on whenever they are not resisted. I presume you are only waiting for the tortoise [Rommel] to stick his head out far enough before chopping it off. (47: 48)

Wavell replied:

> I have to admit to have taken a considerable risk in Cyrenaica after the capture of Benghazi, in order to provide maximum support to Greece …Result is I am weak in Cyrenaica at present, and no reinforcements of armoured troops, which are the chief requirement, are at present available.(47: 21, 44: 49)

With a war on four fronts – North Africa, Greece, Somalia and Eritrea – it would take time to remedy this situation. The consequences would soon become clear.

The capture of El Agheila was only the prelude to a much larger attack on British fortifications in the region of Mersa el Brega along the coast road by the tank regiment of the 5th Leichte Division on 30 March. The underlying reason for this attack was that aerial reconnaissance and intercepted radio messages showed that the British were digging in and building reinforcements. The first attack on Mersa el Brega stalled, but in the evenings of the same day the 2nd MG Abteilung succeeded in unbalancing the defenders by means of a flank attack. The British fled in panic, abandoning fifty armoured cars and thirty trucks.

> The local Arab population, meanwhile, saw which way the wind was blowing. When Fenck, the 20-year-old gunner of a PzKpfw III, called his comrade Hohenecker – who was taking a walk – from the turret of his tank, this had an unexpected effect: 'The call "Hohenecker" had remarkable results, because it was repeated from a neighbouring house in a foreign accent, at first tentatively and then more and more loudly in unison, until happy and excited Arabs were dancing around the Panzer with hands held up high, all shouting "Hohenecker!" They had evidently taken the word to signify peaceful intentions, and the call ran around the town like a wildfire. But Hohenecker himself turned up, looking somewhat sheepish. The commandant of a scout car, too, was looking rather dubiously down at some Arabs grinning at him and roaring, "Hohenecker!"' (14: 43)

The rapid advance confronted Rommel with a dilemma: he had been explicitly instructed not to advance towards Mersa el Brega until the end of May after the arrival of the 15th Panzer Division, but this order had been overtaken by events, and with the conquest of Mersa el Brega the way to Agedabia was open. Not advancing any further would give the British the opportunity to bring in reinforcements and dig in again. Rommel was clever enough not to give the order to go further east himself, but left the decision to Streich. The latter ordered his second MG battalion, the 8th MG Abteilung under Colonel Ponath, to attack and conquer Agedabia. This battalion began its advance on 2 April under constant British pressure, but Agedabia yielded the same day. With this town in German hands, the way to the next target, El Vigilie, lay open, and the other units of the 5th Leichte Division regrouped east of Agedabia for the assault.

Rommel was constantly in line with his view on leadership at the front:

> It is very important for a commander to understand the positioning of his units and that of his opponent on the battlefield. It is often of greater importance to have an accurate picture of the developments on the battlefield than to have more theoretical knowledge or more experience. This is especially so in a situation where developments cannot be predicted. A commander must see things with his own eyes because reports from second hand cannot serve as a basis for important military decisions. (36: 68)

His observations confirmed the impression his intelligence unit had given: the British were retreating rather than fortifying. This was in accordance with Wavell's order to withdraw in phases and in an organized manner. Based on intercepted Enigma messages, he assumed that there was plenty of time for this, since Rommel had been ordered not to launch an offensive until the end of May. But he had not taken into account the character of his opponent. Rommel had smelled success and aimed to launch a large-scale offensive towards Tobruk as soon as possible.

Rommel's plans provoked understandable objections from the Italian commander Gariboldi, technically Rommel's superior, who pointed to the precarious supply situation and the fact that Rommel had ignored orders from the OKW. Gariboldi demanded that

Rome authorize such an action, but just as the discussion reached a climax, a message from the OKW arrived, in which, at least Rommel so claimed, Hitler gave him a free hand in whatever action he wished to take. In reality, it was an order from the OKW *not* to continue the offensive.

This was a good example of how Rommel's relationship with his Italian superiors and the OKW would develop in the coming period. He largely went his own way, falling back on the OKW whenever it suited him or, in extreme cases, on his special relationship with Hitler. Rommel placed himself outside the existing hierarchy by paying little attention to orders from above and acting at his own discretion. He could afford such an attitude because of his success, the support of 'his' (German and Italian) men and officers, and in the last instance, his relationship with Hitler. With Gariboldi he would over time develop an excellent working relationship.

Command structure Axis troops first phase

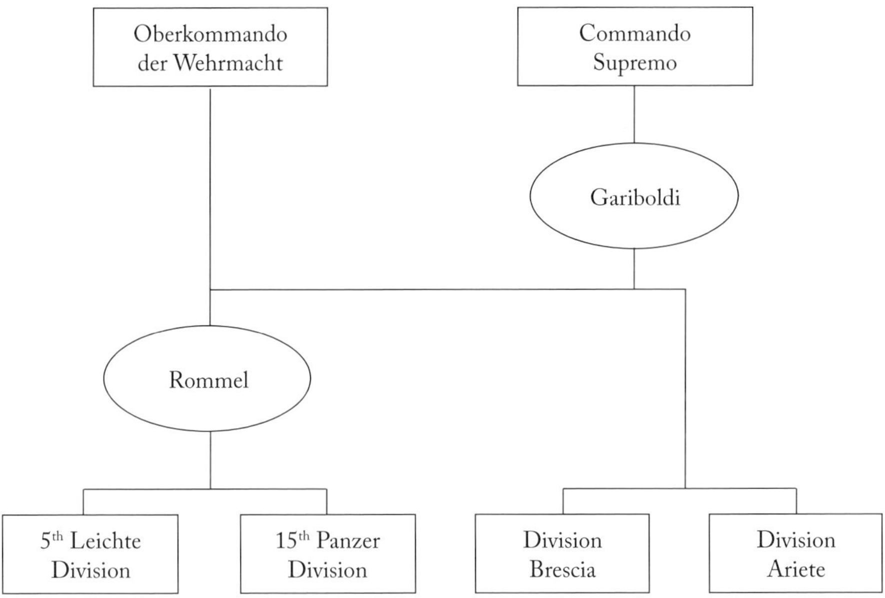

The commander of the 5thLeichte Division was Streich. The 21st Panzer Division was commanded by von Prittwitz, who was killed at Tobruk and succeeded by von Esebeck.

2.7 Rommel's first offensive

Gariboldi was not alone in objecting to an offensive; Rommel's own commanders were also hesitant. Streich, for example, demanded that his division be given four days to re-supply. This, however, was unacceptable to Rommel, who wanted to keep up the pace. He ordained that all trucks of the supply units should be emptied to pick up ammunition and fuel in a 24-hour operation from Arco del Fileni, where the Afrika Korps' supply dumps were located. The tank crews would function as reserve drivers. Streich warned in vain that during this period his division would be unprotected. However, Rommel believed the guess based on his assessment of British intentions to be a responsible one.

The offensive which Rommel now envisaged consisted of an attack along three axes:

- A left Kampfgruppe consisting of the Brescia Division led by the reconnaissance battalion of the Leichte Division would advance along the coast road to Benghazi
- A middle Kampfgruppe led by Streich, consisting of his tank regiment, other units of the Leichte Division and the Ariete Division, would push through in the middle
- A right Kampfgruppe headed by von Schwerin, consisting of the Leichte Division and a reconnaissance battalion of the Ariete Division,would advance through Cyrenaica via Ben Gama and Bir Tengeder and then turn north towards Derna to cut the retreating British troops off at the pass. This last Kampfgruppe had to travel 450km to execute this outflanking manoeuvre through unexplored desert terrain in temperatures which reached 50°C during the day and freezing at night.

In this action Rommel made large-scale use of Kampfgruppen for the first time. They played an important role in the North African theatre, as we shall see. The character of the battlefield was ideal for the type of mobile warfare of which the Germans were true masters and where a variable composition of combat units was the key to success.

In addition, German combat units smaller than a Kampfgruppe would over the coming months increasingly turn into self-supporting formations made up of tanks, anti-tank units, supply and salvage units. These combinations went into combat as one integrated force and held together as a fighting force even under the severest enemy fire. This explains the capacity of the German units to remain operational for extended periods of time and to carry out difficult manoeuvres over large areas, without losing contact with supply units and in keeping large numbers of tanks operational. The *Crusader* battles examined later are a good example of this. (3: 189)

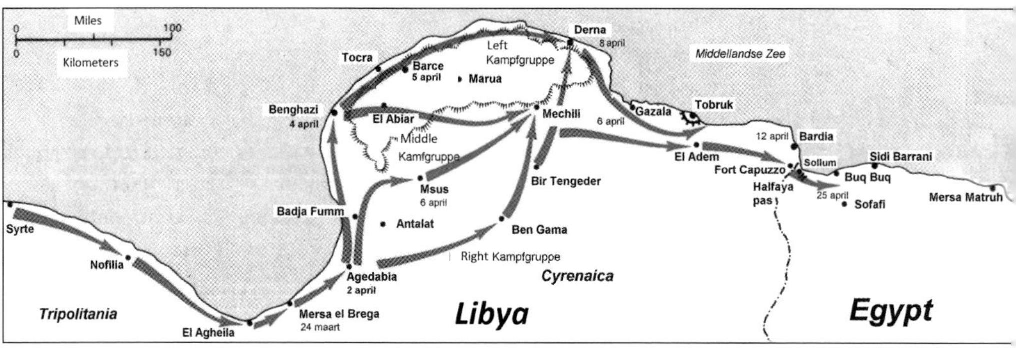

The advance of Rommel.

The offensive was launched on 4 April and then events unfolded fast. The left Kampfgruppe conquered Benghazi that same day, Barce on 5 April and Derna on the 8th. The middle Kampfgruppe took the British fuel dumps at Msus on 6 April and advanced rapidly towards Mechili. Meanwhile, the right Kampfgruppe completed the outflanking manoeuvre through the desert, to the surprise of the British, who assumed that the Germans had too had little knowledge of the terrain to achieve such a feat.

What is described above as a simple operation, however, turned out to be a tough confrontation with reality of the rocky desert terrain for the middle and right Kampfgruppen. Moreover, Streich was ordered by Rommel to get underway with his Kampfgruppe before the trucks of the supply units were back with fuel and ammunition. At nightfall on 4 April drivers with no experience except on European roads left the Via Balbia and turned off into the desert, with the result that all vehicles without tracks quickly became stuck. Streich's tanks were manned by inexperienced men, since the real tank drivers were on the road with fuel and ammunition. In addition, the route had been strewn with mines by the Italians during their retreat some months before. Most vehicles got stuck within hours, scattered across the desert. The temperature in the ensuing days caused engines to overheat, atmospheric disturbances made radio traffic impossible, and units and their commanders lost all contact with each other.

> Joachim Sänger was twenty-two years old, a radio operator* in the company commander's PzKpfw III, and like the rest of the crew had no combat experience whatsoever. His tank got stuck in a salt flat during the journey, was fired on by British anti-tank guns and then ran aground in a minefield, where one of the crew of another tank stepped on a mine and was killed. Under the scorching sun they had the tracks of their tank repaired and now they were on their way again. 'They were driving downwind so that each vehicle was running in its own dust. They closed the hatches and put their gasmasks on; but the dust penetrated everywhere and the blistering heat drove everyone onto the deck behind the turret armour. Sänger took his mask off his face; he felt he was suffocating. He cried with exhaustion and helplessness and was very ashamed of himself. But then he noticed tearstains on the dust-covered faces of the others. And so they drove behind their regiment to Mechili, weeping for Greater Germany.' (14: 42)

Rommel *an der Spitze* (in the lead)

Meanwhile, Rommel drove his men forward, flying in his Fieseler Storch ahead of the forward elements of his troops. If commanders did not move fast enough, he dropped notes threatening to personally take command. During the advance to Mechili Rommel constantly reconnoitred the terrain from his plane. During one of these flights he was welcomed with gunfire by Italian Bersaglieri. When a little later he wanted to take a closer look at a lonely 88mm Flak gun about two to three kilometres away from a column of British vehicles, his plane landed with its nose in a sand dune. The Flak commander told him that the gun was damaged and the driver was fetching help with the half-track. As the British column drew closer, Rommel and the Flak commander realized that all the ammunition had also gone with the half-track, but they and the gun crew managed to escape capture in a second half-track. This was the first of a series of adventures of Rommel, including becoming an unexpected guest in a New Zealand field hospital and finding his command vehicle in the middle of a British column.

* When his tank hit a mine, Sänger had warned the other tanks of the company by radio. However, these tanks continued to drive and many were brought to a halt by mines. Only later did it become apparent that the radio frequencies had been changed after departure from Germany. Because the radios had not been tested, and they had been operating in complete radio silence, the company had not yet noticed this.

Ponath's motor units rest en route to Mechili. (*Photo BTM/von Esebeck*)

The chaos reached a temporary climax when on 6 April Rommel landed with his plane far ahead of his troops and ordered Streich and von Schwerin to storm Mechili. Streich opposed this order, saying that he had only two trucks with light anti-aircraft guns and von Schwerin only had a unit with a few machine guns. Rommel was furious and searched in vain with his Fieseler Storch for other units, but it was not until 8 April that the first tanks appeared after a gruelling journey of hundreds of kilometres through the desert, and the various units were able to regroup.

Rommel gave them no rest. On the same day, 8 April, the middle and right Kampfgruppen attacked Mechili. The entire communication and command structure on the British side collapsed, and the British units were unable to offer any effective resistance. This in itself should not have come as a surprise: most of the available radio equipment had been shipped to Greece, field telephones were largely absent and troops had to rely more and more on the civilian telephone network. At their wits' end, the British had started to extract radio equipment from captured and stranded Italian vehicles, but without much effect. Communication between units and headquarters was ultimately largely based on chance encounters and rumour. A well-organized retreat was therefore impossible, and the British began retreating eastward in a disorganized manner. Many units would reach Tobruk or the Egyptian border in the following days via a variety of adventurous routes.

> Captain Armitage, commander of a battery of 25-pounder howitzers, found himself without his guns in Mechili when the Germans attacked. He and his colonel decided to break out and set out with the staff car and three trucks, first south, then east, toward Egypt. 'There was no moon, the stars were bright. A few of them stood remarkably low on the horizon. Before Armitage could recognize them as the side lights of approaching vehicles, they had virtually run into the Germans.' The British prepared for a fight, 'But the German column drove by them at speed – evidently

> they were just as frightened ...Minutes later, they had to run for it again, when they met another column, which luckily wanted to have nothing to do with them either. 'Traffic like Piccadilly Circus', remarked the colonel ...They drove for another half hour; nothing happened. Suddenly they became aware that they were driving through a German camp. Vehicles stood scattered about ... Armitage accelerated ... and concentrated on not hitting any of the trucks. Not a shot was fired.' The Germans were probably as exhausted as the British, and Armitage's small group eventually reached the Egyptian border. (14: 63)

After the capture of Mechili, parts of the right Kampfgruppe were given the order to move on to Derna, which was captured the same day. The rapid advance had taken the British by surprise, and the Kampfgruppe captured *en passant* three British generals, including Neame and O'Connor.* The latter was the only British commander with any experience of desert warfare. Together with the British generals, three command vehicles (4x4 AECs) were captured, which will play a role in various places in the near future.

> Brigadier John Combe, until recently commander of the 11th Hussars, was asked because of his specific knowledge of the area to accompany General Neame in the withdrawal of the British troops. General Neame's car, however, ended up at Derna behind a British column. 'A moment before, John Combe had dismounted to find out what was happening ahead, and suddenly he heard un-English voices shouting instructions in the darkness. He turned uneasily to General Neame's driver. "What the devil's that?" he asked, and the soldier with philosophical resignation replied, "I suspect it is one of them Cypriot drivers, Sir." But unhappily it was something very different, for scarcely were the words out of his mouth before the car was surrounded by Germans pointing sub-machine guns.' (21: 72)

The reconnaissance battalion was then ordered to advance with the 8th MG Battalion under Lieutenant Colonel Ponath as fast as possible via the Via Balbia to Tobruk. There, 15km from Tobruk, the lightning offensive of Rommel came to a standstill under heavy artillery fire from the British. For the next few days Rommel would try in vain to take Tobruk by storm. These attacks were executed in an uncoordinated way, with troops deployed in order of their arrival, instead of waiting for units that could form a force to carry out a concentrated attack. (14: 99) One of the victims of this was the commander of the15th Panzer Division, von Prittwitz. Just arrived in North Africa and knowing neither the terrain nor his men, he was given command of the attack on Tobruk. Rushed into it by Rommel, his staff car ended up in no-man's-land, and he was killed within 24 hours of arrival. Streich was so shocked at the way in which von Prittwitz, in his eyes, had been sent to his death that he went after Rommel in a captured British staff car. This almost got him killed, too: Rommel's *Gefechtsstaffel* (combat squadron) was about to open fire when they recognized the Panzer commandant. Rommel was furious at what he considered to be a rash act and told Streich he had been lucky he wasn't shot. 'In that case', replied Streich, 'you would have killed both your Panzer commanders in one day.' (17: 78)

* O'Connor had been recalled by Wavell a few days earlier to replace Neame.

As Rommel advanced rapidly to the east, new units were constantly being brought in via Naples: an SdKfz 7 tractor and a 150mm howitzer in the hoists. (*Photo S. Klein*)

Men of the 8th MG Battalion ride towards their doom on a tank.

The journey of the various Kampfgruppen through virtually impassable terrain had had disastrous effects on their vehicles. The combat strength of the 5th Panzer Regiment was broken not by enemy fire but by the resulting damage to their tanks. A report on 5 May 1941 from the Werkstatt Kompagnie of the 5th Panzer Regiment states that 83 of the 155 tanks had suffered severe damage to their suspension, shock absorbers and engines. The engines of fifty-eight tanks had to be replaced completely; their air filters were unable to cope with the fine desert dust. In addition, parts of the suspension and the shock absorbers had to be replaced in sixty-five tanks. The result was that only a small number of the regiment's tanks could eventually be deployed at Tobruk. (18: 102) To make things worse, it turned out that sand also caused the turrets of the tanks to jam. All in all, the fighting force with which Rommel aimed to conquer Tobruk and the eastern area was effectively decimated.

To frustrate the retreat of the British and to be able to advance quickly towards Egypt and the Nile Delta, Rommel sent the 2nd MG Abteilung, with anti-aircraft guns and other artillery, to the eastern side of Tobruk. He also sent the 3rd *Aufklärungsabteilung*, reinforced with the newly arrived sidecar combinations of the 15th Panzer Division, further east to the passes leading to Egypt. This left Rommel for the attack on Tobruk only the few operational tanks of the 5th Panzer Regiment, some light and heavy 88mm Flak guns, eight pieces of field artillery almost without ammunition, some engineer units and the 8th MG Abteilung.* Based on his experience in May 1940 in France, he wanted to take

* The 8th MG Abteilung was also part of Rommel's division, the 7th Panzer Division, in 1940.

a gamble with this small force; after all, the year before, he had forced the British 51st Division to surrender at St Valery, taking 12,000 prisoners of war including four generals.

The attack was launched on 11 April by the 8th MG Abteilung, supported by twenty tanks. However, when the tanks encountered a tank ditch they turned back and left the MG Abteilung behind. The engineers failed to reach the tank ditch, and for the next few days the MG Abteilung remained pinned down under the blazing sun on the hard ground between the two lines. On 13 April the MG Abteilung finally succeeded in crossing the tank ditch at night and cleared the barbed-wire barriers for a subsequent attack with tanks. However, the battalion had unwittingly ended up between well-entrenched British defenders, who waited until the morning to strike. The German tanks were repulsed by British artillery fire and air raids, and for a second time the MG battalion was left to its fate. In the ensuing fierce fighting, the British defenders inflicted heavy casualties on the Germans. Out of 500 men only 116 succeeded in withdrawing the following night to the German lines; the rest had been killed or captured. The 88mm Flak battery, which had given artillery support, lost almost all of its equipment and many men, and the crews of the 20mm Flak guns were massacred. Half of the tanks were knocked out, while the turrets of the other half were stuck. Rommel was stunned and furious. He demanded that Streich launch another attack the same evening to support the survivors of the MG Abteilung. However, Streich and other officers refused to carry out this order, stating that if the British made a sortie from Tobruk they could easily overrun the 5th Leichte Division and the Afrika Korps headquarters. Rommel had no choice but to accept this refusal, and he had to be content with taking the positions at Ras el Madauer from the British; he intended to use this area as a springboard for a later attack on Tobruk. But the units found life very difficult: the hard ground made it impossible to dig in properly, thus daytime movements were virtually impossible. The men were plagued by continuous artillery fire and thousands of flies, and almost all suffered from dysentery. Between them and the British in Tobruk a certain live-and-let-live would develop during the months ahead: both parties admitted medical personnel and came to various other understandings.

The Germans, meanwhile, pushed further east, captured the important Halfaya Pass on 25 April and drove the British back on 26 April to a line between Buq Buq on the coast and Sofafi inland.

> In these last days of April, Tim Palmer and Jock Campbell of the 7th Armoured Division became acquainted with the versatility of the 88mm flak gun at Caouzzi. They had watched, full of admiration, from a distance of 2,500 metres, how this heavy artillery piece behind a half-track was quickly positioned by its crew and chased off a British bomber which was attacking the convoy the gun guarded. Campbell's driver had followed his officer by car, throwing up a large cloud of dust, and was now clearly visible parked on the ridge. 'But the greatest surprise still awaited them … Incredulously, the two officers watched while the great gun barrel, like an enormous finger, swung around in a single, flowing movement and pointed at the truck. The whipcrack report of the shot came a little while after the hit, which set Campbell's vehicle on fire. In utter confusion the driver threw himself in the dust.' Campbell was furious because his belongings were going up in flames in front of his eyes; Palmer was shocked because he had argued time and again, without success, for deploying British anti-aircraft guns against ground targets such as tanks. Now he saw it put into practice, by Germans. (14: 92)

The net result of this first offensive of Rommel was that by the end of April all British troops had been expelled from Cyrenaica, except for those besieged in Tobruk. In the following months Tobruk would receive fresh units, tanks, ammunition and other supplies by sea, an operation that would continue throughout the siege.

The other side of the coin for the Germans was that after this rapid advance their troops were at the end of a very long supply line, and Tobruk had not yet been taken. Tripoli to Tobruk was more than 1,700km via the Via Balbia, roughly the same distance as Hamburg to Rome (!) In addition to logistics, Tobruk would continue to pose other problems for Rommel over the following year. Rightly so, the British regarded Tobruk as one of their first victories over the Germans. Rommel would become obsessed by Tobruk over the next few months, losing sight of all other fronts.

Tobruk

Tobruk was of great strategic importance to Rommel for two reasons. Firstly, it was the best port in Cyrenaica, with a capacity that Rommel needed to press home his offensive into Egypt. The use of Tobruk harbour could have alleviated the often precarious supply situation for the Axis troops, who required a minimum of 50,000 tons per month, while the port of Tripoli had a capacity of only 29,000 tons. Without Tobruk, men and materiel had to travel 1,700km overland on the Via Balbia, a very heavy burden on the logistics apparatus.

Secondly, Tobruk's sizeable garrison could launch a flank attack on Rommel's troops at any time and blocked twenty-two kilometres of the Via Balbia. This meant that the German supply lines had move eighty kilometres inland to a desert track, built by Italian engineers in the scorching heat and under enemy fire. However, this route, too, could easily be cut by the Tobruk garrison.

Effectively, Tobruk saw mobile combat become static positional warfare, to which the Germans, with their emphasis on mobility, did not immediately have an answer. However, it perfectly suited the British, who came into their own in a relatively static situation.

Tobruk Fortress

Tobruk was a solid fortress. It had a 54km-long defensive ring built by the Italians in the form of a semicircle, consisting of two lines 500m apart with a total of 128 overlapping fortifications. These were of concrete and each was equipped with a mortar or anti-tank gun, a light or heavy machine gun and a small garrison of fifty men. The first line of defence was surrounded by a tank ditch 3.5m deep and 6m wide.

In addition, there were extensive barbed wire barriers, and at each side of the ring two natural obstacles in the shape of *wadis* leading into the sea: Wadi el Sahal in the west and Wadi es Zeitun in the east.

The besieged British forces consisted of two Australian brigades and the remnants of the 3rd Armoured Brigade, a total of 34,000 men, equipped with their tanks, including the dreaded Matildas, and artillery.* (17: 82) In other words, this was a formidable force,

* To be precise: four Matilda tanks, twenty-five Cruiser tanks, fifteen light tanks, thirty Marmon-Harrington armoured reconnaissance vehicles, eighteen 6-pounder (light) and 18-pounder (medium) guns, and seventy-two 25-pounders. (14: 70)

Rommel during unloading in Tripoli: logistics would prove to be the Achilles heel of his time in North Africa. (*Photo S. Klein*)

larger than the Afrika Korps at that time (!), and one to be reckoned with, as Streich had pointed out earlier.

For the next eighteen months this force would be supplied from the sea by the Inshore Squadron, a strange collection of small ships, including A-lighters, the first tank landing ships. The Squadron's losses from air attack and later submarines were great, but Tobruk's lifeline was never completely cut.

Only after the first attacks had come to naught did the Italians produce detailed drawings of the defence line. This delay infuriated the Germans, who until then had underestimated the strength of Tobruk's fortifications.

2.8 Crisis at the top

The failure of the offensive at Tobruk was one of the reasons for a serious crisis of confidence between Rommel and part of his officer corps. This centred on Streich who, according to Rommel, had shown too little initiative. Other officers, such as Olbrich, commander of the 5th Panzer Regiment, were accused of not adhering to orders, which in Rommel's opinion had caused the offensive to bleed to death. They, in turn, accused Rommel of having continued the offensive against the will of the OKW and the Italian High Command and without proper preparation and clear orders, resulting in the tragic loss of the 8th MG Abteilung.

The shockwaves from this crisis soon reached Berlin, where the offensive had caused great concern in the General Staff. Chief of Staff General Halder sent his Adjutant, Lieutenant General Paulus, to Libya to evaluate the situation and write a report. He also gave Rommel explicit instructions from the OKW that his primary goal was to preserve

Cyrenaica. During his stay in North Africa, Paulus became increasingly worried about Rommel's hyper-activity and his tendency to take action on his own initiative then justify it afterwards. The relationship between the two lieutenant generals was unusual; Paulus, who was the senior, albeit only by one month, used this seniority on 1 May, a few days after his arrival, to force Rommel to call off an attack on Tobruk that had started two days earlier. Paulus found the losses unacceptably high: 1,200 dead, wounded or missing in just two days, an unprecedented casualty rate in this war.* (17: 88). In addition, ammunition stocks had become dangerously low, a first sign of the supply problems which would plague the Germans in the coming years. The aim of taking Tobruk in the near future was tempered by these events. Looking back, Rommel bemoaned the fact that he had not been given the time to get better acquainted with his men; in his view, a lack of training in static warfare explained the failure to take Tobruk:

> The heavy casualties during the attacks from the south-east were not least due to lack of training. Even during skirmishes, tactical skills can be used to reduce casualties as much as possible, and these must be taught to the troops in thorough training. In some situations they reacted too quickly while they should have acted cautiously. In other situations they were too careful while they should have acted boldly. With infantry tactics there is one rule: maximum caution coupled with boldness, and that at the right time. (36: 70)

To remedy this weakness, a special training school was established in Acroma. However, none of this detracted from the fact that the men of the Afrika Korps were completely under Rommel's spell, just like the Geister Division in May 1940. They knew he ate the same food as them and lived under the same conditions; they knew that whatever he asked of them, he demanded more of himself. He was devoted to his 'Afrikaners', and they would do anything and go anywhere for him.

The Italian troops also had great admiration for Rommel: they had never before seen a general who mixed with his men, and they loved the way he dealt with the Italian high command.

OKW and OKH

Rommel would have to deal with two important institutions in the next two years, namely the *Oberkommando des Heeres* (OKH) and the *Oberkommando der Wehrmacht* (OKW). Until December 1941, the OKH was more important for him. General von Brauchitsch was the commander-in-chief (*Oberbefehlshaber*), with General Halder as his chief of staff. Von Brauchitsch advised Hitler and was responsible for all parts of the Army, especially personnel, the *Feld Heer* and the *Ersatz Heer*. As we have seen, the role of the *Ersatz Heer* under General Fromm was crucial to recruitment and selection, training, the purchase of weapons, all kinds of administrative matters and the Army in Germany itself. Halder as Chief of Staff in charge of the Army in the field was responsible for combat operations, intelligence gathering, troop movements, etc. In addition the General Staff came under his jurisdiction, as did all sorts of other more specialized departments.

* Compare this with the losses suffered by Rommel's units in the six-week campaign of 1940: 682 officers and men killed, 1,646 wounded and 296 missing. The price paid for fighting First World War-like static warfare is clear.

In competition with the OKH was the OKW, which encompassed the Army, the Luftwaffe and the Kriegsmarine, with Hitler at its head and Keitel as chairman (sometimes called '*Lakeitel*' [lackey] to indicate his relationship to Hitler). The OKW rarely met with Hitler – only three times before the end of 1941 – since

Hitler preferred to settle things in bilateral consultations, but its influence grew over time. From September 1939 to early 1941, the OKH planned its campaigns with the help of the other two military branches. When in 1939 the OKH planned the May 1940 campaign, the OKW was given responsibility for the invasion of Norway and Denmark. In the spring of 1941, when the OKH planned Operation *Barbarossa* against the Soviet Union, the OKW was given responsibility for all 'quiet' fronts, including North Africa. In the period after that, the OKH focussed on the Eastern Front, while the OKW with Chief of Staff General Jodl was responsible for all other theatres.

The influence of the Army slowly dwindled, and after the forced departure of von Brauchitsch at the end of 1941, more and more issues, for example all personnel matters, were transferred to the OKW. Finally, at the end of the war, the General Staff also came under the control of the OKW. The existence of these parallel structures did not pose any major difficulties, however, because all staff officers within the Heer were trained by and part of the General Staff organization, ensuring unity in thought and action.

In line with this, the main point of contact for Rommel during the campaign in North Africa shifted from the OKH to the OKW. Informally, he kept a line open via Berndt (see below) with Hitler. (48: 27–31)

3.9 The men

High morale would be crucial in the coming years under the often harsh conditions of North Africa. Since the decision to send German troops to North Africa had been taken ad hoc, there was no time to prepare the men properly. They were vaccinated against cholera and typhus but were given nothing more than the standard medical examination. Only from spring 1941 was the medical examination adapted to the specific requirements of North Africa. (45: 10–11)

Training

It was not possible to train the first batch of troops in advance for the conditions they could expect to meet. They did receive a number of lectures by specialists in tropical diseases and by officers who had travelled in the region and had some idea about local conditions. These lectures underestimated the effects of heat, sand, insects and disease, although the instructions on hygiene in the tropics were good. Troops deployed later to North Africa also failed to receive any special training, partly because they were often dispatched at short notice. (45: 11)

Due to the *Erfahrungsberichte* system, combat tactics for the front in North Africa were continuously adapted by the General Staff, and formed part of the training of the various units. In addition, the system of *Ersatz* and *Feld Heer* ensured that experience was passed on to new arrivals by units that had fought in North Africa.

Acclimatization

The first men sent to North Africa were given no acclimatization period, although some replacement troops did have a chance to get used to warmer temperatures in southern Italy or the Balkans. In practice, however, it turned out that an acclimatization period did not really improve combat efficiency, since losses were also due to poor food and combat conditions. Deploying fresh troops during the summer turned out to be very unwise, partly because of the many flies in that period. The physical resistance of men dropped during their first year in North Africa but improved thereafter, and their combat efficiency followed the same path.

Food supply and disease

Illnesses plagued the troops constantly. A simple cut on the hands or legs, caused by digging or by the sharp spines of desert plants, could lead to months of ulcerated wounds. Lips and noses would blister in the sun, and men were constantly bothered by gastrointestinal complaints. Their diet was monotonous: biscuits, olive oil, canned sardines, coffee, jam, soft cheese and unidentifiable canned meat of supposedly Italian origin. Fresh vegetables, eggs, ham, milk, etc., were all lacking, which led to scurvy-like symptoms. The Germans looked enviously at the British, who were given mineral water, canned meat and fruit, the spoils of war in years to come. Officers were not spared these hardships; they fell ill en masse, and Rommel himself, ravaged by jaundice, was forced to go to back Europe by the end of 1942 to recover.

A typical example of what could go wrong was the case of the Fallschirmjäger Brigade Ramcke, which was transferred from Europe to the rocky terrain around El Alamein in July 1942. It was an elite unit, but soon 50 per cent of the men had fallen ill as a result of the combined effects of heat, local conditions and poor food. Shortly after their arrival, many men were found to be suffering from stomach complaints such as dysentery, from jaundice and from ulcers that healed only slowly. These were caused by brackish water and a diet which consisted almost exclusively of canned food. Blond, red-headed and pale-skinned men were more likely to fall victim to these diseases; their darker fellows recovered relatively quickly after an initial period of illness. However, this knowledge was not taken into account in later missions. (45: 12)

Italian troops

A not insignificant number of the troops in North Africa were Italians, who in the coming eighteen months would be mainly deployed under German leadership and in combination with German units, as in the mixed composition of the reconnaissance units and Kampfgruppen. Rommel repeatedly said that Italian soldiers were made from the right stuff, but that they were ill-led and ill-armed, which affected their self-image:

> The Italians had developed a serious inferiority complex. That was not surprising, as their infantry had almost no anti-tank weapons and their artillery was obsolete. Their training did not meet modern requirements, so that we increasingly had to deal with all kinds of problems in the deployment of Italian units. (36: 70)

If well led, armed and trained, he believed their ability was similar in some respects to that of German soldiers. In particular, however, the officer corps caused him problems, some

The Autoblinda 41, the Italian equivalent of the armoured reconnaissance car. (*Model J. Tainton*)

of which arose from the fact that Italian cadets were trained in institutions and special units consisting solely of officers. They met their men only after they had completed their training, so team building could not take place and a gulf arose between officers and men. It looked as if representatives of a higher class were giving orders to an anonymous mass of workers. Rommel also thought that Italian officers also had a misguided attitude to war:

> Many Italian officers see the war as an amusing distraction. They are bitterly disappointed by its reality and if they are not willing to face the harsh realities of warfare they will face the consequences. (36: 70)

Differences in food supply and other matters also exacerbated the gap between German and Italian units. (14: 101)

2.10 Evaluation of the German Army

The strategic dimension

From a strategic point of view, it is clear that the deployment of German troops in North Africa was motivated by political reasons. While the *Wehrmacht* was preparing for the invasion of the Soviet Union (Operation *Barbarossa*), the North African campaign served to frustrate British ambitions and keep the Italians in the Axis alliance. The front in North Africa was considered to be a sideshow. The consequence of this was that Rommel never received the quantities of men and equipment he asked for. However, after the first offensive, appreciation grew of the propaganda effect of Rommel and his troops in North Africa.

This was not in line with the views of the OKW, which clearly disapproved of the way Rommel handled matters, quite apart from the fact that he sometimes simply ignored explicit orders. But things could have turned completely differently. After all, it was not obvious that the British had wanted to strengthen their forward positions in Cyrenaica and defend them to the utmost. These positions could easily be circumvented by means of a flanking movement. The British themselves had done the same with success against the Italian positions in February. The British retreated not so much under the threat of a German-Italian offensive, but because they realized that occupying terrain in itself did not yield any strategic advantage. If Rommel had not acted so fast and against the explicit orders of the OKW, thus posing a clear threat to British interests in Egypt, British troops would have retreated at a leisurely pace to the east and regrouped to face the new threat in Greece. As we have seen, the maps in the British headquarters in Cairo were literally changed. In this scenario, perhaps what the OKW intended, Rommel would have launched his offensive a few months later; with the British gone he would have had the territory all to himself and, moreover, would have had the additional combat power of the 15th Panzer Division. The British troops shipped to Greece would no longer have had any strategic significance in the end, like the troops already in Greece: it was not possible to evacuate them after the German invasion on a large scale and they could thus be considered lost. If this was part of a grand strategy at the OKW level, it was not understood by Rommel. Now for the next eighteen months Rommel's freedom of movement would be determined by the presence of a large number of enemy troops in Tobruk, troops he personally had driven into this fortress. (18: 102)

The tactical dimension

Tactically, the Germans had fallen short of what they were taught and should have put into practice. In principle, the operating method of the Afrika Korps did not differ from 'standard' tactical doctrine. The big difference in North Africa was that there were no clear front lines, and occupying territory was of relative unimportance. The campaign therefore had the character of war of manoeuvre, with all the specific requirements that entailed, and the side which was able to deal with it in the most flexible way had the advantage. Since creating chaos and deploying troops in a mobile fashion were central elements of the doctrine of the German Army, it was no surprise that the Germans clearly had the upper hand at this stage of the conflict. Their mission orientation and the quality of their C3I structure meant that it was easy for them to hold the initiative. However, the German armoured troops did not always adhere to the guidelines of their own tactical manual. On 2 April, for example, German tanks attacked British tank units head-on instead of pinning them down under fire and then attacking swiftly from the flank. This action led to unnecessary losses on the German side. (18: 101)

The first attacks on Tobruk were launched with far too few men, without good artillery support and without proper reconnaissance of the terrain. The 8th MG Abteilung and the 88mm and 20mm Flak guns were deployed in a role for which they were not suited. All were sacrificed to the ambition of Rommel, who envisaged a second St Valéry. He covered this up later by talking about the deployment of the Afrika Korps in general terms and not about the units actually deployed. This, incidentally, was in serious violation of *Erfahrungsberichte* rules.

In addition to Rommel's failure, the first attacks on Tobruk also demonstrated a long series of blunders by the 5th Panzer Regiment: they went into action without having sufficiently reconnoitred the terrain, advanced parallel to the enemy's defence lines, did not

The devastating effect of the 25-pounder howitzers: the gun turret of this tank has been completely torn away from the hull. (*Photo IHC*)

use the tactics of *Verbundene Waffen* and, to top it all, left the infantry behind. The latter, in particular, was tactically a deadly sin, leading to the demise of the 8th MG Abteilung.

Moreover, on 14 April the Panzer Regiment attacked a British artillery battery of 25-pounders* head-on, instead of making a flanking move. They had to retreat after an intensive artillery duel, recognizing the superiority of the British howitzers, only to be attacked in the flank by a second battery and then in the rear by Cruiser tanks. The Regiment completely lost control over events due to incorrect execution of the attack on the first battery, despite the fact that this was just the type of attack that they had undoubtedly practised many times in training. In total, seventeen tanks were lost in this engagement.** (18: 116)

The *Erfahrungsberichte* read like a manual for how tanks should not be deployed. It was no wonder, therefore, that Rommel was dissatisfied with the leadership of the tank regiment. Perhaps the OKW drew its own conclusions from these *Erfahrungsberichte*, and this is why they sent Paulus to investigate.

The German troops had great difficulty in coping with the defences of Tobruk. Their strong suit was mobile warfare, and they had forgotten how to deal with such Great War-style defence lines. The British were right to claim their first victory over the Germans at Tobruk. It was a humiliating situation for Rommel, who would take almost a year to capture the city.

Also during this period, the German armoured troops hesitated to attack Mark II Matildas, although in the following months they developed a successful tactic of using PzKpfw IIIs to take out these feared tanks from very close range (300m). *Battleaxe* in the

* The 25-pounder howitzers used HE shells and not the AP shells which are much more deadly to tanks.

** Of the seventeen, two were burnt out and the rest were damaged but could not be recovered because they were in British territory. This was a heavy loss for the 5th Panzer Regiment, especially since among the losses were five PzKpfw IVs.

next phase would show that the combination of tanks, 88mm Flak and anti-tank guns worked well against Matildas.

The losses at Tobruk also illustrate how rapidly casualties can mount in a switch from mobile to static warfare. Rommel described this as follows:

> In a mobile war, materiel is the essential tool for combatants. The best soldier is powerless without vehicles, tanks and supplies. If one manages to take out the opponent's tanks, one has actually knocked him out without much loss of life: he is no longer able to take action.
>
> The opposite is true for static warfare. Here the soldier with his rifle and hand grenades takes centre stage as long as he can be protected by anti-tank guns and other obstacles to oppose the enemy tanks. His goal is to take out the infantryman on the other side. It follows that static warfare is always aimed at killing people, while in mobile warfare the key to success lies in the destruction of the adversary's equipment. (36: 70, 44: 57)

2.11 Evaluation of the British Army

The strategic dimension

The North African theatre was of great strategic importance to the British. If the Germans succeeded in driving them out of North Africa, then their centuries-long presence in this area, on the pivot between the home islands in Europe and the colonies in Asia, would come to an end; hence all the political attention, certainly after the advance of the Germans through the Balkans to Greece, which was devoted to this arena. This meant that the freedom of movement of Wavell, C-in-C Mediterranean, and his successors was relatively limited, because Churchill and the War Cabinet in London followed everything so closely. In other words, it was no longer the general in the field who decided where and when to engage in battle, but Churchill or the War Cabinet. Political considerations played an important role in every part of the campaign, and diplomats had almost as much influence as the military. Because the C-in-C Mediterranean was part of a complex, long-standing, political-administrative organization, he was forced to attune all military activities to this organization, work through all sorts of channels, take into account the opinion of many parties and fall back on all kinds of advisers from the various ministries and Army and Navy units. The military had to take into account all existing political and administrative frameworks, sensitivities and preferences. This hampered their planning and decision-making throughout the campaign. (3: 188)

In addition, Wavell had to wage war on four different fronts: North Africa, Greece, Eritrea and Somalia. His campaigns against the Italians on the last two fronts were successful, but Greece and North Africa were a disaster. The problems that this caused on the strategic level diverted all attention from serious tactical and organizational shortcomings of the British forces.

Rommel's position was simpler, since his only political concern on the ground was the relationship with the Italian High Command.

The tactical dimension

At the tactical level, too, things did not work out as they should have for the British. First, there were no clear objectives. Wavell had told Neame not to focus on holding territory, but to withdraw if necessary. He did so, but at an ever increasing pace and in an increasingly chaotic way. This was seen in the actions of the 2nd Armoured Division. Instead of delaying actions, with a flexible deployment of materiel and unexpected counter-attacks, they offered little more than rearguard activity. At no time were the British units a serious threat to the advancing German troops, nor did their tanks offer effective resistance. In the only serious tank-versus-tank engagement on 2 April, the British resisted bravely but could come up with nothing more creative than a line-up of all available tanks.

Maintenance was an issue for both sides in the harsh desert climate: dust, the hard surface and the great distances made constant repairs necessary. (*Photos S. Klein*)

In addition, it turned out that individual tanks, squadrons and infantry units were not allowed to take new positions without the permission of the next-ranking officer. This centralization of command limited the flexibility of British units to a great extent. This, combined with a low level of training, the inexperience of commanders in mobile warfare, logistical problems and the technical condition of the materiel, mean the British were no match for the Germans.

An important reason for the limited British resistance, moreover, was undoubtedly the fact that their already weak C3I structure had collapsed completely after the onset of battle, a problem that the British would fail to solve in the coming years. British deployment was ultimately determined by rumour, chance encounters and personal initiatives, and the effect was that their entire organization disintegrated into smaller units, each of which drew up its own plan and fought its own war. The literature generally provides a romantic image of inspiring officers and courageous combat units, who confront the Germans with typical British humour and a great deal of understatement, but this does not really reflect the rapidly unfolding drama on the battlefield in North Africa and elsewhere.

The technical condition of British materiel was a major concern. In this first round of combat, all but ten of the tanks of the 2nd Armoured Division were lost due to mechanical defects. This was not a new experience for the British: in the May 1940 campaign, half of their tanks were not operational due to technical defects, and in Greece all of the fifty-two Cruiser Mark II tanks were lost due to mechanical failure. This problem cast its shadow ahead, as we shall see in the next chapters.

Chapter 3

Operations *Brevity* and *Battleaxe*

Under great political pressure, Wavell would attempt to throw the Germans back to the west in the coming months – but without success. The two British offensives of this period, *Brevity* and *Battleaxe*, ended in victories for the Germans.

Before we discuss these offensives, we will consider a number of issues that were of great importance in North Africa in the following two years. First, we will look at the tanks and tank divisions of both sides, since these weapons largely determined the style of battle from now on. Then we will consider orientation in the desert and the C3I capacity of both sides – crucial elements in being able to deploy the right units in the right place at the right time. We will also consider in more detail the logistical requirements of the German Army, a constant issue during the North African campaign.

3.1 Tanks

After his first offensive, Rommel had two tank divisions at his disposal: the 5th Light Division and, after May, the 15th Panzer Division. We will discuss the organizational structure of these divisions and the tanks they had at their disposal, and will look at the same subjects in describing the British Army. First, however, we will consider a number of critical factors that play a role in the successful deployment of tanks, relating to their effectiveness and employability. By effectiveness we mean the extent to which the use of tanks actually leads to results. In the coming chapters we will see that this depends on:

- Applying a clear, proven doctrine
- Crews that are sufficiently trained and have internalized the doctrine
- Concentrated deployment of tanks
- Control and coordination in battle
- Communication between tanks
- Speed, armour and armament of tanks
- Cooperation with other weapon systems

By employability we mean factors such as:

- Operational range
- Supply options during battle
- Recovery options during and after battle
- Repair and overhaul options during and after battle
- Technical reliability, including the service life of the various components, especially the engine.

All these factors determine the extent to which tanks and tank divisions can operate successfully. These will be discussed one by one in the coming chapters.

German Panzer Divisions

The standard structure of a German tank division is shown in the diagram below. The 5th Leichte and 15th Panzer Division had a similar structure.

Structure of a German Panzer Division 1940: 1st Panzer Division

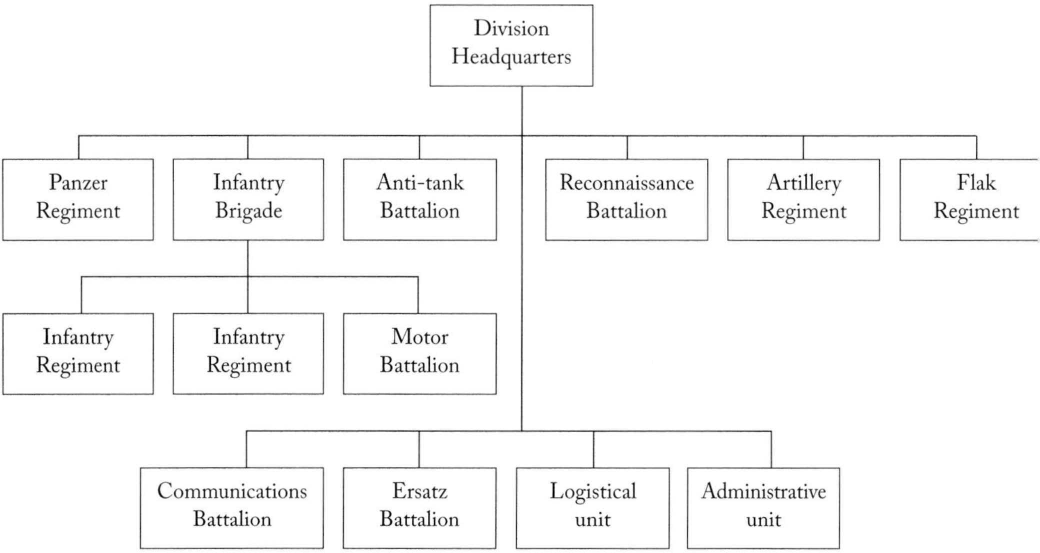

The core of the Panzer Division was the Panzer Regiment, structured as follows:

- *Regiment Stab* (regimental staff), with:
  - *Nachrichtenzug* (communications unit)
  - *Leichter Panzerzug* (light tank platoon for reconnaissance missions)
  - *Panzer Abteilungen* (two tank battalions)
  - *Panzer Werkstatt Kompagnie* (field workshops and recovery units)

The two Panzer Abteilungen were made up as follows:

- *Abteilungs Stab* with:
  - *Nachrichtenzug*
  - *Erkunderzug* (reconnaissance platoon)
  - *Leichter Panzerzug*
  - *Pionierzug* (engineer platoon)
  - *Fliegerabwehrzug* (anti-aircraft platoon)
- 2 *Leichte Kompagnien* (light tank companies)
- 1 *Mittlere Kompagnie* (medium tank company)
- 1 *Leichte Kolonne* (supply column)

When the Afrika Korps arrived, the Panzer Regiment consisted of two Abteilungen with three Kompagnien each. In 1942 this was changed to three Abteilungen with three Kompagnien.

The Abteilungen could attack in two waves or independently. In battle formation (*see* also the next chapter) one light company advanced in front, the other at the rear or on the flank, both covered by the medium company. This medium company was also the unit that would ultimately attack and attempt to break through the *Schwerpunkt* in the enemy's line with the full weight of its tanks. (18: 70)

In accordance with the principle of *Verbundene Waffen*, an infantry brigade with two regiments and a motorcycle battalion, an artillery regiment and an anti-tank battalion formed an integral part of the tank division. The division numbered approximately 10,000 men.

German tanks

Rommel could deploy the PzKpfw III and IV, two reliable, robust, well-armed and well-armoured tanks, which had proved their value in previous campaigns. These would be produced with minor changes until the end of the war, and even then they represented world-class tank design. Sensibly, the hull and turret were designed in such a way that, as the war progressed, heavier guns could be installed in them. In early 1941 there was no Allied tank on the Western Front that could compete with them.

These tanks had a reliable 300hp Maybach engine, armour plating 80–90mm thick and a sturdy chassis. They had the same top speed of 60–70kph, so they could operate together, in contrast to the British Matilda and Cruiser tanks, which could not cooperate due to their great difference in speed. The PzKpfw III and IV also complemented each other in terms of artillery. The PzKpfw IV, which had a short (L/24) 75mm gun and used HE ammunition,* was especially intended to silence artillery and infantry reinforcements after a possible breakthrough and was to some extent a form of mobile artillery. Despite its low muzzle velocity of 385m/sec, its effect at 1,000m was comparable to that of the British 2-pounder, thanks to the weight and explosive power of the shells. The PzKpfw III had a (L/42) 50mm gun of lower calibre, but with a higher muzzle velocity** of 685 m/sec. At this speed its AP*** shells could pierce Cruiser tank armour at 1,500m. This tank often led the way in forcing breakthroughs; the PzKpfw IV would then follow to clear artillery and reinforced positions.

German tanks always fired from a stationary position, whereas British ones were usually moving, harking back to their cavalry tradition. A stationary position offers easier aiming and a higher chance of hitting the target. It is important to note here that neither tank was in fact suited to the role they were assigned in North Africa, namely in tank-versus-tank battles. Tanks played a major role in the Germans' offensive concept at the breakthrough phase: after eliminating enemy resistance through artillery and bombing, the tanks' role was to advance quickly behind the enemy's lines to eliminate his C3I capability. Enemy tanks had to be neutralized by anti-tank guns, not primarily by tanks themselves. No matter how superior the German tanks were, they still had to get close to their opposing tanks to

* HE = High Explosive: ammunition especially suited to destroying artillery and infantry reinforcements.

** Speed at which the shell leaves the barrel.

*** AP = Armour Piercing: ammunition specifically for penetrating armour.

actually eliminate them. Most tanks in North Africa were neutralized by anti-tank guns. Only in the course of 1942 did a variant of the PzKpfw IV become available carrying a 75mm gun with high muzzle velocity. This tank, the PzKpfw IV F2, was specifically designed for tank-on-tank confrontations, and the gun had appropriate AP ammunition for the role. These tanks were cherished by the Germans and seen as one of the answers to the increasingly heavily armed and armoured Allied tanks. (14: 98)

Anti-tank guns (*Panzer Abwehr Kanon* or PAK)
German anti-tank guns constantly adapted to the changing demands of the war. The standard infantry anti-tank guns at the beginning of the war were the PAK 36/37mm and the PAK 38/50mm. The latter remained in use throughout the war and played an important role in North Africa. In addition, the Germans made use of captured French and, later in the campaign, captured Soviet anti-tank guns. The most widely used was the Soviet 76.2mm gun which was renamed by the Germans the 7.62cm PAK 39 (r). This gun was used in both anti-tank and artillery roles.

In North Africa the Germans used the same vehicles as in Europe. These were, with the exception of the halftracks, civilian vehicles not suitable for the terrain in which they were deployed. In this respect they were inferior to the British vehicles, the design of which was based on years of experience in the region, with high clearance, large, single tyres and often four-wheel drive. Captured British vehicles would become a welcome spoil of war for the Germans, who never received the number of vehicles they actually needed. Around the time of the Battle of El Alamein, 85 per cent (!) of the German fleet consisted of British vehicles, which understandably made mutual recognition very difficult.

No vehicles with diesel engines were used, to avoid having to carry two different types of fuel. All vehicles had specially developed air filters and additional equipment such as driving plates and ladders to place under the wheels if they got stuck in the sand. Double tyres could not be used because stones could become trapped between them. Volkswagens, which were widely used, were equipped with an air intake inside the vehicle and large aircraft tyres, which proved to be ideal.

British tank divisions

British tank divisions differed from the Germans' in many respects. First, in line with British tank doctrine, they played a purely independent role on the battlefield, separate from the infantry. They had no infantry attached, only a number of ancillary units such as artillery, engineers, etc., in a so-called Support Group. In practice, this Support Group was often unable to keep up with the tanks and quickly lost contact with them. The Armoured Divisions were committed to this independent role as successors to the cavalry, and their tanks were also specifically developed for this role. They were the heirs of such illustrious cavalry regiments as the Hussars, the King's Dragoon Guards and the Queen's Bays. Some, like the King's Dragoon Guards, had been introduced to tanks for the first time just two years earlier. Culture, attitude and tactics in these regiments were strongly determined by the past.

In 1938 General Hobart trained the tank units that would later form the 7th Armoured Division. He described the experience to his wife:

> I had the cavalry COs in and laid my cards on the table. They are such nice chaps, sociable. That's what makes it so difficult. But they are so conservative of their spurs and swords and regimental traditions ...so easily satisfied with an excuse if things aren't right, so prone to blame on the machinery. And unless one upsets all their polo ...it's so hard to get anything more into them or any more work out of them. Three days a week they come in six miles to Gezirah Club for polo ...Non-polo days, it's tennis or something. (28: 111)

This culture and attitude gave them a feeling of superiority to the infantry and other units. In the field of tactics, tank units had an unstoppable tendency to attack on sight and to seek out and fight individual duels. Robert Crisp, a participant in the first confrontations in Cyrenaica, described the actions of these units as follows: 'Other officers told me how they had seen the Hussars charging into Jerry tanks, sitting on top of their turrets more or less with their whips out ...It looked like the run-up to the first fence at a point-to-point.' This was typical of a number of the early encounters involving cavalry regiments. 'They had incredible enthusiasm and dash, and sheer exciting courage which was only curbed by the rapidly decreasing stock of dashing officers and tanks.' (28: 111)

It would take a long time for these attitudes to become a thing of the past.

Infantry Divisions, in turn, were supported by the Royal Tank Regiment with tanks specifically developed for this role, such as the Matilda. The Armoured Divisions looked down on the men of the Royal Tank Regiment, and the two type of tank division had never trained together, nor had Armoured Divisions trained with Infantry Divisions.

Structure of a British Armoured Division

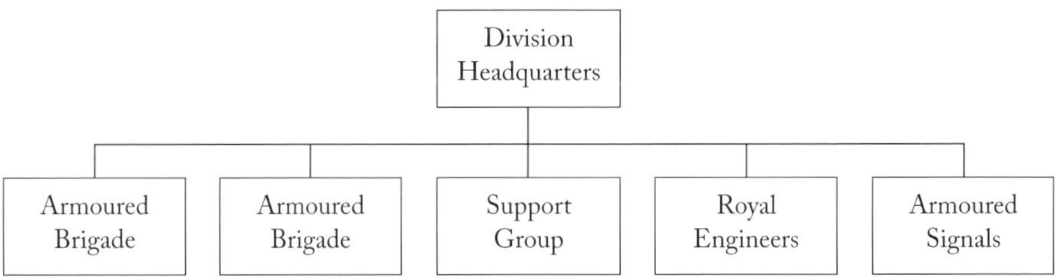

The core of the Armoured Division consisted of the two Armoured Brigades, each consisting of three Armoured Regiments. These regiments had the following structure.

Structure of a British Armoured Regiment

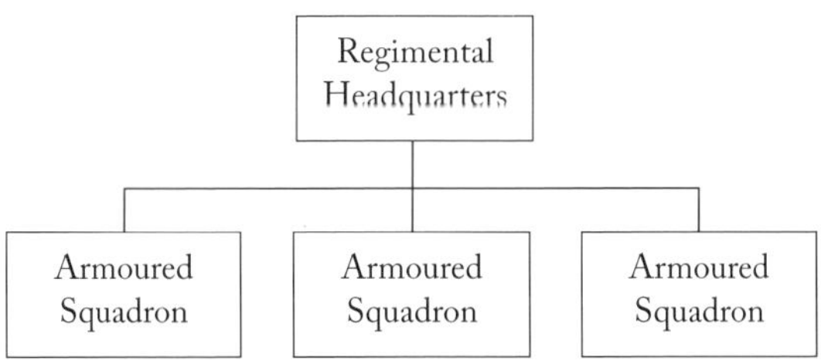

Each Armoured Squadron consisted of:

- Squadron headquarters (four tanks)
- Four troops (three tanks each)

Each squadron therefore had sixteen tanks; the regiment with the four tanks of the Regimental Headquarters had fifty-two tanks at its disposal. Three such regiments formed one Armoured Brigade with a total of 165 tanks. We will encounter these Brigades in particular in later chapters.

The Support Group consisted of:

- Headquarters
- A Royal Horse Artillery regiment with two batteries of eight 25-pounder guns
- An anti-tank and anti-aircraft gun regiment with two anti-tank batteries (each with twelve 2-pounder guns) and two anti-aircraft gun batteries (each with twelve 40mm guns)
- Two motorcycle battalions

The Royal Engineers unit consisted of:

- Headquarters
- A field squadron
- A field troop (with 3,016 mines)

An Armoured Division with its two Brigades had a total of 330 tanks. (18: 61) British Armoured Divisions were therefore larger than German ones (approximately 13,000 men as against 10,000).

During Operations *Brevity* and *Battleaxe* we will only encounter the Armoured Brigades; other important elements such as the Support Group will play a more prominent role in the next phases, for example in the attempts to relieve Tobruk during Operation *Crusader*.

British tanks

The British, as we have seen, had light reconnaissance tanks, tanks supporting infantry and tanks of the Cruiser variety.

Infantry tanks, of which the Mark II Matilda and later the Valentine were active in North Africa, were developed to support the Infantry Divisions and were housed within the regiments of the Royal Tank Corps. The Matildas were slow (to keep pace with the infantry), armed with a 2-pounder gun and, above all, heavily armoured. The Germans respected them because they could withstand almost every type of anti-tank gun available at the time. Only the 88mm Flak gun could deal with their armour at a safe distance. Rommel had already experienced this type of tank near Arras, when a breakthrough by them was only foiled at the last minute by deploying 88mm Flak guns. The British, on the other hand, were much less happy with this tank, mainly because of its downsides, low speed and weak armament. For unclear reasons, the 2-pounder gun was only suitable for AP ammunition instead of HE, with delayed ignition to disperse as many deadly splinters as possible for use against infantry, machine-gun nests, etc.

Cruiser Mark IVA with a 2-pounder gun and a 7.92mm Besa machine gun, fast but lightly armoured. (*Photo BTM*)

Cruisers were housed within the Armoured Divisions and developed for an independent role in quickly and effectively attacking the enemy's flanks and rearguard. They had many variants in North Africa, namely the Mark I, Mark II A, Mark IV A and VI (later called 'Crusader' after Operation *Crusader*). Cruisers were fast, but lightly armoured, relatively lightly armed and mechanically unreliable. This made the Cruiser tanks relatively easy to counter, the only problem being the high speed of the Cruiser Mark VI (50–60kph due to the use of the Christie suspension system); however, they could not escape the long arm of the 88mm Flak gun.

Due to the aforementioned differences in role and speed, the two available tank types could not be used in combination in large peripheral movements or deep breakthroughs. There was also no satisfactory system to supply fuel and ammunition for troops who had advanced a long way, and equipment for recovery units was only sparsely available. (37: 172) Moreover, the large number of technical defects in these tanks limited their operational deployability.

The level of training of tank crews was also a problem for the British in this phase of the conflict. Many crews had not driven tanks since February, and others were assigned to tank types they were unfamiliar with. Some regiments did not receive their tanks until the end of May, leaving no time for practice. In addition, cooperation between larger units could not be practised at Brigade, let alone Division, level. No new tactics had been developed, let alone practised, and infantry and tanks had not been able to train together. All this meant that the British were not well prepared to fight German units that had become very well attuned to each other in recent months. (37: 172)

The Christie Suspension System

Colonel Giffard Martel, Assistant Director of Mechanization at the Ministry of Defence and specifically responsible for tank development, was impressed by the BT-26 tank during a visit to the Soviet Union in 1936. This used the suspension system of the American designer Walter Christie which made it possible for the tank to reach very high speeds. The characteristics of this tank, a 37mm gun and a speed of 54kph, seemed to make it a suitable successor to the Vickers Medium, a reconnaissance tank. However, Martel's superior, Lieutenant General Sir Hugh Elles, Master-General of Ordnance, rejected his proposal and ordered Vickers to produce prototypes for a successor to the Vickers Medium. These were the A-9 and A-10, the first so-called 'Cruiser' tanks. However, Martel still wanted to realize his ideas, and he managed to acquire Walter Christie's last prototype for the British Army in 1936 and persuaded Lord Nuffield, head of the Morris Group, to buy Christie's patents. The Morris Group then designed a prototype at its own expense in 1937, the A-13 or Cruiser Tank Mark III. This had a 2-pounder gun, 14mm of armour and a speed of 45kph.

3.2 Italian units

While North Africa was the ideal terrain for mobile operations, the mobility of the Italians lagged far behind that of the other combatants involved. This was in line with the Italian principle of 'people over machines', which gave pride of place to the infantry. Tanks had to support the infantry, and the importance of good cooperation between infantry and artillery was emphasized.

It should therefore come as no surprise that in mid-June 1941 Italian units had a ratio of motor vehicles to troops of 1:21, a proportion that would hardly change in the coming period. In comparison, the Germans had a ratio of 1:3.6. The speed of Italian infantry divisions was therefore determined by the walking pace of the men involved. The speed of motorized infantry divisions was no better, and infantrymen could only fight on foot, because protection in the form of armoured vehicles was lacking. As a result, a single enemy armoured car could cause great confusion in the ranks of an Italian infantry division. The deployment of Jock Columns by the British against the Italians at the end of 1940 thus had a devastating effect. Anti-aircraft defences were also largely absent, giving enemy fighter-bombers free rein to paralyze entire divisions. Italian tank divisions were weak in comparison with the Germans and British at every point. Tanks such as the M-13 and M-14 were too light in terms of armour and armament, and technically unreliable. (25: 124–8) Of the hundred brand new M-13 tanks delivered to Tripoli in 1941, only ten survived the journey to Tobruk during the first offensive. (14: 99)

The relationship between training and combat effectiveness was not considered by Italian tank divisions in 1941. Little attention was paid to training, and it was assumed that intuition and personal courage would be decisive in battle. 'On the job' training was common, and armoured units at the front were sometimes given drivers and gunners who had never driven a tank, let alone practised with the infantry or artillery. (25: 144) The same applied to the infantry divisions, with the exception of the German-trained Folgore paratroop division, which particularly distinguished itself at El Alamein.

A high proportion of the officer corps in the Italian Army consisted of reserve officers.* There were no adequate selection criteria for these reservists: they simply had to be physically fit, and the army leadership itself described their training as completely inadequate. Professional officers, in turn, often opted for jobs in the safe bureaucracy of the Army, further reducing leadership capacity and experience among officers at the front. (25: 146) This also applied to the regular non-commissioned officers: limited career opportunities meant that at the beginning of the war many of these important leaders could be found in administrative jobs. (25: 146)

Italian divisions were relatively small: 7,000 men in an infantry division (against 17,000 in a British one), and 8,600 men in a tank division (versus 13,000). These low numbers can be explained by the supply concept of the Italian Army in which one central supply unit behind the front, the *Intendenza*, provided all the units on the front line with food and ammunition on a daily basis. The other combatants operated a different logistical structure. For example, German transport columns, an integral part of the combat units, collected supplies for their own units from the storage depots behind the front and formed an integral part of the combat unit when on the move. The Italian system had already proved to be highly unreliable during quiet periods, but during combat the lifeline with the *Intendenza* located far behind the front was generally broken at an early stage, and units were then dependent on the supplies they already had or could obtain on the battlefield. This could lead to a rapid disintegration of combat ability.

Low-loaders and recovery vehicles were also deployed by the Italians to tow stranded tanks and trucks from the battlefield for repair behind the front. The large number of vehicle types and the lack of a reliable spare parts service system subsequently made the repair of salvaged vehicles a challenge in itself. This led to a vehicle availability ratio of 60 per cent on average throughout the entire campaign. (41: 124–8)

All in all, the mobility and fighting power of Italian units was very limited. The Germans tried to overcome this by having Italians operate as much as possible around a core of German units. Furthermore, they tried to move the Italian units as much as possible on paved roads such as the Via Balbia. For example, the retreat of Italian units during the *Crusader* offensive took place via this Via Balbia, protected by German units in the more difficult interior.

3.3 Orientation and C3I capacity in the desert

Maps and good C3I capacity** were essential to operate effectively in an environment without reliable landmarks and with large numbers of mobile units.

Maps

The British had a clear advantage here, having already intensively mapped the terrain before the war.*** During the conflict, the Long Range Desert Group in particular, in addition to their primary tasks of gathering intelligence and carrying out sabotage actions, collected further information about the terrain. (45: 2)

* 90 per cent of lieutenants and 66 per cent of captains in 1942.

** Command, Control, Communications and Intelligence capability.

*** See, for example, the film *The English Patient.*

The position on the German side was completely different. Siegfried Westphal (we will meet this brilliant staff officer in the next phase) spoke in 1959 during a lecture to the Anglo-German Association about his position in the Operation Section of the General Staff in Berlin in the late 1930s. When one day he was approached by an officer who asked whether, in addition to maps of West, East and South-east Asia, there was also a need for maps of the Scandinavian countries and North Africa, he had immediately replied in the negative – a view that was supported by his superiors at the time. No one then considered the possibility that Germany might one day have to fight in the desert. After all, Germany had no possessions outside Europe.

Years later, the same man was serving as transport officer responsible to Westphal for transport to Libya. Not without some triumph in his voice, he pointed out to Westphal that he had been right in asking for desert maps. In the months that followed, Westphal and his colleagues had to make do with improvised maps which often deviated sharply from reality. (11: 75)

The Germans supplemented captured British maps with information from their own military geological unit, consisting of two geologists and ten other staff. The thorough explorations carried out by this unit were combined with existing information and resulted in maps on which the accessibility of different areas was clearly shown.

The information collected was used intensively by the Germans to plan attack routes and the like. Collecting this information took time and could only be done in areas controlled by the Germans. This explains why Rommel took such trouble to personally acquaint himself with the terrain during the first period of his stay in North Africa.

German C3I capacity

Communication between the various combat units in the desert was also of great importance to coordinate actions. The Germans had excellent means of communication, since they saw this as an essential part of their concept of mobile warfare. Guderian, with his experience in liaison formations, had always been keen to provide them with optimal communication resources. At his insistence, tanks were equipped with radios, and special armoured command cars with the correct numbers of radios were developed for the different levels of command in tank divisions. (35: 42)

Given the German Army's emphasis on mission-orientation, personal initiative and fast decision-making, C3I capacity within the hierarchy was not used to control units in detail (micromanagement), but to gain a global picture of the position of units on a fast-moving battlefield. The German Army was also less vulnerable in the area of C3I capacity, because commanders and men were trained to achieve their objectives (their *Auftrag*) at their own discretion.

In combat, three important lines of communication could be distinguished:

- Between tank crew members
- Between tanks and other vehicles involved in the battle
- Between the commander on site with his mobile command unit and the division headquarters and staff officers further behind the front

Communication in tanks

This line of communication is of great importance during combat. The turrets of the German tanks provided space for three people to function as a team. During the campaign of May 1940, this turned out to be one of the advantages of the German tanks over, for instance, the French Char Bs. The single-person turrets of those tanks led to constant miscommunication between the commander and the other members of the crew, resulting in unfocused fire and the use of incorrect ammunition.

Communication between tanks

Communication between tanks plays a role in optimally concentrating forces during an attack. Properly coordinated, several tanks can target the enemy and eliminate opposing tanks one by one. (35: 65) There were generally three types of radio for this line of communication:

- Fu. Spr. Ger. F. vehicle-to-vehicle contact
- FuG. 8 or FuG. 12 (with or without frame antennas) for contact with the division headquarters
- FuG. 7 for Luftwaffe support

However, communication in the desert was at times made impossible by atmospheric disturbances. In addition, batteries drained quickly. Normal transmitting equipment was used, but larger aerials were mounted on all kinds of vehicles, as we have already seen with the *Aufklärungsabteilungen*. The tubular frames were fixed on top of the *Panzerspähwagens*, while on tanks these (smaller) frames were placed on the aft deck.

Communication between the different echelons

The situation was different with regard to the second line of communication. By remaining in direct contact with his regimental commanders on the front line, a divisional commander was able to gain a good picture of the course of the fighting and, if necessary, take control himself. However, radio did not always prove to be the most efficient means of maintaining contact with staff at division headquarters behind the front, due to the need for coding and decoding. It was more practical for the divisional commander and his chief of staff to sit around the table together in the morning to plan and in the evening to evaluate the day. Once objectives for the various units had been determined, they had a great deal of room for manoeuvre (*Auftragstaktik*), and the emphasis was more on communication within the units and less on communication with divisional headquarters. (36: 41)

However, problems persisted with regard to air-ground communications. Romantic though it was, Rommel could only communicate with his commanders on the ground by means of notes thrown from the window of his plane. The fact that he was actually able to land his Fieseler Storch – and sometimes did so, to the horror of his commanders – to communicate with a commander in person does not alter the fact that there were clear shortcomings in the German communications systems.

All in all, however, the Germans had a well-oiled C3I structure at their disposal which made it possible to obtain a clear picture of their actual position and the situation on the ground of the various units, to monitor the enemy's movements (the I component) and to respond alertly. They could thus maintain control and coordination at all times and deploy their units in a concentrated manner. The only disruptive factor within this whole was Rommel himself, who often manoeuvred audaciously outside the C3I structure, as we will see in the next chapters.

British C3I capability

The order-orientation, hierarchical command structure and emphasis on more or less detailed plans meant that in theory British C3I capacity was used for strict planning and control of the various levels of command and units. In practice, in North Africa, British communication capacity often proved to be completely insufficient. The result was that, on the one hand, the various headquarters had no idea how the fighting was developing and, on the other, that units received no or outdated orders, causing them to remain passive and to delay. In other words, the British Army was particularly vulnerable in terms of C3I capability, and its loss led to paralysis of the entire organization or its disintegration into smaller units, each fighting their own battle. It was only the fact that the British were very steadfast fighters which partly compensated for the shortcomings in their C3I capacity and often prevented them from being overrun.

Between the two world wars, the British had paid relatively little attention to communication by means of radiotelephony. The Royal Tank Corps can be seen as one of the pioneers in forcing the Royal Corps of Signals to purchase radio installations that could be used in moving vehicles. Very few officers had experience of using these at the beginning of the Second World War. Although the number and quality of radio installations increased between 1940 and 1942, conversations over more than a few kilometres were often impossible, and the enemy could listen in. Using Morse code or coding took a lot of time, so this was not a realistic alternative. This mainly affected communication between headquarters and the lower echelons, and the alternative was for the various commanders to meet in person. In practice, this partly determined the daily schedule of British commanders: the day started with carrying out reconnaissance to determine where the enemy was located. If this was known, the divisional commanders could sit round the table with the corps commander (who may have had to short-circuit some things with the commander-in-chief) to discuss the actions for the day. The divisional commanders then met with their brigade commanders to plan possible actions. Only then could plans actually be put into force.

A lot of time was lost in this way on travelling and meetings. Troop movements could only take place after all findings had been coordinated. After all units had been put into position and everyone had been informed of the new orders or the attack plan, the day had often come to an end. A whole day could be lost in this way without any action being taken. During combat, the divisional commander had the choice of remaining at his headquarters, at the risk of being overrun by rapidly advancing or cruising enemy units, or driving around at the risk of losing all contact with his own men. (3: 144)

The poor quality of British C3I capacity, especially in the period up to El Alamein, meant that British commanders were often in the dark about the current situation at the front. As a result, alert response and rapid execution of manoeuvres were not possible, nor was the concentrated deployment of units. This had major consequences for the course of the various offensives, as we will see.

3.4 Rommel as a manager

It is interesting to consider Rommel's – sometimes explicit – views on management, which help to explain his success in the coming period:

One of my first lessons in the field of motorized warfare was that speed and reaction time are of decisive importance in combat operations. The units must be able to carry out their missions with the greatest possible speed and without delay. As a commander you cannot settle for the average, but you must constantly raise the bar as high as possible and demand the utmost from your men, because the one who puts in the greatest effort is the fastest – and the fight is always decided in favour of the fastest.

In my view, the commander's task is not limited to staff matters. He must not only concern himself with the details of the preparation, but also be at the front of the line, for the following reasons:

- Correct implementation of the commander's plan by his subordinates is of great importance. It is naive to assume that every officer can understand the meaning of his specific assignment within the bigger picture. Most will quickly choose the easiest path: an excuse will soon be found why pre-set goals cannot be achieved. The fact that they realize that their commander is present at the front contributes to the fact that they will not quickly drop out. The commander must be the driving force on the battlefield. The men must realize that he is the one in control.
- The commander must strive to ensure that his troops are always informed of the latest developments in the field of tactics and their practical applications on the battlefield. Junior officers must be taught to respond quickly and adequately to sudden events. A commander must ensure that his troops receive good training, because this prevents unnecessary casualties.
- It is also important that the commander is well acquainted with the situation at the front and the problems his men are confronted with. He must keep this knowledge up to date and test it against the current situation on the battlefield, because otherwise he would conduct battles purely based on theory and with his limited knowledge of reality, as if they were a game of chess. In other words: a true leader is someone who constantly tests his own views and ideas against the circumstances in which his troops find themselves, instead of going into battle from a fixed framework and with rigid rules.
- The commander must remain in contact with his men. He must know their feelings and think like them. The soldier must have confidence in him. There is an absolute rule of thumb here: one must always be sincere towards the troops and never try to fool them for any reason. The soldier has an excellent nose for what is the truth and what is a false representation. (36: 113–14)

These management precepts are still powerful, and as we will see, they were a guideline for Rommel in the coming period.

We will now go on to describe the next series of battles.

3.5 *Brevity* and *Battleaxe*

The Axis forces were now partly in Egypt, and their main strongholds were at Sollum, the Halfaya Pass, Musadi, Fort Capuzzo and Sidi Omar, the so-called 'Sollum Front'. The passes at Halfaya and Sollum were of great significance because these were the only places where tanks could easily cross the desert plateau and gain access to the Libyan plain beyond. The troops on the Sollum front were led by Colonel von Herff, who in the first weeks of May had waged an aggressive and mobile defence against British troops and raided deep into the Egyptian hinterland. Von Herff had a total of 6,000 men at his disposal, spread over various places on the Sollum front. His task was to 'prevent certain operations by the opponent', while Rommel's mobile units were to provide 'adequate opposition to any offensive action directed against the Tobruk front, and at the same time to repel any attack by British motorized units east of Sollum.' Rommel had also given orders to build up defensive lines further west, at Gazala, like those at Tobruk, because these 'proved to be so eminently resistant to modern methods of attack.' (11: 120)

Von Herff was still busy strengthening the positions on the Sollum front when Wavell, under pressure from Churchill, decided to launch the offensive codenamed *Brevity*. Beresford-Peirse had, meanwhile, taken command of the British units from Neame, who as we have seen had been taken prisoner; the offensive itself was carried out by units under General Gott. The objective of *Brevity* was to recapture the Halfaya Pass, and the offensive focused on three points, namely the pass itself, Fort Capuzzo and Sollum. The British under General Gott attacked on 15 May, quickly capturing the Halfaya Pass and, after heavy fighting, Fort Capuzzo. However, Von Herff had let the British pass then successfully attacked them in the flank on 16 May. This was a good example of fluid defence, in which the German units repositioned themselves to open the counter-attack while maintaining cohesion and avoiding chaos. The British were driven back to the Halfaya Pass, where they managed to hold out for some time but were the victims of a surprise attack by von Herff on 27 May. They withdrew in disorder, leaving much materiel behind.

The recaptured places were reinforced, and the remarkable Captain (and ex-pastor) Wilhelm Bach was put in charge of the so-called Halfaya detachment. The fighting force

An 88mm Flak gun with SdKfz 7 tractor of the 1st Battalion/33rd Flak Regiment on the way to the Hafidh Ridge. (*Photo S. Klein*)

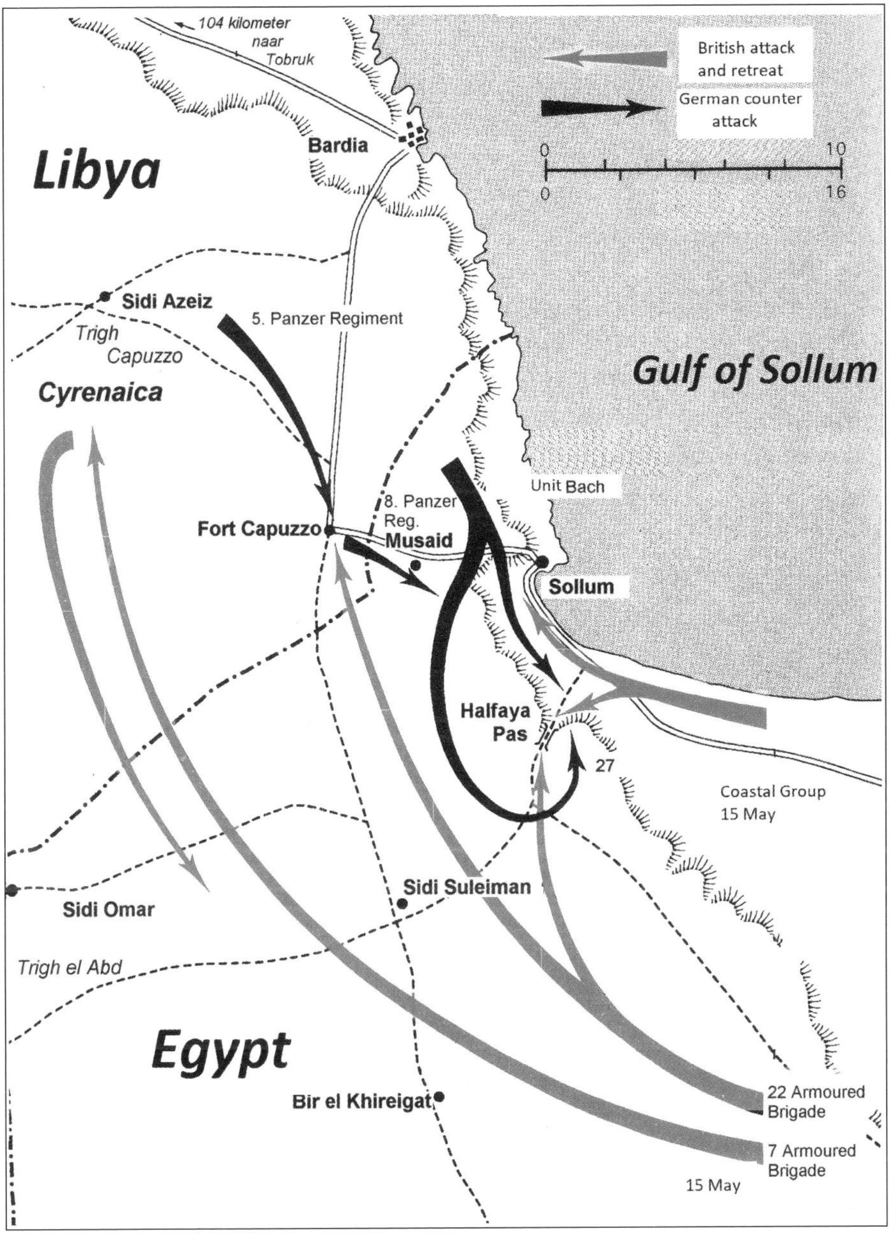

Overview of *Brevity*, 15–17 May 1941

there consisted of 500 German and 400 Italian troops, with five well-entrenched and effective 88mm Flak guns and a battery of French 155mm guns.

The other points on the Sollum front were also reinforced in the course of the following weeks. At the Hafidh Ridge, four 88mm Flak guns were dug in, and another four were assigned to the 15th Panzer Division, which was positioned as a strategic reserve behind the Sollum front. The new Pak 38/50mm anti-tank gun, a welcome improvement on the Pak

36/37mm, was placed at other points on the front. Meanwhile, Rommel had done his own reputation no good by sending hourly messages to the OKW in Berlin during the first attacks on 15 May, giving a very inconsistent and chaotic picture of the course of the battle. This earned him a reprimand from Field Marshal von Brauchitsch, Commander-in-Chief of the Army, who urged him to report clearly and consistently in future and not to be guided too much by the emotion of the moment. Rommel was clearly offended and wrote to his wife Lucie:

Bach and Rommel with the Halfaya Pass units.

> Yesterday evening [25 May] I got a good telling off from Berlin, from the OKW, for reasons that are completely unclear to me. It seems to be 'that my reports on the current situation at the front were not well received by the gentlemen up there. The result is that we will become silent here and will only report the absolute necessities. (36: 72)

If von Herff had not been so successful in parrying the British attack, Rommel, after the failure at Tobruk, would probably have been relieved of his command. Success on the Sollum Front led Rommel to ask the high command to show greater confidence in him. The question was irrelevant, however, since Rommel's fame was spreading like wildfire through Germany. (17: 93–4)

Both sides received reinforcements in the following weeks. Rommel could look forward to the phased arrival of the 15th Panzer Division, which came in three convoys at the end of April and beginning of May. The first units on motorcycles were, after a forced march, just in time to participate in the advance to Tobruk. The core of this division was the tank regiment with a total of 146 tanks.* After a long, phased journey along the Via Balbia, the division joined the DAK, and Rommel now had two tank divisions at his disposal, namely the 5th Leichte with its 5th Panzer Regiment and the 15th Panzer Division with its 8th Panzer Regiment. The 15th Panzer Division replaced the 5th Leichte Division on the border and began to strengthen the defensive line there with, among other things, 88mm Flak guns.

Rommel also used this period to get rid of officers he did not like. The commander of a tank battalion was court-martialled because during the assault on Tobruk in early May he had broken down in tears and had refused to attack the 'unbeatable' Matilda tanks.

* The 8th Panzer Regiment had at its disposal forty-five PzKpfw IIs, seventy-one PzKpfw IIIs, twenty PzKpfw IVs and ten PzKpfw *Befehlspanzer*.

The commander of the 5th Panzer Regiment of the Leichte Division, Olbricht, was sent on sick leave and Streich* was informed that he, too, was being replaced.

In the meantime, Wavell also received significant reinforcements on 12 May with the arrival of the Tiger convoy.** In mid-March Churchill had ordered this convoy of five fast ships to sail through the Mediterranean, despite the risks – indicating the importance the British attached to the North African theatre. Churchill's instruction to Wavell was clear: 'If this consignment gets through the hazards of the passage …no German should stay in Cyrenaica by the end of the month of June.' (44: 59) And on 17 May he asked with interest, 'What are your dates for bringing Tiger Cubs into action?' (3: 23) Wavell replied that this could not take place before the end of May 'and it would be better if they [the newly arrived units] could be given more time.'

Under increasing pressure from Churchill to deploy the 'Tiger Cubs' as quickly as possible, Wavell prepared a new offensive, named Battleaxe, with the newly arrived reinforcements. Its aim was to break through the German lines on the Egyptian-Libyan border, then relieve Tobruk and advance further west to Derna and Mechili. The attack had two axes:

- A frontal assault by infantry aimed at the Halfaya Pass
- A southward flanking movement by tank units towards Hafidh Ridge, Fort Capuzzo and Point 206

If these were successful, the British could break through to Sollum on the coast. The frontal attack would be carried out by part of the 4th Indian Infantry Division*** supported by Matilda tanks. The flanking movement would be carried out by the 7th Armoured Division with the 4th Armoured Brigade (Matildas), the 7th Armoured Brigade (Cruisers) and the remaining part of the 4th Indian Division. Various types of Cruiser tanks and a large number of Matildas would be deployed in this attack.**** Given their lack of speed, the latter would be deployed in the 'inner bend' of the southward flanking movement, followed by the infantry of the 4th Indian Division. The Cruisers would be responsible for the 'outer turn' of the movement and cover the flank of the Matildas and the infantry.

Because the unloading of the tanks went extremely slowly and some of them needed overhauling,***** the crews (and maintenance units) were ultimately only able to train for five days on tanks that were new to them.

* Upon his departure, Rommel remarked that Streich was too concerned about his troops. Streich replied that as a divisional commander he could not imagine a greater compliment.

** Tiger was a so-called fast convoy and carried a total of 238 tanks (!) – 135 Matildas, the rest Cruiser and light tanks – and fifty Hurricanes. A ship with sixty tanks was lost during the voyage. The Tiger convoy brought four different types of tank, bringing the total of tank types in North Africa to eight. Due to the inefficient unloading of the ships, it took until the end of May before all the tanks reached the troops. (40: 157)

*** Messervy commanded the 4th Indian Division, Creagh the 7th Armoured Division, and within this division, Gatehouse the 4th Armoured Brigade and Russell the 7th Armoured Brigade.

**** More than 100 Matildas.

***** The engine life of the Cruiser Mark IVA was only 1,600km. The tanks supplied by the Tiger convoy had already covered an average of 1,100km and were therefore of limited use.

This, along with a number of other reasons, made Wavell less than optimistic about the outcome of *Battleaxe*. 'The measure of success', he said, 'which will attend this operation is in my opinion doubtful.' (3: 23)

But *Battleaxe* continued, and on 15 June the British attacked. This first day of their offensive produced success in the southern flanking movement at Hafidh Ridge, Point 206 and Fort Capuzzo, but northwards the attack stalled at the Halfaya Pass. Bach's German/Italian detachment there, with its well-entrenched 88mm Flak gun, managed to repel the British frontal attack by eighteen Matildas. An artillery battery of 25-pounder howitzers, which was supposed to assist the Matildas in attacking the German position, had become stuck in the sand. Due to the lack of joint command and control, the tanks had advanced without their supporting artillery. They needed this because without artillery or air support the deployment of these tanks against well-protected positions was pointless, since the Matildas did not have HE ammunition. (29: 130)

> The friendly Captain Bach stood with his stick and cigar at the Flak 88 position. There is hardly a more nerve-racking sound imaginable than the growling and rattling of approaching tanks. But Bach said softly in his Baden accent, 'More than enough time …' At a signal from Bach the guns fired with their characteristically fierce sound, overwhelming the screeching of incoming shells. The Italian guns also started firing. The effect of the 10kg shells was devastating. The Matilda tanks exploded or came to a stop belching heavy smoke, some with their turrets leaning from the force of the impact. The remaining tanks desperately sought cover in the flat terrain to protect themselves with their toy guns …The carnage lasted for hours …The gun crews worked undisturbed as if they were on training. (29: 130–1)

Repelling this attack meant that an important part of Wavell's plan fell through. Further south, the 4th Armoured Brigade captured Point 206 and Fort Capuzzo on the same day,

The first encounter: tensely awaiting the arrival of the British tanks at the Hafidh Ridge. Note the aiming devices of the battery. (*Photo S. Klein*)

and a force of eighty Matildas advanced past these positions. The 7th Armoured Brigade, meanwhile, cornered the detachment at the Hafidh Ridge which was slowly but surely running out of ammunition.

> During the advance to Capuzzo, Major R. 'Jock'* Holden, commander of a squadron of the 4th Armoured Brigade, saw his Cruiser tanks on his left side carrying out a charge in the best traditions of the cavalry against the position on the Hafidh Ridge. 'They had the same luck as the cavalrymen of the First World War, whose commanders had refused to take cognizance of the invention of the machine gun. One tank after another flew apart, hulls shattered, turrets torn off and belching black, oily smoke. An entire squadron was wiped out in a matter of minutes. (29: 131)

After a final attack on the Hafidh Ridge had died down, Rommel made a southward detour with the 5th Leichte. A fierce tank battle broke out between the 5th Panzer Regiment and the 7th Armoured Brigade which continued on 16 June, after which not a single British tank remained operational (!)

Meanwhile, a second tank battle was raging between the 8th Panzer Regiment and the 4th Armoured Brigade. During the night of the 15/16th, the 4th Armoured Brigade had entrenched itself well and dug its tanks in, which meant that the German tanks had to come within range of the 2-pounder guns. This led to considerable losses, and at the end of the morning only thirty of the original eighty German tanks were still operational. On the British side, too, many Matildas were no longer operational, mainly due to mechanical defects.

In one incident during the battle a Sergeant McGinniley was asked by a sergeant major and two stretcher-bearers to stop firing because a wounded man was lying between the lines:

> The men had a large Red Cross flag, and the German panzers, too, immediately held their fire. The three men proceeded to bring in a sergeant of McGinniley's unit who explained that his tank had been knocked out the previous evening by one of the Panzer IVs. Since he himself had been wounded in the knee, the Germans had given him a blanket and told him, 'You'll be all right; by tomorrow morning, at the latest, your bearers will be here to fetch you.' Immediately after he was carried away, the armour-piercing ammunition began to whine again all over the place. (29: 136)

Despite the successful repulsion of both attacks, there remained the threat of a British breakthrough by a concentrated attack with their remaining tanks. That is why Rommel made the decision to attack the British from the flank, something they had always feared. Rommel had his two tank divisions advance to cut through the British flank towards the Halfaya Pass, with the aim of relieving Bach and ultimately surrounding the British. Seizing the initiative, he threw the British force off balance; they were surprised and began to withdraw to the south-west at Point 206 and Capuzzo, with the Matildas covering the retreat of the infantry. When the two tank divisions arrived at the Halfaya Pass late in the afternoon of 17 June, it appeared that the majority of the British troops there had withdrawn.

---

* According to old English custom all Scots were known as 'Jock'.

Relief: German servicemen breathe a sigh of relief as the first German tanks arrive at the Halfaya Pass. (*Photo TM/von Esebeck*)

The result was that although the British attack had been repulsed, an encirclement of the British troops had failed. Rommel was incensed by this, especially because the surrender of Capuzzo by the British had been reported at an early stage by reconnaissance units, but no immediate follow-up had been ordered.

Typically, during these encounters, Rommel was always to be found wherever the action was. Due to the key role that staff officers played at the (static) headquarters in the rear, he could move freely around the battlefield with his *Gefechtsstaffel* (combat squadron) to inspect the progress of his troops at the front. The *Gefechtsstaffel* consisted of a number of armoured personnel carriers, staff cars, Volkswagens and two of the three AEC 4x4 Mammoth Armoured Command Vehicles (ACV) captured from O'Connor and Neame. Rommel thought these were comfortable vehicles and christened them 'Max' and 'Moritz'.* He made the third Mammoth available to other commanders. For crossing open terrain he used his SdKfz 250, called 'Greif'. For optimal communication with the (static) headquarters behind the front, radio vans with transmitting equipment were added to the *Gefechtsstaffel*. However, practice showed that, especially in the follow-up phases, when Rommel advanced very quickly, the radio vans were often so far behind that contact with him was sometimes impossible at critical moments. Incidentally, the headquarters had its own unit, the *Kampfstaffel*, to protect against surprise attacks or enemy troops appearing

* *Max und Moritz* is a German illustrated tale from 1865 by Wilhelm Busch. Max and Moritz are two naughty boys who torment their village by pulling seven pranks, the last of which ends fatally for them. Its black humour made the story controversial.

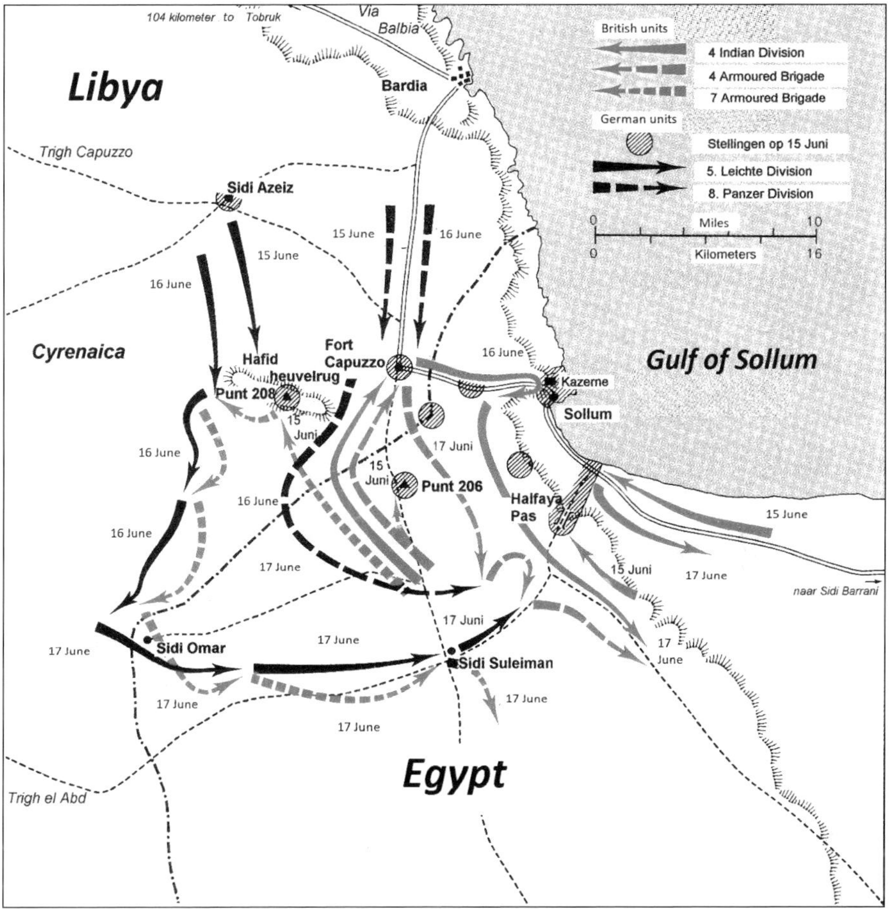

Overview of *Battleaxe*.

by chance in the open desert. At this stage the *Kampfstaffel* was the size of a company, but because of the unpredictable nature of the fighting it was later increased to the size of a battalion. However, this could not prevent the DAK headquarters from being completely overrun by British units during the *Crusader* battles (see next chapter).

The final losses of the British were around 200 tanks,* while only twelve German tanks could be considered a total loss. The fact that the Germans were left as masters of the battlefield meant that they were able to recover their damaged tanks and make them operational again. In terms of casualties, the British lost 1,000 men and the Germans 700. Better tactics and better training, combined with Rommel's daring, formed the basis of this victory. The fact that so many tanks, including Matildas, were destroyed contributed to the myth of the superiority of the German PzKpfw III and IV; the British did not realize that due to the tactic of *Verbundene Waffen* many tanks had fallen victim to anti-

* They were accounted for by 1,680 88mm shells, roughly twenty per tank. The 2cm Flak knocked out three tanks with a total of 13,500 shells.

Rommel in his SdKfz 250 'Greif'. The large tubular frame served for radio communication. (*Photo BTM*)

tank guns rather than tanks. The use of the 88mm Flak (anti-aircraft) gun as anti-tank weapon was unthinkable to them.

A good example of the effectiveness of German anti-tank artillery is the failure of the frontal attack by Matilda tanks on the Halfaya Pass during Operation *Battleaxe*. A captured British major, who asked which gun had knocked out his tank, described the use of anti-aircraft guns as anti-tank guns as 'unfair'. The high silhouette of the guns was a drawback that was partly remedied during 1941. In addition, they were fitted with an armour plate to protect the crew, and better aiming equipment, and the muzzle velocity was increased. In desert warfare the Flak was often used in transport positions during mobile combat actions. In such cases it was not fixed on the ground, but disconnected from its tractor, usually an SdKfz 7, on a special trailer with side supports folded out for stability. Its speed of deployment and greater mobility outweighed its high profile and instability.

The 88mm Flak gun

The 88mm Flak gun had once again lived up to its fame on the battlefield and also offered relief against the heavily armoured Matildas. After *Battleaxe*, the Flak Regiment 33 claimed a total of ninety-two disabled armoured vehicles* (of which eighty-two were tanks), and the 8th Panzer Regiment 'only' sixty-four disabled armoured vehicles (18: 188). However, the number of artillery pieces available was very limited, five at the Halfaya Pass, four at the Hafidh Ridge and four at the strategic reserve. This experience certainly undermined British confidence in the inviolability of their Matildas. After *Battleaxe*, the British considered these tanks to be too slow and too lightly armed.

What is remarkable is the way in which the troops of the various Flak units adapted to their new role. Instead of static anti-aircraft guns, they operated as highly mobile *Panzerjäger*, something for which they were neither selected nor trained.

* About half due to enemy action, the other half to mechanical failure. (3: 25)

Explanation of the battle at the Hafidh Ridge. S. Klein is directly behind Rommel in dust goggles. (*Photo S. Klein*)

In the form of the 3.7-inch (approximately 94mm) anti-aircraft gun, the British had a weapon with essentially the same potential as the German 88mm Flak gun. But due to an incomprehensible resistance to learning from the enemy, the use of this as an anti-tank weapon was prohibited by the Army leadership, to the anger of the soldiers in the field. This illustrates the way in which the regimental system and the resulting strict separation into armed forces units frustrated the development of tactics and the adequate deployment of weapon systems. It may have been a big step to use anti-aircraft guns as anti-tank guns, but it had been common practice on the German side for several years. It is interesting to note in this context that the Germans described taking out tanks as '*abschiessen*' (shooting down).

In practice, the British used their excellent 25-pounder (approximately 90mm) field gun, greatly respected by the Germans, as an improvised anti-tank gun. At the time of *Crusader*, in addition to HE ammunition, AP was also available for this gun, significantly increasing its effectiveness. On the other hand, using the gun in this role removed it from the role in which it was most effective, namely that of regular artillery.

The failure of the two offensives cost Wavell and Beresford-Peirse their positions: Wavell left for India, General Auchinleck replaced him and General Cunningham became the new commander-in-chief of the Eighth Army on 2 July. The following months were characterized by relative calm at the front. Units were sent deep into the enemy hinterland by both sides, but nothing more than pinpricks were dealt.

3.6 Logistics management: the other strategic dimension

The first confrontations with the British were decided in favour of the Axis, but now Rommel was confronted with a new strategic problem, namely logistics. In the coming years, he would constantly complain about the amount of materiel he received, and on several occasions he accused the Italian navy of a lack of commitment to transport to North Africa. This last accusation was not justified by the statistics. During the campaign, the Italian navy did its utmost to help supply the troops – each transport ship had on average more than one naval vessel as an escort.

After Rommel's first offensive in early 1941, there were approximately 164,000 German and Italian troops in North Africa. They had over 15,000 vehicles (and over 5,500 horses and mules) and needed about 70–80,000 tons of supplies per month. The troops at the front alone needed 1,500 tons per day. The great variety of vehicles and weapons systems (for example, the very large number of different German trucks) exacerbated the problems of supply and logistics.

These logistical demands exceeded the capacity of the ports of Tripoli and Benghazi, which is why they were enlarged over time and eventually better protected with anti-aircraft guns. (11: 120) With regard to logistics, two phases can be distinguished:

- Transport to North Africa via the Mediterranean
- Transport over land in North Africa itself

The following diagram gives an idea of the first route.

Overview of tonnage

	Shipped	Arrived safely	Percentage
Men	206,402	189,162	91
Fuel	599,338	476,703	80
Trucks/tanks	275,310	243,633	85
Weapons/ammunition	171,060	149,462	87

Rommel's units received 80 per cent of the fuel and 86 per cent of the other supplies that had been shipped to them. (17: 17) His reproachful comments about the Italians were therefore unjustified. It was true, however, that, given the priorities of other fronts, Rommel received much less than he asked for.

A second logistical dimension, however, was transport within North Africa itself. Depending on where the supplies were landed, in the most extreme cases they had to be carried over approximately 1,700km, roughly the distance between Hamburg and Rome, often over a limited number of roads, of which the coastal route, the Via Balbia, was the most important. In addition, some supplies were carried by the Luftwaffe's transport fleet.

With regard to logistics, four periods can be distinguished:

February–May 1941

Convoys were able to cross the Mediterranean from Italy to North Africa with relative ease. After the capture of Benghazi, the flow of goods shifted to this port, although its capacity was limited. Submarines were used to unload fuel at Derna for the forward units of the DAK. Smaller ships were used for coastal transport.

June–December 1941

During this period, many men and much shipping capacity and materiel were lost due to actions by the Royal Navy. Air transport was arranged as an alternative, and tanks and spare parts were ferried over by naval vessels. Bardia, a port close to the front, could not be used due to the constant attacks on it by the RAF. The situation was so serious in December 1941 that even Italian battleships had to be deployed to protect the convoys.

January–June 1942

Air transport was relatively unhindered during this period, as the Luftflotte 2 (Air Fleet 2) under Kesselring managed to gain air superiority. Between 93 and 99 per cent of supplies reached the ports. By keeping the British under constant pressure on Malta, the convoy system ran smoothly and losses were few. During this period the Italians and Germans had sufficient equipment and supplies for the limited offensive that would almost take them to Egypt, as we shall see. Additional supplies were also built up for six to eight weeks in anticipation of an offensive aimed at capturing Malta.

However, on 10 May Kesselring decided that the threat from Malta had been neutralized and transferred two *Gruppen* of bombers and two *Gruppen* of fighters to the Eastern Front. Almost at the same time, Malta received reinforcements in the form of fighters, enabling the British to regain local air superiority.

July 1942–May 1943

The successful offensive in May had taken Rommel far from his supply dumps in Tripoli and Benghazi; transport over land was virtually impossible given the distances involved, and coastal shipping was severely hampered by the RAF. Luftflotte 2 came to Rommel's aid and set up bases in North Africa to support Rommel on the spot. As a result, the German grip on Malta loosened, allowing the British to recover and, thanks to new bombers with radar, paralyze the convoy system. As a last resort, an air bridge was set up from Crete, but its capacity was far too small to support the *Panzerarmee*. After El Alamein, the logistical situation deteriorated dramatically, and in late 1942 and early 1943 North Africa was completely cut off from Europe by Anglo-American superiority. The end of the German-Italian presence in the area was now only a matter of time.

What is striking about the logistical movements is their high degree of asynchrony: when Rommel operated in the west, this often coincided with a favourable logistical situation, which made an eastward offensive possible (spring 1941 and summer 1942). This then led to a situation in which the entire logistical system became overstretched due to the great distances involved and British actions put further pressure on supplies (winter 1941 and autumn 1942). As a consequence, the British were able to launch counter-offensives which often led to logistical problems on their side. (45: 14–15)

The British in turn were often forced to shift their attention to other fronts with a higher priority immediately after successful offensives. In early 1941, after Wavell's offensive, the situation in the Balkans and Greece demanded all their attention. A year later, after the *Crusader* offensive, the advance of the Japanese in the Far East led to a shift of attention to that region, which in turn led to new priorities in the areas of men, materiel and logistics. All these changes gave the conflict in North Africa its strongly oscillating character.

3.7 Evaluation of the German Army

Tactical dimensions

Brevity, and in particular *Battleaxe*, demonstrated clearly the way in which Rommel would engage the British in the coming period. During *Battleaxe*, the German tank units operated as a single entity; the units of the two tank regiments were never deployed separately. Moreover, by concentrating the power of both regiments, Rommel proved able to take the initiative and dictate the course of the battle. Defensively, the Germans were also able to repel the British offensives by deploying anti-tank guns and 88mm Flak guns. In addition, German tanks repeatedly succeeded in luring British tanks into ambush by anti-tank guns. The British then became stuck, after which they were attacked by tank units advancing rapidly from behind the gun line: this 'sword and shield' tactic would be used often and successfully by the Germans in the coming period. Choosing the right moment to take the initiative was also important, as Rommel said:

> The decisive moment had arrived: the halting of the British attack, followed immediately by the joint advance of both armoured regiments to the Halfaya Pass. One can often turn a battle to one's advantage by simply shifting the focus of the battle. (36: 72)

Tanks

After this first round of tank battles, the Germans evaluated the performance of their tanks. Not surprisingly, they concluded that the PzKpfw I was completely outdated, while the PzKpfw II had fulfilled its role as a command and reconnaissance tank adequately. The PzKpfw III was initially a problem child with a large number of weak points. However, after modification, this tank functioned perfectly and formed the backbone of the German tank regiments throughout the campaign, together with the PzKpfw IV. These tanks were given wider tracks and a new air intake inside the crew compartment. Before that, their engines constantly sucked in dust and had to be overhauled every 1,500 to 2,000km (!), as against a normal service period of 6,000 to 7,000km. The filters in the new air intake had to be closely monitored and cleaned regularly, preferably every 40km (!), when travelling through the desert. The PzKpfw IV was rated as 'very good' and did not require any modifications. (18: 188)

In the meantime, the British had also subjected several captured PzKpfw IIIs and IVs to testing. Although the PzKpfw IIIs were completely dismantled, the British overlooked the specially hardened steel plates that had been welded onto the tanks as additional armour and made these tanks immune to the 2-pounder gun. Training Memorandum No. 2 from October 1941 reported that 'numbers of each type (PzKpfw III and IV) have been knocked out in Libya and Greece in a variety of methods, and penetration performance of British weapons against these tanks is very good indeed ...The myth of German invincibility of material, when submitted to the cold light of engineering fact, makes a very sorry exhibition.' (18: 112) Technically, therefore, these tanks should not have been a problem for the British, despite their constant references to the superiority of German material. It did not yet occur to them that superior German tactics might have played an important role in the enemy's successes.

The Germans had also learned some lessons about waging war in the desert:

- All units had to be motorized
- A much higher percentage of tanks and anti-tank weapons had to be deployed than on other fronts, since these were the decisive weapons

In addition, there was a need for:

- Water units with equipment to dig wells and instal pumps and desalination plants
- Water transport columns. However, there were no separate tankers available for this (as on the British side) so jerry cans had to do the job. These had to be filled separately, loaded onto trucks and distributed: all in all, an extremely inefficient method of transport. (45: 8)

The British did have tankers for transporting water, but they encountered other problems. Their four-gallon fuel cans were so light in construction that they fell apart easily, and British petrol trucks could therefore leave an explosive trail on rough terrain. Petrol loss during transport could amount to 40 per cent (!)

The Germans formulated a number of additional tactical precepts. For example, reconnaissance units had to be deployed far ahead in the desert, since experience had shown that accurate target recognition was only possible in the early morning hours, because once the sun was up the outlines of tanks and vehicles were completely confused by heat vibration in the atmosphere. Troops who were new to North Africa had to be continuously trained in estimating distance; due to the combination of good visibility over long distances, the aforementioned heat vibration and the lack of orientation points, new armoured troops tended to overestimate the distance to their targets by between two and three kilometres. New *Panzerjäger*, on the other hand, often underestimated the distance. This led to an undesirably high consumption of ammunition. (18: 188–9)

Men

The health of German troops in North Africa soon became a source of concern. In the summer of 1941 *Oberarzt* (senior physician) Dr Fahndrich visited Libya and found that the troops were short of essentials such as butter, eggs, milk and easily digestible carbohydrates. Of the 50,000 men in North Africa, about 10 per cent were chronically ill. After dysentery, jaundice was the most dangerous disease: men suffering from it could often be seen walking with an arm over their swollen livers. The treatment of dysentery in particular worried Fahndrich greatly. Dysentery patients were generally transported quickly far behind the lines, so that the field hospitals at the front could focus on men wounded in battle. However, many of these dysentery patients were severely ill and died in transport. Dysentery could strike quickly: in a hospital in Derna he saw rows of patients who had arrived in North Africa only four weeks earlier. Incidentally, he himself was struck down immediately upon arrival, but he recovered quickly, since dysentery is in fact easily curable.

The equipment and food supply in the field hospitals, on the other hand, were excellent. Many were located in *wadis* because they were then easy to camouflage against air raids and protect from the sun. However, these *wadis* also formed the natural drainage to the sea, and when it rained the field hospitals were often flooded, sometimes drowning patients. (29: 166)

Rommel

It is now time to look more closely at Rommel himself, especially since he had been exposed to so much criticism during the first two phases – as he would be again later.

Rommel's leadership seemed omnipresent in North Africa. He overwhelmed his subordinates and the OKW with his often daring plans and frequently ignored orders completely. Miraculously, many of his decisions turned out well, although the question remains whether he paid enough attention to preparation, direction and coordination. There was clear resistance to his methods among commanders such as Streich, but none were strong enough to offer genuine resistance. Only in the later phases of the conflict did Rommel have to deal with personalities such as Crüwell, Bayerlein and Westphal who were not so easy to convince. Rommel came across – to the despair of officers such as Streich – as a general who paid little attention to the opinions of his subordinates, was impatient and stuck to his own interpretation of events. If things did not go as expected, he did not hesitate to blame others. On the other hand, he always enjoyed the support of his men (including the Italians) and was consequently able to motivate them at all times. In addition, Rommel showed himself to have a number of very special qualities: he sensed the intentions of his opponents exceptionally well, and he understood the desert.

3.8 Evaluation of the British Army

What is striking in this and later phases of the conflict is Churchill's continued involvement. It was he who forced Wavell to attack as soon as possible after the arrival of the Tiger convoy, while some of the equipment was not yet ready and crews had hardly had time to get used to the new tanks. They were also not given the opportunity to practise at brigade or division level, so were forced to operate in relatively small units.

Incidentally, Rommel was impressed by Wavell and called him the only British general who 'showed any form of genius'. He analysed *Battleaxe* and Wavell's role as follows:

> Wavell's strategic planning of the offensive had been excellent. What distinguished him from the other British army commanders was his great and balanced strategic insight, which made him concentrate his forces without having to take into account the moves of his opponent. He was aware of the necessity of preventing any manoeuvre which would enable his opponent to break through his line, isolate his formations and destroy them one by one by creating a local superiority. But he was at a great tactical disadvantage owing to the low speed of the Infantry tanks, which made it impossible for him to react alertly to the movements of our faster vehicles. (44: 68)

Tanks

The combination of Cruiser and Matilda tanks proved to be unfortunate, due to the great difference in their speed. The Matilda also proved to be far less invulnerable than initially thought: new German tactics meant that they fell prey to German anti-tank guns, particularly because they were so slow.

A number of other points are striking. During the assault on the Hafidh Ridge, the British attacked head-on, with the tanks advancing in a single line at right angles to the German positions, then turning 90 degrees and driving along the German positions while firing. This was an incomprehensible and dangerous manoeuvre that seems to have been blindly copied from the navy (the so-called 'crossing the T'*), but was not evaluated as such. British reports also show that they did not realize that they had to fundamentally change their tactics if they wanted to be able to take on the Germans on equal terms. They also failed to realize that the majority of their tanks were being destroyed by anti-tank guns, particularly the 88mm Flak guns, and not by tanks. This perpetuated the myth of German tank superiority. (18: 187)

On the German side, the actions of British Cruiser tanks during *Brevity* and *Battleaxe* were seen as swift and bold,** particularly because they were often carried out against a numerically superior force. Contrary to British custom, the tanks attacked the flanks and rear of German units, instead of frontally. The British, however, operated their tanks in small parcels, without much mutual direction and coordination and without anti-tank guns, a structural failing that would come back to haunt them many times. While the Germans emphasized the concentration of striking power, the British forces were thus divided. This meant that Rommel did not have to worry about a 3:1 British versus German tank superiority in the later stages of the conflict. He assumed – not without reason, as will become apparent – that the superior tactics of the Germans, combined with the tank regiments' integrated supply and recovery system, meant that the British were no match for his tanks.

With regard to the Matildas, it is noticeable that at Point 206 and Capuzzo they were used as a kind of mobile artillery for the infantry, which was very vulnerable and could not protect itself in hostile terrain. The digging-in of these tanks at Capuzzo did give them protection, but it also made them completely static, despite the rule that tanks must always be able to operate in a mobile fashion on the battlefield.

The performance of both British tank types once again confirmed the rule that the success of a tank is determined by a combination of armour, armament and speed. These elements were unevenly distributed over the British tanks and that put them at a disadvantage compared to their German opposite numbers.

Artillery

The British increasingly questioned the effectiveness of the 2-pounder gun mounted in most tanks. Opinions vary, but in general this gun is considered less effective than the one mounted in the PzKpfw III and IV.*** Doubts about it are reflected in the discussion, which had been raging since 1938, about replacing it with a heavier-calibre gun. However, due to shortages, no new type was developed in the following two years. It was not until April 1940 that the design for a heavier 6-pounder (57mm) gun was ready for testing.

* In crossing the T, a squadron steams at right angles to the opponent's ships. The squadron can only use the forward guns of the leading ship, while the opponent's ships can fire with all their guns broadside. The only way to prevent this is to make a 90-degree turn to be able to fire broadside as well.

** There was no shortage of courage on the British side at this stage of the conflict, a feature which had everything to do with the mentality and morale of the units involved.

*** Compared to the 88mm gun, the 2-pounder was indeed a 'plug shooter', as the British called it. The shells weighed 0.91kg compared to 10kg for the 88mm gun. The kinetic energy of the 88mm shells had such great destructive power that they could penetrate 150mm of armour (the frontal armour of a Tiger I tank) at a distance of 2km. The 2-pounder gun with the same muzzle velocity, on the other hand, was only able to penetrate 56mm at 500m.

The dramatic events of May 1940 once again underlined the need to put a 6-pounder gun into production in the short term, but the decision was initially made in favour of the 2-pounder (37mm) gun, which was easier to produce and in larger quantities. Production of the 6-pounder got underway at the beginning of 1941, and in November of that year the first pieces reached the front in North Africa. In 1942 the British had about 100 6-pounder guns at their disposal (37: 175), and by then the development of an even heavier 17-pounder gun for tank and anti-tank guns had already begun. The first production examples of these appeared in January 1943.

Innovation in the British Army

The British 3.7-inch (94mm) anti-aircraft gun had characteristics similar to those of the German 88mm Flak gun. The potential of this gun had already been recognized by the men in the field, and Wavell personally ordered it to be tested in the winter campaign of 1940 against the Italians, when General McIntyre was given the opportunity to use it to break down the defences at Tobruk. Tim Palmer saw the pillboxes around Tobruk being shot to pieces one by one over a distance of 2,500m by crews untrained in this type of shelling. McIntyre was nicknamed 'Mad Max' by the traditional officer corps for his ideas and left the North African theatre a few months later; Wavell was then relieved of his command and sent to India. In the months that followed, all the 3.7-inch guns were used against the Luftwaffe, and any use of the guns in an anti-tank role was rejected. Churchill was constantly preoccupied with the subject of tanks and anti-tank guns. Despite a continuous stream of notes and memoranda from him on the subject, no bridge was built between the political elite and the young officer corps with front-line experience. The 3.7-inch gun continued to play the same role, that of an anti-aircraft gun. (14: 95–6)

The Germans were in awe of the way British tanks and mobile artillery operated together. The British artillery was very accurate, even in mobile situations, and at this stage of the conflict the Germans had no mobile artillery that could advance with their tanks. In their evaluations of combat, the Germans warned of British trucks with a field gun mounted on the loading platform and shooting over the cab. These were often difficult to distinguish from normal trucks, but their effect was very limited; few tanks were damaged because only HE ammunition was available. German tank crews generally found British artillery fire exasperating, because it meant they had to close the hatches of their tanks. Later in the conflict, the fear of British artillery would grow, when AP ammunition became available in addition to HE.

In the eyes of the Germans, the fire of British tanks themselves was ineffective because, in line with cavalry tradition, shots were often fired while moving. The Germans, on the other hand, always fired from a stationary position and their shooting was much more accurate. (18: 188)

According to German evaluations, the British also proved to be very adept at carrying out reconnaissance and raids behind the front line using Jock Columns, in which, in addition to fast armoured cars, infantry and artillery on trucks were deployed. These were at first less effective than during actions against the Italians in 1940, but they would show their destructive power again during *Crusader*, the next phase. Small tank units also

Artillérie portée

Using guns on trucks was not a British innovation. As early as 1915, the French mounted their famous 75mm guns on trucks to enable them to manoeuvre more quickly and to reduce their dependence on horse traction: they had calculated that in a prolonged conflict there would soon be a shortage of horses. Part of the truck's cab was removed to make room for the gun barrel. During the course of the war, the number of '*artillérie portée*' units grew from two batteries in 1915 to thirty-three regiments in 1918. These had a total of approximately 8,600 vehicles (trucks and others) and a total complement of 44,000 men. In this way, the French developed extremely mobile, formidable and effective artillery units. Their only drawback was the mechanical reliability of the trucks.

carried out operations far behind enemy lines, forcing the Germans to be constantly on their guard. The disadvantage was a fragmentation of men and materiel over the various units, especially the artillery, the most effective part of the British armed forces.

The British did not allow tanks and infantry to operate together, and these units did not train for joint operations. Nor did they have armoured personnel carriers for the infantry to operate with tanks. Without such vehicles, the infantry was defenceless in terrain without natural shelter such as bushes or houses. Unsurprisingly, both sides considered the destruction of the enemy's materiel to be of great importance: without tanks, armoured vehicles or trucks, combat in the desert was impossible. British tanks also lacked the protection of anti-tank guns operating with with them. These two factors largely determined the great differences in effectiveness between British and German tank units.

Tactics

In terms of tactics, the British did not yet realize that they had to make a number of fundamental changes if they wanted to offer effective resistance to the Germans other than by achieving overwhelming superiority in men and materiel. In the coming episodes we will see that the British applied various organizational and tactical concepts, but without ever achieving satisfactory results. Only Montgomery would reduce these ideas to a number of starting points which formed the basis for his success. But that was yet to come.

With regard to command, it became apparent that the lack of sufficient knowledge and experience in armoured warfare among key figures would lead to ineffective deployment of the tank units. This sometimes also related even to basic elements such as frequently used terms and concepts and the technical abilities of tanks. In addition, commanders generally stayed far behind the front, and communication between the various levels of command was often very slow due to the lack of effective means of communication. (44: 66)

All in all, the British had a long way to go before they could tackle the Germans on equal terms.

Chapter 4

Operation *Crusader*

4.1 A new formation and a new structure: *Panzergruppe Afrika*

After June, there was a lull in the fighting which would last until September while both sides reflected on their situation and received reinforcements. By the start of Operation *Barbarossa* (22 June 1941), it had become clear to Rommel why he had not received more men and equipment in the preceding period. In the eyes of the OKW, however, Rommel's position in North Africa had acquired a heightened strategic priority. There was a concept within the OKW of a grand strategy in which Rommel, after the capture of Tobruk, was to advance westwards through Egypt and Turkey in order to eventually make contact with German troops advancing from the Caucasus. He was given the task of developing the necessary plans for such a move (17: 102) In the meantime, he had been promoted to *General der Panzertruppen* on 1 July, and from 15 August the troops under his command were called *Panzergruppe Afrika** and consisted of the DAK and the Italian XXI Corps. Lieutenant General Crüwell, specially transferred from the Soviet Union in September, was the new commander of the DAK, which consisted of:

- The 5th Leichte Division (after 21 October the 21st Panzer Division) with the 5th Panzer Regiment under the command of Major General von Ravenstein
- The 15th Panzer Division with the 8th Panzer Regiment under the command of Major General Neumann-Silkow
- The *Afrika Division zur besonderen Verwendung* (consisting of troops already present in Africa, supplemented with new arrivals), after January 1942 renamed the 90th Leichte Division, under the command of General Sümmermann

The XXI Corps under General Navarrini consisted of:

- The 17th Division Pavia
- The 25th Division Bologna
- The 27th Division Brescia
- The 102nd Division Trento (motorized – on paper, not in practice)

---

* It was not entirely clear what was meant by a *Panzergruppe*. It was certainly smaller than an *Armee*. On the other hand, Rommel had been promoted to general, the rank that went with command of an *Armee*. Rommel was in doubt whether he was an *Oberbefehlshaber* or just a *Befehlshaber*. In September, his pay slip showed that he was indeed paid as an *Oberbefehlshaber*, and that his Gruppe was therefore more or less an *Armee*. Incidentally, these reflections had not prevented him from issuing the first order of the *Panzergruppe* on 15 August as '*Armee Befehl Nummer 1*'.

These Italian divisions were generally not motorized, and poorly armed. The only motorized Italian units could be found in the mobile Italian XX Corps (Corpo d'Armata di Manovra) under the command of General Gambara. They were:

- The 132nd Ariete Tank Division
- The 101st Trieste Motorized Division
- RECAM (Raggruppamento Esplorante)

In addition to a number of light tanks, Rommel had approximately 170 larger tanks (135 PzKpfw IIIs and 35 PzKpfw IVs) in two tank divisions at his disposal. Gambara had 146 M-13 tanks, which had a poor reputation. In addition to ninety-six Pak 38/50mm guns, Rommel had twenty-three 88mm Flak guns at the front and twelve as a general reserve for the DAK.

In theory, Rommel, like Gambara, was answerable to the Italian Commander-in-Chief in North Africa, Marshal Bastico. However, Rommel had built up such a reputation, with his Italian subordinates as well as his own men, that he could generally afford to ignore the Italian.

A new staff was also appointed for the Panzergruppe, with Gause* as chief of staff and a new staff officer for operations, the brilliant Colonel Westphal. The latter would be Rommel's right-hand man during the eighteen months of his stay in North Africa. Westphal was nominated twice by Rommel for the Knight's Cross and was finally awarded the German Cross in Gold in December 1941 and the Knight's Cross in November 1942. We shall see, however, that in the course of the coming months the relationship between Westphal and Rommel was not entirely smooth.

Another arrival was Alfred Berndt, a fervent supporter of Hitler with a high position in the Nazi hierarchy. Berndt was attached to the Ministry of Propaganda and was responsible for the PR of the DAK and of Rommel personally. He performed this task excellently and promoted the legend surrounding Rommel, ensuring that the DAK and Rommel remained in the public eye and being responsible for the direct line between Rommel and Hitler. This explains the attitude that Rommel sometimes adopted towards his superiors in the OKW: he knew that if push came to shove he could always fall back on Hitler, via Berndt. It was also Berndt who, via Hitler and Goebbels, ensured that Rommel was promoted to general after the establishment of the *Panzergruppe Afrika*, much to the dismay of the High Command and the General Staff.

At the end of October, Colonel Bayerlein, with his experience on the Eastern Front under Guderian, strengthened the ranks of the DAK as Chief of Staff. All in all, Rommel was very pleased with these changes to the staff of the *Panzergruppe Afrika*.

With regard to the Italian units, it became clear that Rommel, despite the pressure he put on Marshal Bastico, whom he referred to as 'Bombastico' – in theory Rommel's supreme commander – could not control the XX Corps under Gambara. His relationship with the Italian supreme command did not improve as a result.

---

* Gause had been sent by Halder to North Africa to be attached to the Italian High Command in order to keep an eye on Rommel. He arrived on 15 June at the beginning of *Battleaxe* and was immediately impressed by the way in which Rommel led the fighting. He placed his entire staff at Rommel's disposal: 43 officers, 20 civilian technicians, 120 soldiers and 46 vehicles, and was then promptly recalled to Berlin by Halder for consultations.

Despite this difficult relationship with the Italian supreme command and Marshal Bastico, Rommel got along well with the various Italian commanders. He was convinced of their dedication and commitment and trusted them completely. He found that Italian soldiers, if well trained and well led, were of excellent quality, but he knew their limitations and thought it was irresponsible to give them impossible orders. He accused the Italian supreme command of having given its soldiers poor equipment, partly of First World War vintage, which made them no match for their British opponents.

The crisis rages on

The dossier on Rommel compiled by Halder had grown steadily. An impressive list of officers had complained about their boss,* many of whom had been interviewed by the General Staff on return from North Africa. Their complaints were diverse but all serious: letting the battle at Tobruk get out of hand, resulting in a kind of mini-Verdun; taking grotesquely inappropriate decisions; giving unpredictable orders; operating a form of purely 'proletarian' leadership. Furthermore, Rommel's use of courts martial for officers who did not properly follow orders was seen as not in keeping with the traditions of the Army. Incidentally, these courts martial usually acquitted defendants accused by Rommel, including the battalion commander mentioned above, who had been nominated by Rommel for a high decoration a few days earlier. Rommel was accused of giving impossible orders and then just as rapidly revoking them, or insulting officers and then flatly denying he had done so.

This all led to a reprimand from Field Marshal von Brauchitsch on 9 July, which made no impression on Rommel. He stated, not entirely without reason, that his successes and rapid promotion had aroused a great deal of jealousy among other officers: promotion from lieutenant colonel to general in two years was, after all, exceptional. (17: 103)

In order to avoid his plans being blocked, Rommel had sought and found political cover behind Bastico's back by getting both Hitler and Mussolini to support the idea of first capturing Tobruk, before any further advance towards the Nile.

Rommel devoted the summer months of 1941 to training the troops under his command, with an emphasis on improving communication and coordination between the various units. Training was very intensive, with live ammunition since blanks were not available. In addition, all key points in the Sollum Line were fortified, and Rommel ensured that the units there had access to enough ammunition and food for at least eight days of fighting. In preparation for an attack on Tobruk, he trained his men in the art of trench warfare and infantry tactics, partly based on his own experiences as described in his book *Infanterie Greift an*. The German Army, with its emphasis on mobility, no longer paid attention to training in this method of warfare from the past, but it would play a crucial role in breaking through the lines at Tobruk.

* One of these officers was Von Herff, the defender of the Sollum front. He complained that his regiment had lost 1,000 men during the campaign in the west, another 250 in the crossing to North Africa and 450 in the uncoordinated attacks on Tobruk. He found Rommel's orders to be impulsive and unclear.

Command structure (second phase) of Axis troops

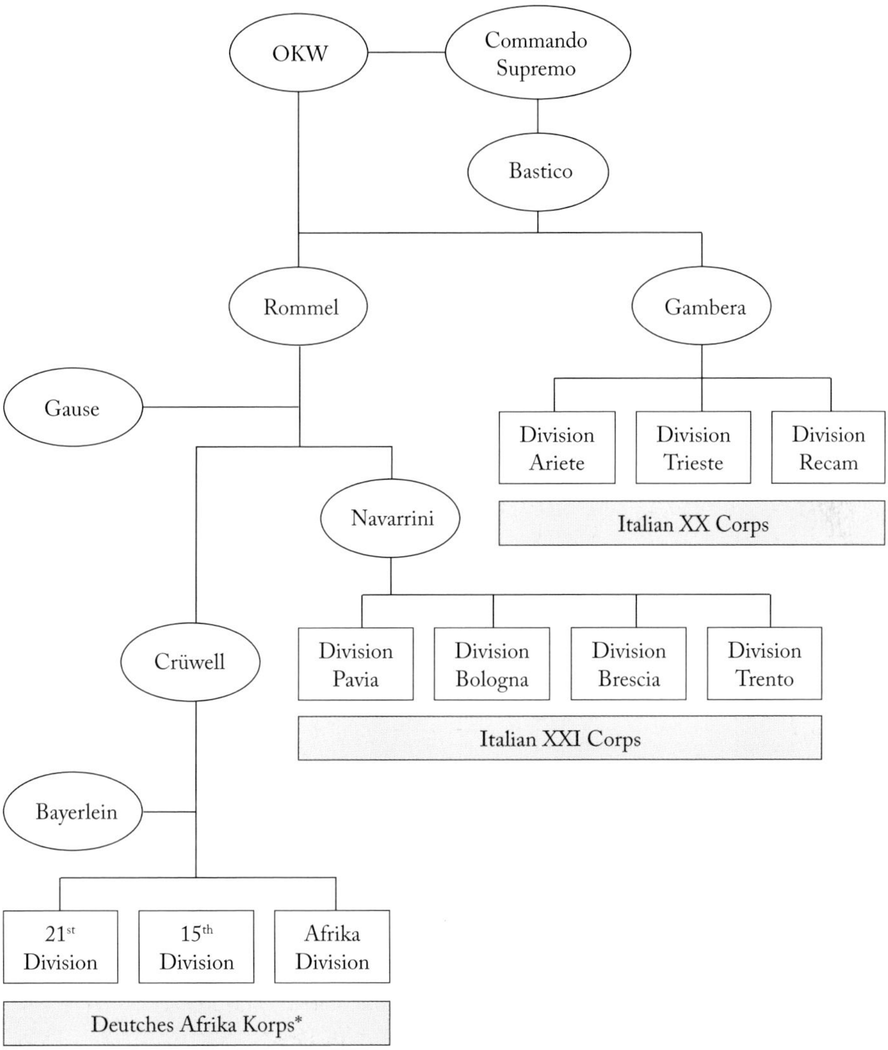

* The 55th Division Savona also fell under the DAK. All artillery elements were placed in the Artillerie Kommando 104 under Major General Böttcher.

Rommel also emphasized once again what he considered to be the most important principles in the field of mobile warfare:

1. One must concentrate one's own fighting force in place and time, while at the same time one must try to spread the deployment of enemy units over a larger area and in greater time, so that they can be neutralized one by one at different times and places.
2. Speed of manoeuvre and organizational cohesion within one's own fighting force are the decisive factors in the battle and require specific attention from

> commanders. Any sign of a decrease in cohesion must be solved as quickly as possible by organizational adjustments. (46: 120)

In September, he established the headquarters of the Panzergruppe at the front in Bardia and not in Beda Littoria, the place the Italians had in mind for it, 300km behind the front.

Later, he moved his headquarters even further east to Gambut, between Tobruk and the Egyptian border and within range of the British guns in Tobruk; this was where the confrontation between British and Germans would take place in the near future. In Gambut the Germans and Italians built large, well-camouflaged field workshops equipped with heavy lifting equipment, machine workbenches and plentiful spare parts. In these workshops, trucks and armoured vehicles, no matter how badly damaged, could be sent directly from the battlefield to be completely overhauled within a few days.

Rommel with his men. The PR value of visits like this was keenly exploited. (*Photo LKK*)

From Gambut, Rommel visited his soldiers every day in his Mammoth; he was still the *General der Soldate* (the soldier's general). Men knew that Rommel would put his men first and never spare himself; they saw him in their midst and recognized him as the ultimate leader. Somehow he even managed to give them the feeling of being immortal, remarking once in front of the propaganda unit's cameras, 'Tell your men to shave off their beards. We want to see young soldiers – we will never grow old!' The reality was that almost all units were operating below their nominal strength, and many men were suffering from the various diseases that prevailed in the desert climate. (17: 109) Logistics continued to worry Rommel during this period. After the start of *Barbarossa*, the Luftwaffe had shifted the focus of its activities to the Soviet Union. Although Benghazi was now available as a port in addition to Tripoli, albeit with limited capacity, in August and September 25 per cent of ships crossing from Italy were lost. On 16 October a last convoy reached Tripoli. The OKW and Hitler also saw the threat posed by the rapid build-up on the British side and the possibility of having to face a swift attack. Hitler therefore decided in October to transfer an entire Luftflotte to the Mediterranean to restore the balance of power. The brilliant Luftwaffe commander, Marshal Kesselring, became commander-in-chief of this Luftflotte, responsible for all air operations in Southern Europe and North Africa. In addition, two dozen U-boats were moved, under protest from the Kriegsmarine, from the Atlantic to the Mediterranean. All this, however, could not prevent an Italian convoy with 40,000 tons of supplies from being sunk on 8 November. As a result, the Italians temporarily halted the convoys, and it was not until mid-December that ships would reach North Africa again.

Despite warnings from various quarters, Rommel's attention was focused less on the possibilities of a British offensive than on the question of how to take Tobruk. His plan was as follows. After a days-long artillery bombardment, the infantry division of the DAK would force an opening for the 15th Panzer Division in the south-eastern sector of the defences. The flank would be covered by the Italian XXI Corps under the command of

Navarrini. The division would then advance to the port, upon which the British would have no choice but to surrender. Rommel assumed that this would not take more than two days. This fixation on Tobruk led to increasing unrest among the commanders of the Panzergruppe and the German and Italian high commands. Jodl and Hitler, among others, pointed out to Rommel the build-up of resources on the British side and the possibilities of an offensive in the near future. Rommel replied that he was keeping the 21st Panzer Division as a mobile reserve. Strengthening the Sollum Line would force the British to make a detour lasting at least three days. By that time, Tobruk would have fallen, and he would have his hands free to face any British offensive.

The final discussion of his plans with Mussolini and the Italian Supreme Command took place in early November. The OKW gave permission for the attack on 6 November, provided there was sufficient air cover.

4.2 A new formation and a new structure: the Eighth Army

It was not only Rommel who had expanded his forces; the British had not been idle either. Between January and July, 239,000 troops had landed. In fact, as of 26 September, a completely new fighting unit had been created, named the Eighth Army, made up of the XIII and XXX Corps.

The XIII Corps consisted of:

- The 2nd New Zealand Division
- The 4th Indian Division
- A tank support unit equipped with Matilda Mark II tanks

The XXX Corps consisted of:

- The 7th Armoured Division
- The 1st South African Infantry Division
- The 22nd Guards Brigade

As a general reserve, the Eighth Army had the 4th Armoured Brigade at its disposal.

In addition to a new supply of Cruiser and Matilda tanks, the British could look forward to the arrival of the first American M3 Stuart tanks – an interim provision until a new generation of American tanks was available. The M3 effectively filled the gaps caused by the substantial losses of tanks in the preceding period. The 4th Armoured Brigade was the first to be equipped with these new Stuart tanks (or 'Honeys' as the British crews called them):

> At the start of the first test, the crew, used to Cruisers, were sceptical when they took their place in the tiny contraption. They went tearing through the desert, enjoyed the powerful acceleration, and dropped their speed carefully before going into a bend, as they were accustomed to do with their Cruisers. The engineers of the US suppliers said, 'Don't worry about going into a bend at full throttle.' Shortly afterwards, you could see a tiny tank tear through the desert like mad, stirring a huge cloud of dust at top speed, full of the joys of life like a fool. When the soldiers climbed out again, the tank commander's face was one huge grin as he said, 'She's a honey.' And the name stuck. (14: 153)

The British had thus built up an impressive fighting force in the past months, consisting of:

- 300 Cruiser tanks (from the very first types to the latest Cruiser VIs, the Crusader)
- 170 Matilda tanks
- 300 American M3 Stuart tanks
- 34,000 trucks
- 600 pieces of field artillery
- 240 pieces of anti-aircraft artillery
- 200 pieces of anti-tank artillery
- 900 mortars

The new commander-in-chief of this army was Lieutenant General Cunningham. As an artilleryman, Cunningham had no experience whatsoever in mobile warfare, but he had proved his skills as a commander in the campaign in Italian East Africa in 1941. With regard to mobile warfare, he could rely on the experience of General Pope, a tank expert, who commanded the XXX Corps. However, Pope was involved in an aircraft accident at the beginning of October and was succeeded by General Norrie. XIII Corps was commanded by General Godwin-Austen.

In the meantime, Auchinleck had his hands full with Churchill. Just after his appointment he received an extensive note from the Prime Minister giving objectives for the coming period as well as a great deal of advice. By the beginning of July Churchill was already becoming impatient and wondering whether Auchinleck was the right man for the job. On 15 July Auchinleck replied to Churchill that he did indeed have 500 tanks at his disposal, but experience had taught him that a reserve of 50 per cent against German units was by

The Cruiser Mark VI Crusader with a 400hp aircraft engine, fast but dogged by mechanical defects. (*Photo BTM*)

no means excessive. In addition, the need for further training meant it was important not to launch a new offensive too hastily:

> Owing to losses of tanks and the number in workshop units, have had little opportunity for training. Would stress importance of time being allowed for both individual and collective training. *Battleaxe* showed that present standard of training is not enough, and we must ensure that team spirit is essential for efficiency. (46: 111)

However, Churchill's confidence in Auchinleck was fully restored after a personal visit at the end of July, and he now agreed to a later offensive:

> He certainly impressed my military advisers with all the detailed arguments he produced. I was myself unconvinced. But General Auchinleck's unquestionable abilities, his powers of exposition, his high, dignified and commanding personality gave me the feeling that he might after all be right and even if wrong he was still the best man. I therefore yielded to the November date for the offensive. (46: 114)

In the weeks that followed, Auchinleck also strengthened his relationship with Air Marshal Tedder, the Commander-in-Chief of the RAF in the Middle East. Tedder would become a trusted partner as well as a close friend of Auchinleck.

A new political problem arose in the course of August: the Australian government asked for the Australians in Tobruk to be evacuated. They had been stuck there for more than six months and had made things quite difficult for the Germans, but the Australian government wanted to have free use of these troops, the best they had, especially now that Australia was increasingly threatened by Japan. Despite Churchill's objections, he could not refuse, and in the moonless nights of September and October these units were evacuated and replaced by the British 70th Division. During this period, Auchinleck received constant advice from Churchill on tactical matters and the way in which, in his opinion, tanks should be deployed. The longer the discussion went on, the more detailed Churchill's advice became. Sometimes the Prime Minister's complaints were not without foundation: while the Germans, for example, were consistently able to unload ships in record time, the British, with their much more extensive port facilities, took much longer, for reasons that are unclear. A particularly irritated comment came in Churchill's letter of 21 October: 'We do not understand why when every day was of measureless consequence it took nearly a fortnight to unload these 150 vehicles from three separate ships.' (46: 135) We have already noted the inexplicably long unloading times in the preparation for *Battleaxe*.

Auchinleck, like Wavell in the previous period, constantly felt Churchill's hot breath on his neck. The only difference was that Auchinleck was able to compel the Prime Minister to agree to a longer preparation period – which he needed, given the state his units were in.

Command structure of the Eighth Army

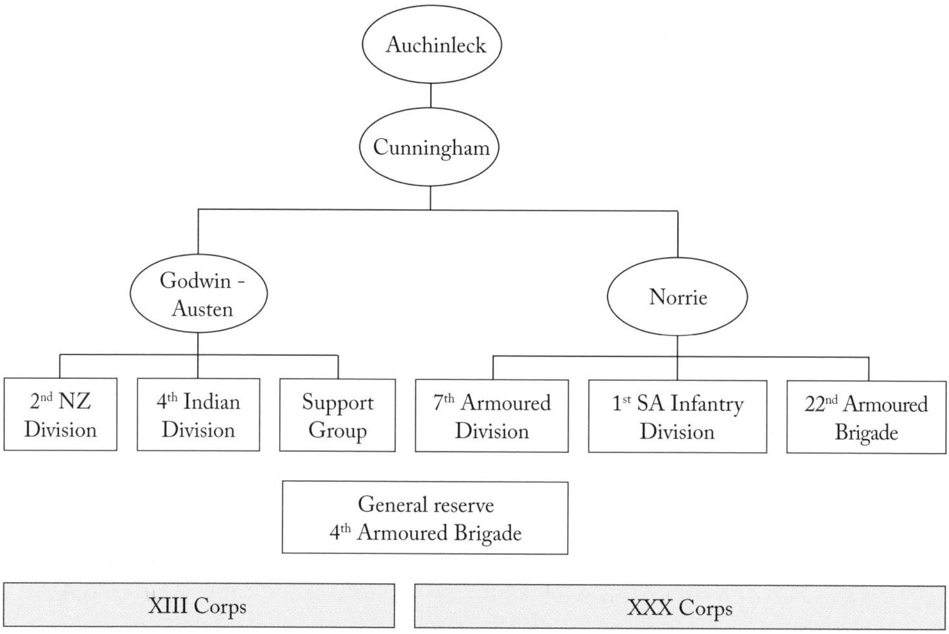

In addition to the above, the 70th Division and a tank brigade were in Tobruk. The composition of the British force was very diverse:

- The 2nd New Zealand Division had recently been repatriated from Crete and other parts of Greece and was not motorized
- The 1st South African Division had dug fortifications at the Mersa Matruh line after a successful campaign in Italian East Africa, was not trained in desert warfare and was insufficiently motorized*
- The 4th Indian Division could be considered the only well-trained division and had proved its worth in recent years. (3: 31)

The British tank units were scarcely in better shape:

- The two regiments of the 7th Armoured Brigade (the 7th Hussars and the 6th Royal Tanks) were experienced units, but their tanks consisted of Cruiser Is (26), Cruiser IVs (71) and Cruiser VIs (also 71). The Cruiser Is were in such a poor state that they had to be transported to the front by truck.
- The 22nd Armoured Brigade had already arrived in July as part of the 1st Armoured Division; the rest of this division would not arrive until January of the following year (!) after a trip round the Cape. The three regiments of the 22nd Armoured Brigade were

* The commander of this division, Brink, was so concerned about the lack of training that he asked Norrie to postpone the upcoming offensive. Norrie then threatened to have the 4th Indian Division take the place of the South Africans. Brink then complied, although the offensive was postponed for a week.

equipped with 158 Cruiser VI tanks, but these had to be adapted to desert conditions on arrival. The regiments of the 22nd Armoured Brigade had no combat experience and had hardly any time to practise because of the necessary adaptations to their tanks.

- The 4th Armoured Brigade consisted of experienced regiments equipped with 165 new American M3 Stuart tanks. The disadvantage of these tanks, however, was their very limited action radius of 60km, and the regiments had little time to practise with them. (3: 32) Other tanks were to be found in support groups of the infantry divisions and at the garrison in Tobruk. With a few exceptions, these were infantry tanks of the Matilda type or the new Infantry tank, the Valentine.

The British prepared a new offensive, *Crusader*, with this force and with the following objectives:

- Neutralizing the German armoured troops
- Retaking Cyrenaica and relieving Tobruk, with as one of the results that the airfields in Cyrenaica would be recaptured and the British would be able to protect Malta from the air
- Recapturing Tripolitania

The order of objectives was crucial: with an unpredictable and tactically skilled opponent like Rommel, the German armoured forces had to be eliminated first before further action was possible.

The basis of *Crusader* was an attack along two axes: a tank offensive to defeat the German tank units, followed by an infantry offensive to relieve Tobruk. After that, the troops would advance further west. The plans were as follows:

- On the first axis, XXX Corps would cross the border between Sidi Omar and Fort Maddelena and then advance north-west to Gabr Saleh. There the British tanks would confront the German tank units at Kilometer 8, defeat them and then relieve Tobruk.
- On the second axis, XIII Corps would advance, leaving the German position on the border at the Halfaya Pass and Sollum on the right, and then lock these troops in from the north.

The 4th Armoured Brigade would operate as a mobile reserve between the two axes and serve as flank cover for XIII Corps, or as reinforcement for XXX Corps.

Before *Crusader* started, however, *Panzergruppe Afrika* would feature one more time in the offensive named *Sommernachtstraum* (Summer Night's Dream).

4.3 *Sommernachtstraum*

The Luftwaffe had noticed during the summer months that the British were growing in strength. At the end of August, four large supply dumps were discovered in the regions of Bir Khiriegat, Bir Diqnach and Bir Habatta. In order to take action again after months of preparation and to replenish his own supplies, Rommel wanted to capture the fuel and ammunition dumps in Bir Khiriegat, 25km into Egypt. In his opinion, these had been built to support an offensive towards Tobruk. In addition, the Germans were always looking for British and American equipment such as Dodge, Ford and Rover trucks, and food in the form of corned beef and tinned butter. They considered British equipment to be superior to their own in some important respects: it was not without reason that Rommel and Crüwell drove around in captured Mammoth Armoured Command Vehicles (ACV). Incidentally, the British also used captured German materiel when it suited them, so that in the heat of battle there could always be confusion about who was friend or enemy.

Kampfgruppe Schütte and the *Kampfgruppe Stephan* were deployed for this raid, with a column of empty trucks in their wake to transport the captured supplies. The 3rd *Aufklärungsabteilung* would provide a diversionary manoeuvre, literally stirring up dust by driving back and forth near the border with heavy radio traffic. On 14 September, the two Kampfgruppen crossed the Egyptian border in search of the dumps and any British troops. They advanced more than 90km into Egyptian territory, encountered resistance here and there, but failed to find any dumps: the British had been warned by intercepted radio messages and had moved them. To make matters worse, some of the Germans' vehicles ran out of fuel and were subsequently attacked by British fighter-bombers. It is unclear what losses the Germans suffered – Rommel's Mammoth was bombed and he himself was hit in the heel of his boot – but they were forced to retreat across the border with their tails between their legs. It was a humiliating experience for Rommel and *Panzergruppe Afrika*. However, the fact that no dumps or troops had been found confirmed Rommel in his view that no attack from the British side was to be expected for the time being. He therefore stuck to his agenda for November: a visit to Rome with his wife Lucie in the first week, a celebration of his fiftieth birthday in the second and the capture of Tobruk in the third. General Sümmermann of the Afrika Division proposed in early October, on the basis of German and Italian intelligence, carrying out a reconnaissance in force behind enemy lines. Rommel rejected this idea, noting that *Sommernachtstraum* had clearly shown that the British were not preparing an offensive. Rommel's staff's suspicions about a possible British offensive were not discussed with the lower echelons, so complete surprise would be achieved by the British a few weeks later. Warnings from both the OKW and the Italian High Command were ignored by Rommel. However, Bastico did warn Cavallero on 11 November that a British attack was to be expected in the near future: he had aerial photographs of supply dumps, airfields full of aircraft, troop movements and reports of intercepted radio traffic, all of which clearly showed that the British were preparing to attack.

German preparations for the assault on Tobruk continued as usual. The two divisions of the Italian XX Corps, the Trieste and Ariete, were moved from Bir Hachim to Bir el Gobi on 10 November; they were to cover the southern flank of the operation. The 21st Panzer Division manoeuvred into attack position 15km south-east of Gambut on 15 November. It was reinforced by *Kampfgruppe Wechmar*, consisting of the 3rd and 33rd *Aufklärungsabteilung*. This Kampfgruppe was to guard the line Fort Maddelena–Sidi Omar deep in Egypt by means of reconnaissance.

The final position of the Axis troops was as follows:

- Around Tobruk: the Italian XXI Corps with the 15th Panzer Division and the 90th Leichte Afrika Division to the east; these units were to attack Tobruk from the south-east, supported by the guns of Artillerie Kommando 104.
- Between Tobruk and the Egyptian border: the rest of the DAK with its headquarters in Gambut and with the function of a mobile reserve. The 21st Panzer Division halfway

towards the border at Trigh Capuzzo and the *Kampfgruppe Weichmar* (the 3rd and 33rd *Aufklärungsabteilung*) which was to cover the area west of Sidi Omar along the Trigh al Abd. If problems arose, the 15th Panzer Division could also be deployed.

- The Libya/Egypt border: mixed Italian/German units including the Savona Division, as well as the detachment at the Halfaya Pass.
- Southern flank: this was covered by the Italian XX Corps on the line Bir Hacheim–Bir el Gobi: the aim was to prevent deep southward encirclement movements.

The attack itself on Tobruk was planned for 23 November.

While the Germans were still busy preparing, and Rommel was on his way back from Rome, on 17 November the British launched Operation *Crusader* with more than 100,000 men and 724 tanks (also 200 in reserve). Rommel could only field 260 tanks (and 154 Italian ones). Of the 260 German tanks, about 200 were the powerful PzKpfw III and IV, while more than fifty were under repair and expected back from the field workshops in the coming period. The situation in the air was even more worrying for Rommel: the British could deploy more than 1,000 planes, while the Axis had barely 300, of which only 120 were German, the rest being partly outdated Italian aircraft, including biplanes. In addition, the Axis airfields had become virtually unusable due to the rain in recent weeks. This meant that the British had complete air superiority.

The balance of power before Crusader

	Axis	Eighth Army
Men	119,000 (65,000 Germans, 54,000 Italians)	118,000
Tanks	260 German/154 Italian	724*
Tanks in reserve	50 back from the workshops	200
Planes	120 German/180 Italian	1,000

* of which 201 Infantry tanks (Matilda and Valentine) and 523 Cruiser tanks, all equipped with the 2-pounder or 37mm (American) gun.

4.4 *Crusader*: first phase

17 November

The first phase of *Crusader* went well for the British. During 17 November, *Kampfgruppe Wechmar* reported from its forward battle position that during heavy sandstorms strong reconnaissance units, including tanks, were crossing the border on both sides of Fort Maddelena towards the Trigh el Abd – a desert track. To be on the safe side, the 21st Division sent several anti-tank units to support the Kampfgruppe. The Panzergruppe staff and Rommel assumed for the time being that it was an enemy reconnaissance in force and as yet took no action. On the evening of the 17th a heavy storm broke out, destroying bridges and roads and flooding airfields. Air reconnaissance was out of the question under these circumstances.

Under cover of this storm, the Eighth Army managed to advance ever further without being seen. In the meantime, Rommel, on his way back to North Africa, had been forced to spend the night in Athens due to engine trouble. He would not arrive until the following day.

Crusader started under difficult conditions: here a British convoy is caught in heavy weather.

18 November

The 7th Armoured Division of XXX Corps advanced further westwards in a southern flanking movement without any significant opposition on this day, turned northwards at Bir el Gobi and advanced towards Tobruk. They had thus moved around the Sollum Line without being noticed, and now threatened the Axis troops at Tobruk from the south-east. During the day, there had already been indications of this manoeuvre when light units of the *Kampfgruppe Weichmar* had come across British troops. These units initially reported an enemy reconnaissance in strength, but towards evening they reported that they were being attacked by 'as many as 200 tanks and armoured vehicles'. Based on this information and other rumours, General von Ravenstein of the 15th Division warned the nearby Afrika Division of enemy action from the south. Meanwhile, aerial reconnaissance revealed that some 1,650 vehicles were getting into position on the other side of the border between

A raid on Rommel

Beda Litteria had been the place the Italians had in mind as Rommel's headquarters, but Rommel preferred to camp much closer to the potential battlefield and turned the building over to his quartermaster staff. The British, not yet aware of Rommel's change of venue, carried out a nighttime raid on his supposed headquarters on 18 November with twelve men. Their assignment was to kill or capture Rommel and Bastico. However, the raid failed completely. Not only were the main targets not there, the attack was repulsed in a short battle by the German officers present. The result was four dead German officers, one dead and one captured British commando. The dead were buried beside each other.

Sidi Omar in the north and Fort Maddelena in the south. While Crüwell and Bayerlein at DAK HQ were now considering a southern flanking movement, their proposal to have the 15th Division's tank regiment advance south via the Trigh el Abd towards Gabr Saleh to meet the British threat was rejected by the newly arrived Rommel, who told them not to be so nervous. Rommel also attempted to reassure Gambara, the Italian commander

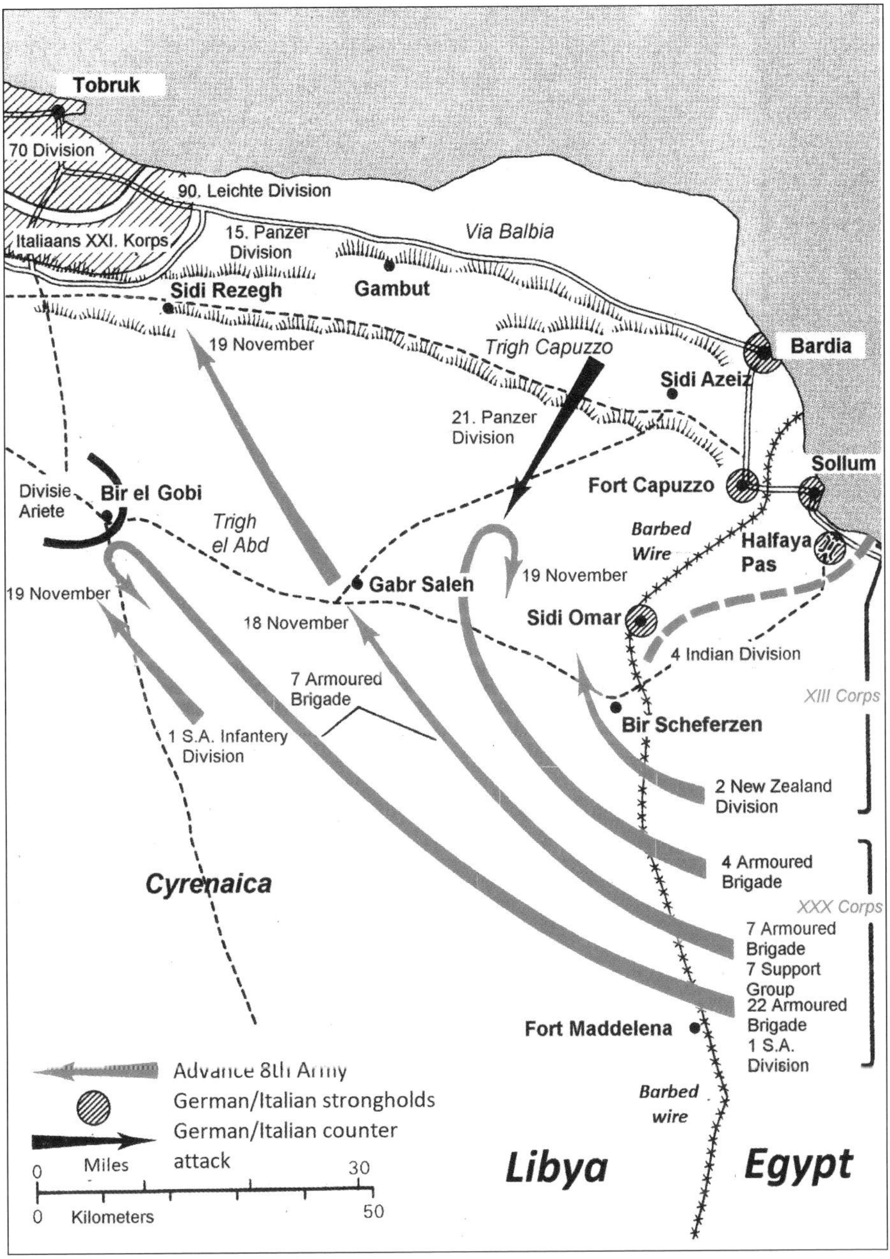

Crusader: first phase.

of XX Corps. Gambara, however, partly on the basis of the information received earlier, immediately put his two divisions, Ariete and Trieste, on high alert – and not without reason, as would become apparent the next day.

19 November

Despite a flood of indications to the contrary, Rommel initially maintained that there was no British offensive of any size on this day. It was not until the afternoon that he realized his mistake and gained a picture of the true size and purpose of the British moves. The tank regiment of the 21st Division was then ordered to advance south to Gabr Saleh, reinforced with twelve light field howitzers and four 88mm Flak guns as *Kampfgruppe Stephan*. Rommel also positioned the 15th Panzer Division south of Gambut to act as a mobile reserve.

However, Rommel's delayed reaction had the unintended side-effect of misleading the British. Norrie, the commander of XXX Corps, was completely at a loss as to why Rommel had not taken action in the previous days, and he had a fearful suspicion that the German commander was preparing one of his famous southward flanking movements. He therefore decided on 19 November to split his armoured forces into three brigades, the largest of which, the 7th Armoured Brigade equipped with Cruiser tanks, was to advance to Sidi Rezegh, just south of Tobruk. Norrie assumed that Rommel would have to defend this place as it provided an excellent base for an attack on Tobruk.

Fearing a Rommel flanking operation, two other Armoured Brigades had to shield the main operation: the southern flank was protected by the 22nd Armoured Brigade, which was to advance to El Gubi, while the northern flank was protected by the 4th Armoured Brigade, which had to advance towards Gabr Saleh. By not reacting, Rommel had thus spread the enemy's resources over three axes. Moreover, the British deviated from the order of the operation that they themselves had seen as essential: first, neutralize the German armoured troops and only then relieve Tobruk.

British and German tank forces compared

A German Panzer Division had one Panzer Regiment, consisting of five companies. The total strength was approximately 120 tanks.

A British Armoured Regiment consisted of three squadrons, each with fifteen tanks. The total strength including the regimental headquarters was fifty-two tanks. An Armoured Brigade consisted of three regiments with a headquarters unit, a total of 163 tanks (29: 195–6) A British Armoured Division had two such Armoured Brigades and could therefore have twice as many tanks as a German Panzer Division (18: 61)

Events then followed in rapid succession. First of all, the 22nd Armoured Brigade encountered the alarmed Ariete Division on the southern flank at El Gubi and was halted there. The Ariete Division lost forty of their 154 outdated M-13 tanks, but managed to knock out twenty-five Cruisers. In the course of the afternoon, under Rommel's watchful eye, *Kampfgruppe Stephan* confronted the 4th Armoured Brigade at Gabr Saleh which was mainly equipped with M3 Stuart tanks, operating on the northern flank. Gatehouse, commander of the 4th Armoured Brigade, had developed a new tactic for his fast but relatively weakly armed and armoured M3 Stuarts:

Consultation in *Kampfgruppe Stephan*. In the background is a Marder 1 tank destroyer. (*Photo S. Klein*)

> Then he lifted up his radio mouthpiece and gave his order. At his command the Honeys did something that tanks don't do in the desert anymore. They charged. It was novel, reckless, unexpected, impetuous and terrific. They charged at speeds of nearly forty miles an hour and some of them came right out of the other side of the German lines. Then they turned and charged back again. They passed the German Mark IIIs and IVs at a few hundred yards, near enough to see the white German crosses, near enough to fire at point blank range and see their shells hit and explode. (29: 92)

Kampfgruppe Stephan. In the background is a mix of vehicles, including a PzKpfw IV, 88mm Flak gun with tractor and a *Panzerspähwagen* SdKfz 222. (*Photo S. Klein*)

During this attack, two German tanks were lost as against twenty-three British ones, showing that the Germans' recent training had not been in vain. The coordination between tanks and heavy guns was excellent, and the tank regiment remained active on the battlefield even after nightfall, which enabled the Germans to tow damaged tanks to the mobile field workshops with their recovery units (the *Panzer Werkstatt Kompagnie*). The British, on the other hand, were no longer in the area but had withdrawn to a night laager (night defensive position).

Meanwhile, the 7th Armoured Brigade on the main axis had been more successful: with other units of the 7th Armoured Division in tow, it had captured the airfield at Sidi Rezegh. This field was only 15km from Gambut, the headquarters of *Panzergruppe Afrika*. However, the fact that the advance to Sidi Rezegh had gone so smoothly made the British high command overconfident. Instead of focusing on the first objective of the offensive, neutralization of the German armoured troops, the *sine qua non* before attempting the second objective, it was decided to relieve Tobruk as quickly as possible. To this end, Cunningham ordered the 7th Support Group to advance to Sidi Rezegh to reinforce the 7th Armoured Brigade, and 21 November was provisionally chosen as the date for the relief of Tobruk.

The Germans also reflected on their next step, and Rommel assessed the situation differently to Crüwell, commander of the DAK. The latter thought that Rommel was reacting too passively to what he saw as a major British offensive. He and Bayerlein, Chief of Staff of the DAK, proposed to Rommel that the two tank divisions should face the enemy together the next day. Rommel therefore gave them free rein to act as they saw fit in the Bardia-Tobruk-Sidi Omar triangle and to attack the various Armoured Brigades one by one with the concentrated power of the two DAK tank divisions.

20 November

The 21st Panzer Division advanced south-east, only to discover that the enemy had withdrawn, but in pursuit of them it ran out of fuel and had no choice but to wait for supplies. The 15th Panzer Division also moved south-east and, after turning south-west at Gabr Saleh, came up against the 4th Armoured Brigade, the victim of *Kampfgruppe Stephan* the day before. Based on the experiences of its sister regiment the previous day, the Germans opened fire at a great distance, forcing the M3 Stuarts to zigzag at high speed to get within range. In the ensuing encounter the Germans knocked out fifty-five of the 165 Stuarts. Surprisingly, the British units refused help from the 2nd New Zealand Division advancing along the main axis. Despite their losses, the command of the 4th Armoured Brigade reported to Cunningham a successful action against German armoured troops. Cunningham interpreted the result as the decisive blow and, with Sidi Rezegh firmly in the hands of the 7th Armoured Brigade, ordered the relief of Tobruk to go ahead.

The 7th Armoured Brigade had received reinforcements from the 7th Support Group during the day, and further infantry reinforcements were on their way along the same route in the form of the 1st South African Division. The troops in Sidi Rezegh had encountered little resistance from the Germans stationed around Tobruk. Everything seemed ready for the relief of Tobruk the following day.

Intercepted British radio traffic and a BBC broadcast announcing a major offensive by the Eighth Army had woken Rommel. That evening, he contacted Crüwell, ordering him to break off the fighting in the south at Gabr Saleh and move the two tank divisions north to the airfield at Sidi Rezegh to attack the British from the rear. With this tactic Rommel cleverly shifted the centre of gravity of the battlefield from south to north.

21 November

This was to be the day of the relief of Tobruk. However, just as the 7th Armoured Brigade was about to move in order to break into the besieged town, it was ordered to stay put; aerial reconnaissance had shown two German tank divisions advancing at full speed towards Sidi Rezegh. The garrison of Tobruk had already begun to fight its way out with Matilda tanks and infantry to El Duda, a weakly defended hill. During the morning, fierce fighting broke out between the 90th Leichte Division in the north and the Bologna Division in the south on the one hand, and the combined strength of the 7th Armoured Brigade and the 7th Support Group on the other. The German and Italian troops at El Duda were in danger of being crushed between the two forces from the north and south, but the British were unable to make contact with the troops at El Duda from Sidi Rezegh, so that no corridor was established between Tobruk and Sidi Rezegh. In the midst of this fighting, clouds of dust on the horizon indicated the arrival of the first units of the two German armoured divisions. These had begun their advance towards Sidi Rezegh earlier that morning and soon came into contact with the columns of the 7th Armoured Division, which were on their way towards Sidi Rezegh. German tanks, artillery and infantry met these columns and pushed them forward, making short work of any resistance. A chaotic scene ensued: burning and fleeing vehicles, guns and men, interspersed with German tanks, 88mm Flak guns – firing from their trailers – and anti-tank guns. Driving alongside the British vehicles, they made short work of any counter-attacks by the more than 100 British tanks. These were not deployed in a concentrated manner, but still in the traditional small formations, which were destroyed one by one by the rapidly advancing Germans.

88mm Flak guns advancing at full speed through the desert. (*Photo S. Klein*)

Sänger, who had been promoted to Panzer Kommandant in the meantime, now experienced his third battle:

> The supply trucks, the transport trucks and the mechanized guns drove aimlessly through each other, kicking up even more dust than usual. Even when they stopped, it was difficult to fire accurately. Radio communication was completely lost – as usual ...Flak guns drove forward, firing as they drove, with their mounts extended so that the whole gun jumped into the air. On the British side, fires broke out and explosions lit up in the dark clouds of smoke. Trucks stopped, burning, drivers ran for their lives, stumbled and fell. (14: 176)

The arrival of both DAK tank formations on the battlefield changed the position of the British in one fell swoop. At the airfield of Sidi Rezegh they were now pinned down by the besieging troops of Tobruk on the one hand and the combined force of the DAK on the other. Meanwhile, a strong screen of anti-tank guns, artillery and the feared 88mm Flak guns of both German panzer divisions prevented the 4th and 22nd Armoured Brigades from advancing from the south to come to the aid of the cornered troops. The familiar 'sword and shield tactics' had made again them easy prey for the German gunners.

Tim Palmer and the 22nd Armoured Brigade were fighting that day with the rearguard of both tank divisions and the anti-tank screen:

> He [Palmer] ordered the driver forward – the range was far too great for the miserable 2-pounder. But then, over to the left, he made out one of these huge guns he had admired on the Egyptian border. It was being towed by a truck, which pulled up sharply. Men jumped down and busied themselves with the gun. 'Let them have it', said Palmer to his gunner. He hit the truck so squarely with his first shot that it blew up.

An 88mm Flak gun of the anti-tank screen prepares for action. The shells are transported in wicker holders. (*Photo S. Klein*)

A little later, his own tank was knocked out and he switched to another:

> He sat on it, next to the driver's viewing slit, to guide the men by hand signals. A crazy idea, but it saved his life. A heavy AP round hit the tank, ricocheted about inside and killed the entire crew. (14: 177–8)

Meanwhile, communication within the British brigades, between brigades, and between the brigades and Division and Corps Headquarters had completely broken down during the day, partly because the communication tanks of the various brigades and of the regimental HQs had been knocked out. The 4th Armoured Brigade was engaged in combat with the German anti-tank shield until the evening; the 22nd Armoured Brigade eventually managed to break off the fighting and advance towards Sidi Rezegh, but due to communication problems it passed the airfield on a north-westerly course towards the mysterious Point 4239, the place where the Ariete Division seemed to have been earlier that day. Meanwhile, at the airfield, Jock Campbell, the father of the Jock Columns, improvised the defence. Tim Palmer also eventually reached the airfield on foot after his fourth tank was disabled, and was immediately put to work by Campbell:

> 'Tim! Catch those bloody guns there and stop them!' A couple of 25-pounders had turned up, running from the steel roller of the Panzers. Palmer grabbed one of those small cars the British call scout cars and the Germans '*Flitzers*' [scurriers] and chased after the howitzers. The gunners were not trying to run away; they simply lacked orders. The name Campbell, already widely known in the Eighth Army, worked wonders. They unlimbered and got their AP rounds out – at that time and for a long time yet, the only effective defence against Panzers. Campbell had driven off again, but he was not away long. The 25-pounders, firing over open sights, halted the Panzers, which stayed at a respectful distance and began to straddle them with high-explosive shells. (14: 179)

A few surviving tanks of the 22nd Armoured Brigade had also reached the airfield in the meantime and were immediately picked up and deployed by Campbell:

> They now came trundling across the airfield, the brigadier's open staff car at their head. Under his fluttering pennant, he was holding on to grab a handle with one hand, while waving the tanks forward with the other like a cavalry officer during a charge. Which was all quite unnecessary but very brave. And which was, perhaps, precisely the sight the exhausted men on the airfield needed for a last effort. (14:180)

Campbell's actions prevented the Germans from taking the airfield that day. In the early evening, the two German tank divisions set up camp in different places, only to break camp during the night and reposition themselves for a final attack on the British at Sidi Rezegh. However, the supply units had lost contact with these tank divisions during the fighting, and it was not until 10.00 the following morning that they could be supplied with fuel and ammunition.

22 November

Rommel knew that the next day would be decisive. The British still had a considerable number of tanks (180), while the tanks of the 22nd Armoured Brigade, which were advancing towards Sidi Rezegh, also had to be taken into account. In other words, the decisive tank battle would still take place at this location.

Rommel changed his plan of attack twice. Finally, in the afternoon, he ordered the 21st Panzer Division, supported by elements of the 90th Leichte and the 155th Artillery Regiment, to carry out a direct attack on the airfield: the tank regiment with its fifty-seven tanks should attack from the west, and the infantry from the north.

In the midst of the heavy fighting, the 22nd Armoured Brigade with 107 tanks appeared from the south to carry out a frontal attack. Before they could throw their weight into the battle, however, the tanks were knocked out at a great distance by the powerful German anti-tank guns. After heavy fighting, the airfield was back in the hands of the Germans, and the remnants of the 7th Armoured Brigade and the 7th Support Group with their remaining ten tanks were thrown back on the positions of the 1st South African Division. The situation for the British would deteriorate further during the night of the 22nd/23rd. At the end of the 22nd Crüwell had sent the 15th Panzer Division westwards, without Rommel's knowledge – the two had been out of contact for most of the day – to track down and destroy the remnants of 4th Armoured Brigade. At the end of the afternoon, the armoured regiment did indeed come across elements of this 4th Armoured Brigade, which quickly withdrew under the protection of darkness. During the following night pursuit, the armoured regiment discovered a night laager (night defensive position) of the Brigade, and in the ensuing battle, fifty armoured vehicles were captured and the British headquarters was overrun.

As a result, the next day, the remaining units of the Brigade moved around the battlefield in groups searching for each other, and only slowly managed to come back together as a single fighting unit.

The death of a tank

Many tanks were put out of action, sometimes when the tracks broke, or the turret got stuck or because there were mechanical defects. The British tanks in particular suffered greatly from the latter. In principle, tanks that were put out of action due to the above-mentioned causes could be made operational again before long, as long as you controlled the area where the tanks were stranded and were able to deploy recovery units.

A tank was permanently disabled if its armour was penetrated and a shell exploded inside it. This often killed the crew and caused secondary explosions when it set off the tank's ammunition. A tank could be rocked back and forth by these internal explosions for some time and burn violently. The aluminium of the engine block and other light materials would melt and form a puddle under the tank.

Ultimately, after four days of heavy fighting, the British could still deploy ten Cruiser tanks of the 7th Armoured Brigade, forty Cruisers of the 22nd Armoured Brigade and a hundred M3 Stuart tanks of the 4th Armoured Brigade. The two German tank divisions, thanks to the efforts of their recovery units, mobile workshops and the workshop at Gambut, still had 150 operational tanks. (29: 195)

On his way to XIII Corps headquarters, war reporter Alan Moorehead got a taste of what would await him the next day:

> Even as we bumped along the uneven track, German armoured cars came in from the west and the east driving in front of them, like stampeding cattle, hundreds of British lorries, ambulances and supply wagons. (29: 95)

23 November

Rommel as Commander-in-Chief of the *Panzergruppe Afrika* and Crüwell as Commander-in-Chief of the DAK had hardly spoken to each other in the past four days and had had no time to sit round the table and coordinate their views. In particular, the British divisions near Sidi Rezegh, the remnants of the 7th Armoured and the 1st South African Division, gave them headaches. The lack of communication between the two generals led to two plans eventually being formulated for the following day, one by Rommel and another by Crüwell.

Rommel's plan was to have the two tank divisions advance southwards and the Ariete Division from El Gubi northwards. The British were then to be trapped and destroyed between the two. The main lines of this plan arrived with Crüwell in the evening of the 22nd. However, the plan developed by Crüwell and his chief of staff Bayerlein involved an encirclement of the enemy by a flanking movement of the 15th Panzer Division, reinforced by a significant part of the tanks of the 21st Panzer Division, to the south-west; another part of the 21st Panzer Division would pin down the enemy at Sidi Rezegh. Crüwell did not agree with Rommel's plan and set his troops in motion at 3.00 am. When Rommel's detailed plan arrived at 4.30 am, he dismissed it as being based on 'outdated' information.

While the remaining tanks of the 21st Division fought bitterly with the 7th Armoured Division, and the Italian Pavia Division prevented a second breakout attempt by the Tobruk garrison, Crüwell with the 15th and the other part of the 21st Panzer Division rushed south. At Haffed el Haiad, far behind enemy lines, the tanks of the two German divisions and the Ariete Division made contact with the 1st South African Division, and in a pincer movement knocked out the South Africans' anti-tank weapons. By 2.00 pm the encirclement was complete, and during the afternoon the resistance of the South African Division collapsed. After very heavy fighting, which cost the Germans their last reserves, they succeeded in forcing a breakthrough towards Sidi Rezegh in an unusual frontal attack with all vehicles. Tanks, mobile guns and infantry in unarmoured trucks advanced on a broad front against the well-entrenched Australian units, and because many officers personally led their troops, many of them became casualties.

Ten kilometres further on, the results of this attack looked like this to Alan Moorehead:

> I was strolling in the sun at Corps and the others of my party were lazily washing in the open when the enemy broke through. We were in a slight hollow lightly studded with camel thorn and salt bush – just fifty or sixty vehicles dispersed about with a few armoured cars to protect us. Into this hollow about a hundred British trucks suddenly burst in a whirl of dust. We looked up wondering. Some convoy perhaps with urgent supplies? Then from another direction several hundred more vehicles, tanks among them, came flying pell-mell across the desert, racing past our stationary

> vehicles without stopping and covering us in great billows of fine sand. This was not an organized convoy. (29: 96)

It certainly was not organized; in fact, the entire HQ then fled. Norrie and Gott were nearly taken prisoner, and Cunningham escaped in his plane just in time (see below). Moorehead and his party hastily joined a group of tanks, cars, trucks and a communications unit from Corps HQ and were rushed among thousands of vehicles into the desert, back to the Egyptian border:

> It was a contagion of bewilderment and fear and ignorance. Rumour spread at every stop, no man had orders. Everyone had some theory and no one any plan beyond the fantastic desire to reach his unit ...It was the unknown we were running away from, the unknown in ourselves and in the enemy. We did not know who was pursuing us or how long they would be able to keep up the pursuit and whether or not they would outstrip us at the end. (29: 97)

After the breakthrough, Crüwell's troops were able to penetrate the last British defensive lines at Sidi Rezegh. Neither Rommel nor Crüwell knew, however, that the mobile headquarters of the DAK with its important communication units had been overrun in the early morning hours by New Zealand units advancing along the northern axis. Communication between the various units of the DAK and the *Panzergruppe Afrika* had thus become virtually impossible. The intervention of these New Zealanders had been a particularly unpleasant surprise.

Casualties among officers

As we have seen before, the Germans placed great emphasis on the presence of officers in the front line. Rommel himself was an excellent (and perhaps extreme) example. The course of fighting in the desert, where one's own position and that of the enemy was often unclear, sandstorms made reconnaissance impossible and mirages led to confusion, meant that commanders often found themselves in unexpected situations. Partly because of this, there were more casualties among senior officers in North Africa than in other theatres of war. For example, during the course of the conflict, seven generals were killed, nine were wounded (including Rommel), one was missing and seven were taken prisoner. Finally, at the end of the campaign, five more generals surrendered. (11: 98)

Corporal Frank, a motorcycle dispatch rider of the 8th Panzer Division, was accompanying three trucks from Bardia to the workshops in Gambut on his BMW motorbike that morning to pick up new tank engines, 'when he saw some strange-looking flat hats appear near Gambut, which immediately disappeared again between the dunes that surrounded the coastal road.' Frank immediately made a U-turn and raced back to the trucks. He was too late, and the three trucks immediately came under fire, but his motorcycle was spared.

> Frank crawled to the motorcycle, tapped the needle of the carburettor, opened the throttle and pressed the kickstarter down with his hand. The reliable BMW immediately came to life. Hanging like a cowboy next to the tank, he sped away without being hit by the machine guns that were being fired at him from the dunes.

He reported the presence of these unknown troops, but it was not until later that day that the significance of this penetrated to the higher echelons. (14: 197)

The balance at the end of the day was that the 22nd Armoured Brigade had been destroyed, as had the 7th Armoured Brigade; in addition, the 7th Support Group and the 1st South African Division had suffered heavy losses. The British communication and supply lines had been cut, and the possibility of direction and coordination by the British High Command had largely disappeared, partly due to the overrunning of the various divisional and corps headquarters. In the coming days, the various units would continue the battle independently of each other, despite attempts by the British High Command to get things under control. Cunningham and the two corps commanders, Norrie and Godwin-Austen, played no role during this period; the initiative lay with the lower commanders. The losses on the German side were substantial, too, and the DAK could deploy only 72 of the 162 tanks with which it had started the battle. It had also lost its headquarters, and the 15th Panzer Division had lost all its communication vehicles, as well as a significant part of its officer corps.

At 7.00 pm hours Rommel was informed that victory had been achieved. He accepted Crüwell's waywardness and made plans for the continuation of this first phase. Based on the course of the battle and the heavy British losses, Rommel concluded that the enemy in the Tobruk region was as good as defeated. He assumed that the British troops, who had been thrown back at Sidi Rezegh and were licking their wounds near Gabr Saleh, would hastily withdraw to Egypt the moment he launched the flanking attack which the British so feared.

Rommel then decided to attack the enemy on their second axis, east of Tobruk. This was XIII Corps, consisting of the 2nd New Zealand Division, the 4th Indian Division and a tank support unit equipped with Matilda Mark IIs. This force had advanced relatively unhindered to the Via Balbia in the past few days, passing the Halfaya Pass and the Sollum Pass on the left. On 20 November, the 2nd New Zealand Division had offered assistance to the 4th Armoured Brigade, which was involved in heavy fighting with *Kampfgruppe Stephan* at Sidi Azeiz. They were now threatening Tobruk from the east. Rommel wanted to cut off this force by first advancing to the south-east via the Trigh el Abd and then launching an attack on Sidi Omar. He assumed that the bulk of the remaining British troops would be there. In this way, the British supply lines would be cut, the New Zealand Division could be attacked from the rear and the road over the Sollum Pass and the Halfaya Pass would be open to targets deeper in Egypt. To achieve this, Rommel had to deploy all his mobile troops, while the besieging and non-mobile troops around Tobruk would continue to invest the city under the command of General Bötchen. However, Rommel completely ignored the fact that after the actions of the previous days, his tank divisions – his main force – only had a limited number of tanks at their disposal.

Not entirely unexpectedly, Crüwell did not agree with these plans; he first wanted all remaining enemy troops in the vicinity of Tobruk and Sidi Rezegh to be eliminated and their equipment to be captured. This was sensible, as the situation on the battlefield was still very unclear and could differ from place to place. In addition, the encirclement of Sidi Rezegh proved not to be watertight; British supply and tank repair units were still reaching the airfield, and wounded were being evacuated.

> And now there were groups of men wandering about, passing through enemy lines again and again. Convoys of vehicles were scattered over a hundred miles of desert, not knowing where they were going. Batteries of guns and groups of tanks were left behind in the empty desert ...Then the enemy in turn would try to carry off his plunder and prisoners, only to find that his own base had disappeared and that he was in the middle of a strong British formation. Prisoners became goalkeepers. Men were captured and escaped three or four times. Half a dozen isolated battles took place. Dressing posts and hospitals took in British, German and Italian wounded impartially, and as the battle went back and forth, the hospitals were sometimes under British command, sometimes under German command. Both sides used each other's captured guns, tanks and vehicles, and absurd incidents occurred. A British lorry driven by a German and full of British prisoners, crashed into an Italian lorry. A platoon of New Zealanders jumped out and rescued our man. Vehicles full of Germans accidentally joined British convoys – and escaped before they were noticed. (29: 98)

Crüwell wanted to put an end to this chaos by bringing the battlefield completely under German control. However, the situation would only deteriorate in the days that followed, as the battlefield was increasingly rendered unsafe by British Jock Columns. These were Auchinleck's answer to the crisis in the British communication and command structure: the high command was no longer able to direct larger units and fell back on the tried and tested concept of small, independent, heavily armed groups. These combat patrols were diverse in composition and could consist of armoured reconnaissance cars, artillery sometimes mounted on trucks, and infantry. Their mission was to track down and destroy enemy units, communication and supply lines, airfields, etc. We have seen earlier that the use of these 'pirates of the desert', in the best traditions of Drake and Raleigh, had always appealed to the British. Within a few days, dozens of these units were active on the battlefield and behind the lines. As the administrative crisis of the Eighth Army deepened during this period, these groups, appearing here and there and sowing death, destruction and confusion, proved to be an extremely effective means of undermining the strength and confidence of the Germans. The supply columns in particular suffered from their attacks: 50 per cent of the German transport capacity was destroyed during this period (!) which largely determined Rommel's later decision to withdraw.

Auchinleck painted a picture of the Jock Columns in a letter to Smith, his superior, on 6 December:

> Our 'Jock' Columns are well-balanced troops of all arms ...and are the most offensive and distinctive. They work with definite objects and are coordinated by superior commanders. They are the kind that fight right into the centre of no man's land, besides being the most valuable suppliers of information. They are in close and continuous contact with the enemy on a broad front, and are constantly shelling his troops and transport, besides taking prisoners. (46: 143)

In addition, in the days that followed, British troops held out tenaciously on all fronts, so that they were slowly but surely able to recover.

24 November

Early in the morning, the 21st Panzer Division, with Rommel at its head, left Sidi Rezegh. Crüwell with his decimated staff followed in his Mammoth at some distance. The 15th Panzer Division was only able to set off in the course of the afternoon after emergency repairs to tanks and the replenishment of fuel and ammunition. Gause, Chief of Staff of *Panzergruppe Afrika*, accompanied Rommel, leaving responsibility for the Panzergruppe with Siegfried Westphal, Chief of Staff for Operations, who remained behind. He was to play an important role in the days that followed, when Rommel seemed to have disappeared from the face of the earth.

The troops advanced eastwards on the Trigh el Abd towards Egypt, causing panic and chaos on the way and driving a large number of British troops ahead of them. Rommel rode up front in his open car, far ahead of his troops. At Gabr Saleh the Germans shot their way through a mass of tanks, lorries and guns; airfields were hastily evacuated, and Cunningham himself narrowly escaped capture.

Brigadier Clifton had driven General Cunningham, who had arrived at Corps HQ in his own Blenheim, to the meeting with Norrie and Gott. Hardly had they sat down to dinner when the whole HQ went into panic as twenty German tanks appeared from the west. General Cunningham was unceremoniously pushed into a car by Clifton, and a wild ride to the airstrip ensued:

> We dodged through the thickening mob of runways, which hurtled across our course, urged on by occasional shell bursts or bouncing tracer …More by good luck than judgment, we hurtled down the strip where the Blenheim was revved up, roaring to go. The commander and his staff officer climbed aboard, and off she bumped, clearing a crossing three-tonner by inches! That was General Cunningham's last impression of the forward situation. Small wonder he believed withdrawal into Egypt inevitable. (21:104)

This incident confirmed Cunningham's conviction that *Crusader* had failed, and he intended to order a general withdrawal to Egypt to regroup. This was very much against the wishes of Auchinleck, who wanted to pursue *Crusader* at all costs. He flew to the front that same day and ordered Cunningham to continue the offensive. His assessment was that the Germans would not be able to launch an offensive in the short term, having suffered too much in the fighting, as had the British. *Crusader* did continue, but Cunningham was eventually replaced on 25 November by Ritchie, Auchinleck's Deputy Chief of Staff. Ritchie was well informed about all the plans, but had no desert experience other than the Mesopotamian campaign in the First World War, and no command experience in combat.

Rommel and Ravenstein, meanwhile, had reached the border at Bir Sheferzen at 4.00 pm. Rommel ordered Ravenstein to move north towards the Halfaya Pass and to position himself south-east of it. However, Ravenstein had at that moment only the lorry he was in; the 2,000 vehicles of his division were still scattered along the Trigh el Abd. An hour later, Crüwell arrived on the scene, shocked to hear from Rommel that units of the 21st Panzer Division had been sent to the Halfaya Pass to encircle the British on the eastern

The Mammoth as saviour

As we have seen, Rommel was always far ahead of any advance. In his mad journey to Egypt he lost all contact with his troops – and, according to some historians, also with reality. It ended with him, his chief of staff Gause, Berndt and a driver becoming stuck on the other side of the border in a broken-down staff car. While they were preparing to endure a cold night, the DAK's Mammoth suddenly appeared with Crüwell and Bayerlein. Rommel was invited on board by Crüwell, and the entire company then tried to get back across the border. This proved more difficult than expected, and even with Rommel at the wheel and after repeated attempts, no passage through the barbed wire barrier could be found. Finally, the company – the entire high command of the *Panzergruppe Afrika*, without any protection – lay down to sleep. During the night, traffic increased, and when they looked out cautiously the next morning the Mammoth was found to be next to a busy road to the front covered in British vehicles.

side; in this way the DAK would be spread out over more than 90km between Gabr Saleh and the Halfaya Pass.

Rommel waited for some time for troops that would never come: the 5th Panzer Regiment with its thirty operational tanks had run out of petrol and ammunition along the Trigh el Abd, the Ariete Division was held up by a South African brigade and the 15th Panzer Division with sixty-five tanks would not arrive at the border until the next morning. The 33rd *Aufklärungsabteilung* was ordered by Rommel to cut off the escape route of the defeated enemy at Habata, but it declared that it had run out of petrol and ammunition, been bombed by the RAF and was unable to engage further.

Rommel and his Mammoth: he used this vehicle captured from the British for his journey across the Egyptian border. (*Photo IHC*)

This did not prevent Rommel from continuing the advance on his own, and after dark he crossed the Egyptian border. Cut off from his troops, his *Gefechtsstaffel* and liaison cars, Rommel raced forward until the steering column of his staff car broke, whereupon Rommel, Gause, Berndt and the driver found themselves stranded in the cold desert night. They were found by chance after a few hours by Crüwell and Bayerlein on their way back in the Mammoth to the DAK headquarters in Gasrel Abid. After trying in vain to cross the border to the west, the entire party spent the night in the Mammoth. The next morning, Rommel was able to rejoin his troops.

4.5 *Crusader*: third phase

25 November

Rommel began to regroup the troops that showed up here and there and dispatched them towards the supposed positions of the British. The 15th Panzer Division was sent north to Sollum to close in on the British from the west, while the supply units were ordered to move around and raise the dust, in order to make the German force appear larger. These were scenes reminiscent of the beginning of the campaign around cities like Mechili. But the situation was now completely different. As the 15th Panzer Division advanced towards Sollum, it was ordered to attack Sidi Omar instead. By this time the division had only twenty deployable tanks, which had to take on well-entrenched British 25-pounder howitzers without supporting artillery and infantry. By nightfall its strength had been reduced to ten tanks, only three of which were actually deployable. Because the supply troops had to simulate an attack elsewhere, there was also no fuel or other munitions. The result was that Sidi Omar remained in British hands.

For the next 48 hours Rommel did not contact Crüwell or the headquarters of *Panzergruppe Afrika*. He was everywhere, however, encouraging his units and giving new orders. This led to misunderstandings and mistakes and was regarded as unnecessary interference.

In addition, the massive troop movements – there were more than 30,000 German and British vehicles in the area – also led to increasing chaos among the German troops. The various units of the divisions had lost contact with each other; the units themselves had become scattered across the battlefield; commanders did not know where their units were; and the supply columns had lost contact with their units. The unarmoured trucks of these supply columns in particular suffered from the resulting situation: on the confused battlefield, enemy armoured vehicles could appear from behind every sand dune and destroy them in an instant. Convoys halted or drove cautiously with lookouts in the cabs, ready to flee at any moment from anything that looked like an enemy tank. Moreover, these were difficult to identify in the desert heat: the Mark IV and the M3 Stuart looked quite similar. To add to the confusion, both sides continued to use each other's vehicles:

> Generally, everything the British so expressively called 'soft-skinned' suffered in the confusion: the lorried infantry and, in particular, the supply columns of both sides, which were not even protected by anti-tank guns. Since everything was milling about all over the place, and since most of the time people were looking for their own combat units, they had a 50-50 chance of attracting the attention of some hostile, steel-splitting, hard-skinned vehicle. Countless convoys of trucks were driving around

> in this way or just stood about in the desert with a sentry posted on the cab, like a group of shy, grazing gazelles, always ready to race off in headlong flight. (14: 201)

There was therefore every reason, as Crüwell fervently wished, to put an end to the advance towards Egypt and to regroup. Meanwhile, at the headquarters of *Panzergruppe Afrika* in El Adem, Westphal had become particularly concerned about the course of the fighting at Sidi Rezegh and the situation around Tobruk. The New Zealand Division had continued its advance from the Bardia region, had taken key positions south of Tobruk and had retaken the Sidi Rezegh airfield. The British troops that had withdrawn at Gabr Saleh had received reinforcements and from there, with Jock Columns, were making the north-west unsafe as far as the Via Balbia. Westphal wanted to attack the New Zealanders from the rear with a tank division in order to relieve the cornered Germans and clear the area of British troops. He tried in vain to contact Rommel by radio, but Rommel's radio car had become stuck in the sand at an early stage. He later tried to reach Rommel with a Fieseler Storch, but it was promptly shot down.

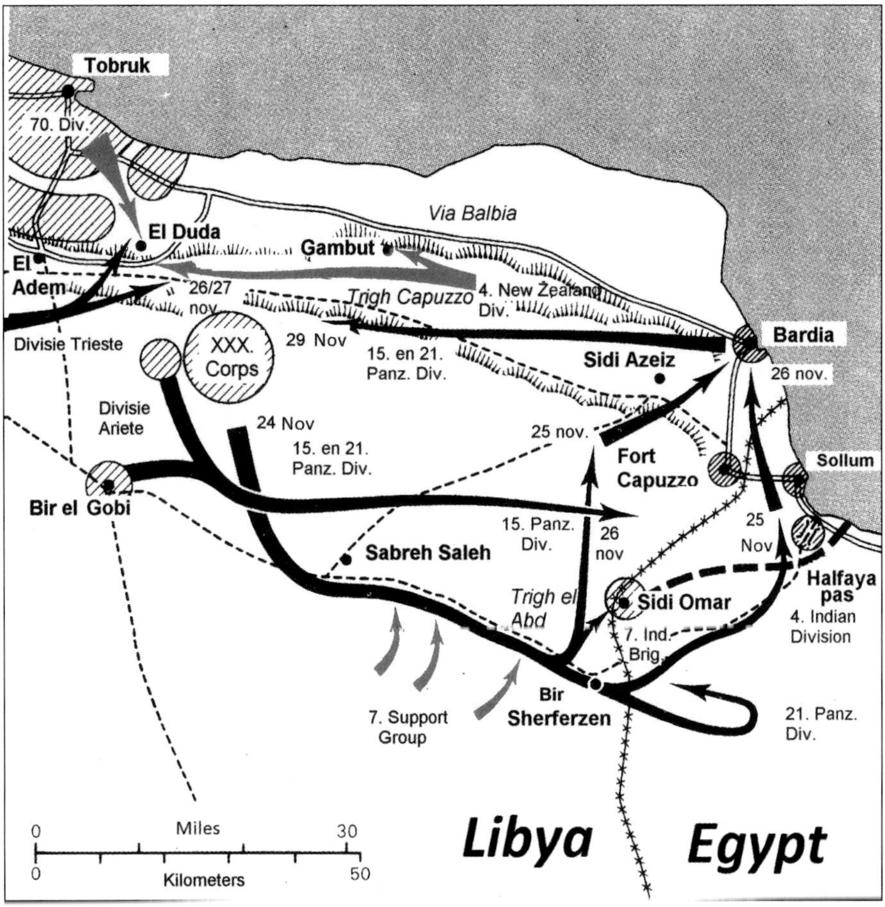

Crusader: third phase.

26 November

Finally, Westphal took the decision at his own discretion to recall all DAK troops to Tobruk. The exhausted and almost tankless 21st Panzer Division did not advance further to Sollum and reached Bardia at the end of the day on its way to Tobruk. The 15th Panzer Division had already arrived there around noon to take on fuel and ammunition. Rommel was utterly astonished and furious on the evening of the 26th to find both the 15th and 21st Panzer Division in Bardia. He assumed that the British had sent a fake signal to trap the DAK.

When a very disgruntled Rommel arrived at Panzergruppe HQ in El Adem, he only had to look briefly at the maps to realize the gravity of the situation and the importance of Westphal's decision. Although everyone expected an outburst on his part, he simply declared that he was tired and wished to go to bed; he knew that his advance on Egypt had been halted.

All in all, however, the first phase of *Crusader* was a success, at least on paper, for *Panzergruppe Afrika*. When this phase ended, the Germans had destroyed an estimated 814 tanks and armoured vehicles and 127 aircraft, had captured large quantities of materiel and had taken 9,000 British prisoners. In contrast, they and the Italians had each lost 4,000 men, but had only forty and thirty deployable tanks respectively. The British still enjoyed a huge superiority in tanks (7:1): the New Zealand Division had eighty Matildas and Valentines, the 7th Armoured Division had 130 tanks after regrouping, and the garrison of Tobruk, which had been able to establish a corridor with the New Zealand Division on 26 November, had seventy tanks at its disposal.

Rommel, on the other hand, could not expect any fresh supplies before January, as the British kept the sea route virtually closed. The result was that in the last weeks of November only one third of the required 120,000 tons of supplies had arrived. Rome had announced that it would not be able to bring in any more until January.

27 November–1 December

Despite the difficult position in which *Panzergruppe Afrika* found itself, Rommel still managed to retain the initiative in the following days. This was partly due to his reputation, but also to the limitations of his opponents. A good example of this was the confrontation between 15th Panzer Division and two Armoured Brigades on 27 November. Early that day, the 15th Panzer Division was on its way to Tobruk with fifty tanks. After about 30km they encountered the 22nd Armoured Brigade with forty-five tanks, and the 4th Armoured Brigade soon joined the battle with a further seventy-seven. Although this was a dire situation for the 15th Panzer Division, the British broke off the encounter and withdrew to prepare for the traditional night laager. The Germans were then able to continue their journey to Tobruk without encountering any resistance.

The 27th was also the day that Rommel and Crüwell sat round the table to address the situation at Tobruk. Once again, there were two options: Rommel wanted to encircle the New Zealanders at the rear, while Crüwell did not want to split his Panzer Divisions for this but suggested chasing the New Zealanders into Tobruk with a concentrated attack from the east. The next day was spent on further discussion, and at 9.00 pm Rommel sent his final plan to Crüwell. Once again, however, Crüwell ignored Rommel's plan, declaring that it had come too late, and summoned the commanders of both his Panzer Divisions, von Ravenstein and Neumann-Silkow, at 8.00 the next day to discuss his own plan. The 21st Panzer Division with nine tanks and the 15th Panzer Division with thirty-one, supplemented with twelve Panzer II tanks, eventually attacked more or less along the lines of Rommel's plan: Neumann-Silkow had in the end decided to follow it.

After two days of heavy fighting the Germans finally recaptured the Sidi Rezegh airfield, and on 1 December the corridor between Tobruk and the New Zealand troops was closed. To reduce pressure on the Sollum front, Rommel sent two Kampfgruppen on 1 December consisting of an infantry battalion supported by anti-tank and artillery guns, one via the Via Balbia, the other via the Trigh Capuzzo. Things ended badly for both Kampfgruppen: the one on the Via Balbia was ambushed and destroyed, while the other was halted by the 4th Indian Division and had to withdraw under heavy air attacks.

Rommel now wanted to deliver a final major attack to relieve the isolated German and Italian troops on the Sollum front. Once again, there were major differences of opinion with Crüwell. Rommel wanted to split his troops: the non-armoured troops of both Panzer Divisions would relieve the garrisons on the Sollum front, while the armoured troops would confront the enemy's tanks at El Duda and further south. Crüwell, in turn, wanted to keep them all together and first seek out the enemy in the south-east. But the offensive launched by Rommel on 3 December was not a success due to the division of forces over three axes of attack, and he was forced to accept reality.

4.6 Rommel's retreat

The events of the last few days forced Rommel to reconsider. Despite all the success they had enjoyed, his units were now at the end of their tether. The supply situation was critical, and fresh supplies from Europe were not expected in the short term. The Panzergruppe's position had become untenable, and the only alternative was to withdraw west. The units at the Sollum Line would have to be abandoned, as would the siege infrastructure around Tobruk. Based on these considerations, Rommel ordered the dismantling of the siege works at Tobruk on 4 December: heavy artillery was moved west, and the facilities themselves were blown up.

The British, meanwhile, had been able to regroup and now advanced towards the remains of the DAK. The two forces met on 5 December at Bir el Gobi, where there was fighting during the following days. But partly due to Gambara's reluctance to deploy the Ariete and Trieste divisions of the Italian mobile XX Corps, Rommel had to make the inevitable decision on 7 December to withdraw the German troops to the west and leave Cyrenaica. *Crusader* had been a real battle of attrition, and while the British were able to continuously re-supply their units, the Panzergruppe was slowly but surely running out of everything. As a consequence, the decision to withdraw was unavoidable.

During the night of 7/8 December the German troops broke off the fighting and the retreat began. The aforementioned Italian divisions distinguished themselves in defending the rear by beating back British troops that had broken through. Marshal Bastico, the Italian Commander-in-Chief in North Africa, was very concerned about Rommel's intention to withdraw from Cyrenaica and made a personal visit to the German general. Rommel, however, took little account of Bastico's opinion, because in his view Gambara had abandoned the DAK at an essential moment of the battle by not deploying the mobile XX Corps. Rommel and Bastico had a heated discussion about the retreat, during which Bastico expressed his wish to deploy one of the Italian divisions under Rommel to defend Agedabia:

> It became a heated debate in which, among other things, I stated that I had no intention of placing any of my Italian divisions under his command and having them deployed by him. In addition, I assured him that I would not hesitate to withdraw through Cyrenaica with only my German units, leaving the Italians to their fate … His Excellency Bastico showed himself considerably more lenient after this.

The Italians recalled this meeting completely differently. They described Rommel as 'very excited and agitated'; he blamed it all on the Italians and was 'particularly hot-tempered and …reacted over-excitedly, shouting that he had been fighting for victory for three weeks and had now decided to withdraw his divisions to Tripoli and to intern himself in Tunisia.' (36: 81)

Now a retreat of 450km with more than 10,000 vehicles began, first to Agedabia, south of Benghazi, which was reached on 25 December, and then to Mersa el Brega, reached on 12 January. At Agedabia a clash occurred between the retreating German troops and the 1st and 7th Armoured Division and 22nd Armoured Brigade. Through efficient use of tanks and 88mm Flak guns, a total of 136 British tanks were destroyed.

During this retreat, Rommel used a very successful strategy: the non-motorized Italian troops withdrew via the Via Balbia, and the DAK and the Italian XX Corps undertook delaying actions to deter the British from any flank operations through the desert. British attacks were always repulsed by a screen of tanks and anti-tank guns, while, whenever the opportunity arose, the weak spots in the British lines were attacked.

The retreat did not always go smoothly. Sänger and his tank, with Chief of Staff Bayerlein as a passenger, were driving through El Adem airport at night when something started rhythmically hitting the side of the tank.

The boys are back in town: British Stuart tanks in Benghazi.

> Outside the tank suddenly there were loud cries and Italian voices shouting, '*Mamma mia*!' and '*Madonna*!' The tank turned out to have driven over a unit of dug-in Italian infantry. Their groundsheets had got caught in the tracks and something was being dragged along by the tank, perhaps an unlucky ally. With each turn of the drive wheels it hit the tank . . . Sänger leaned out and said, 'We are in the middle of a group of Italians. It is an infantry position. We'll grind them to pulp!'
>
> Bayerlein shouted over the noise, 'Drive on! Run over them, I don't care, but we have to get away from here as quickly as possible. I have the bag with all the secret codes with me, can't you see?'
>
> Meanwhile, the Italians, talking loudly, had freed the body from the caterpillar chains . . . They continued westwards, hoping that the invocation of the Madonna and the shouting had alerted their fellows. Nothing came after the tank, except advancing British units. The Italians at the airfield were clearly a forgotten and lost unit. (29: 214)

Benghazi was evacuated on 24 December after the contents of all depots were removed via the Via Balbia. During this period the garrisons on the Sollum Line also surrendered: Balbia on 2 January, Sollum on 12 January and the garrison under Bach on the Halfaya Pass on 17 January. The men of this garrison, marching under escort on their way to captivity, were shot at by units of the Free French Forces, to the dismay of the commander of the 1st South African Division. This was the only notable act by the Free French in this phase of the campaign.

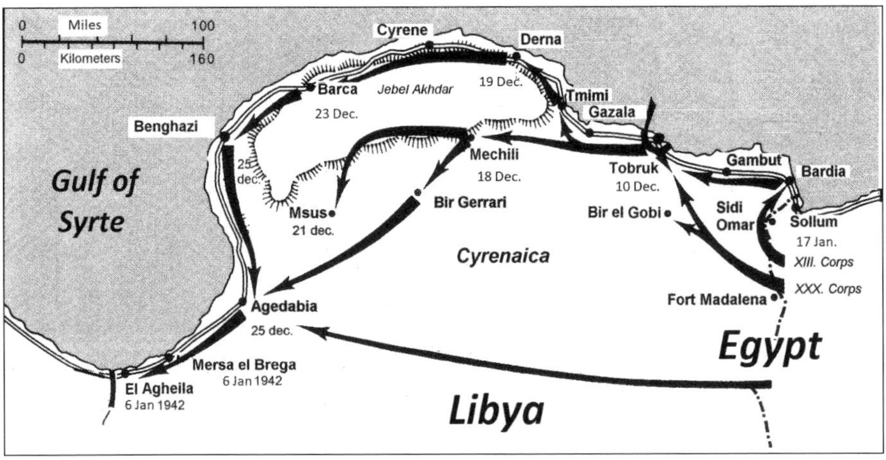

The retreat of *Panzergruppe Afrika*.

The journey of the DAK itself through difficult terrain demanded the utmost from people and equipment. Vehicles became stuck in the sand, there was a shortage of ammunition and petrol, and British fighter planes continued to attack the columns. Rommel's force was not the only one to suffer from shortages: on 20 December the local Luftwaffe commander reported major losses: the day before he had lost twenty Junkers Ju 52 transport aircraft, fourteen of them due to contaminated fuel.

Rommel was constantly to be found along the route of the columns, encouraging men, reorganizing troops and sometimes leading a counter-attack. As reinforcements, twenty-two tanks were unloaded in Benghazi and twenty-three tanks in Tripoli on 19 December, part of a convoy in which two ships with a further forty-five tanks had been sunk en route. These reinforcements arrived too late to turn the tide, but they did form the basis for Rommel's success in the next phase.

The British, in turn, were unable to halt this retreat or inflict serious losses on Rommel. On the one hand, their fear of Rommel's unpredictability and their ever-lengthening supply lines undoubtedly played a role; on the other, this type of encirclement action in mobile situations placed too high demands on the coordination and leadership capabilities of the British.

Rommel managed, however, to hit the British time and again. At the end of December, for instance, Crüwell discovered a gap between the two Armoured Brigades pursuing them which were located closest to Agedabia. The DAK tanks were deployed against one of the two, namely the 22nd Armoured Brigade, and in two smooth attacks this Brigade was stripped of fifty of its tanks, almost two-thirds of the total fighting force. Crüwell's losses amounted to only seven tanks.

Having created space in this way, Rommel fell back even further west, to the Mersa el Brega line, on the border of Tripolitania, which was reached on 12 January. All of Cyrenaica was now back in British hands, and the Axis forces were back to where they had made a flying start in March the year before.

Crusader's balance sheet was ultimately as follows. On the British side, 2,300 men were killed, 7,300 wounded and 7,500 missing or taken prisoner. The Axis powers lost 2,300 men killed and 6,100 wounded, but recorded 29,000 as missing or prisoners of war. At Bardia and the Halfaya Pass alone, 13,800 men had surrendered. However, a not insignificant proportion of these units were Italians, so the combat power of *Panzergruppe Afrika* was not seriously affected. (3: 51) Rommel in fact toyed with the idea of continuing the battle without the Italians, since this would greatly improve his supply situation and relieve him of some of his command concerns.

Although Tobruk was relieved and the Axis powers expelled from Cyrenaica, a sense of failure persisted on the British side. The Axis troops had continually shown themselves to be tactically superior and in particular much better able to maintain control and coordination of their tanks and other units during battle. Moreover, the British were unable to capitalize on their successes and definitively defeat the retreating Panzergruppe. Rommel's retreat, in contrast, had been a fine example of command and control and had often caused more problems to the pursuing units than the retreating Germans and Italians had suffered themselves.

As a result, the British did not get around to the second offensive that they originally had in mind, namely Operation *Acrobat*, although the fighting at the end of December was in fact already part of this offensive. This should have brought the British as far as Tripoli and driven the Germans and Italians out of North Africa for good. However, the Germans had already shown that they could not simply be swept aside, while the supply situation of the British units deteriorated noticeably, as did the balance of power in the Mediterranean as a consequence. In addition, Japan's attack on Pearl Harbor had had an immediate effect on the allocation of men and materiel. In other words, the pendulum had swung back to the Axis side, and Rommel was given a second chance, which, as we will see, he would seize eagerly.

4.7 Evaluation

Crusader provided a clear picture of the strengths and weaknesses of the armies involved, and the operation is therefore worth evaluating in detail.

Evaluation of the German Army

Crusader was not only Rommel's battle, but also the battle of the other commanders of the *Panzergruppe Afrika* and the DAK.

The combination of Crüwell and Bayerlein as commander and Chief of Staff of the DAK respectively came to offer increasing opposition to Rommel. While previously he had been able to bypass Streich, Crüwell and Bayerlein were more difficult to manage. Crüwell, in civilian life a bank manager in Hamburg, had recently gained crucial experience as a reserve officer under Guderian in the Soviet Union; Bayerlein was a very capable staff officer. Both men frequently saw the situation on the battlefield differently to Rommel and openly expressed their reservations about the way in which he wanted to tackle the enemy. This will undoubtedly have made their daily interactions difficult, with Crüwell and Bayerlein trying to restrain the ever enthusiastic and optimistic Rommel – a role that cannot have been easy for them. Moreover, as we have seen, other officers like Neumann-Silkow sometimes made plans based on their own assessments.

Westphal, as staff officer, had in turn made the strategically important decision to have the DAK units abort their eastward attack and return to Tobruk. This meant the de facto end of Rommel's ambitions, just as the continuation of the eastward attack had probably meant the end of *Panzergruppe Afrika*. Westphal's position can also be explained in a different way: Rommel's adventurous approach was not always well received by the OKW and the General Staff. The counter-offensive towards Egypt was a tricky task with the troops that Rommel had at his disposal at the time, even without the British forces still present. In other words, it was an unprofessional, irresponsible decision that neither the OKW nor the General Staff could approve. Rommel could have got away with it in the spring offensive, but he would not have been able to do so a second time, especially if the offensive had failed.

It had also become clear that the commander-in-chief of *Panzergruppe Afrika* had been stranded in the midst of the fighting for a considerable period without his *Gefechtsstaffel* or liaison units; he had been alone in his staff car with Gause and had lost contact with the headquarters of the Panzergruppe and the DAK. This would have had major repercussions for him personally, if helpful hands had not removed the critical pages from the DAK diary. But it remained a bizarre adventure, and Westphal's decision was extremely courageous.

Tactical dimensions

Crusader showed that the Germans were able to keep their tank divisions together during this entire period and deploy them in a concentrated manner against the scattered British units, destroying them one by one while making use of the great mobility and firepower of their own tanks. The German tank divisions were constantly on the move and engaged in fighting almost every day. This highly mobile form of warfare suited the German aim of causing as much chaos and confusion as possible to the enemy. At least as important, but less obvious, was the role of supply columns and mobile workshops, which constantly followed to supply the tanks with fuel and ammunition. These supply troops were also

Rommel and Bayerlein confer, with Rommel already looking ahead. There were extreme differences of opinion between Rommel on the one hand and Bayerlein and Crüwell on the other during this part of the campaign.

The deployment of air power is not a central subject in this book, but it did help to determine the outcome of battles. Here the crew of a Messerschmitt Bf 110 sit in the shade waiting for new orders. (*LKK*)

extremely vulnerable to enemy forces which could appear at any time. It was only in the period from 25 to 27 November that the connection between the tank units and these troops was lost, due to rapid movement, and *Panzergruppe Afrika* was in danger of becoming a victim of its own concept. In addition, these units increasingly fell victim to travelling Jock Columns, a point that has often been neglected. Differences about the extent of the problems this created led to tensions between Crüwell, Bayerlein and Westphal on the one hand, and Rommel on the other.

A very illuminating evaluation of the German way of operating in this phase comes, surprisingly, from the British. It was commissioned by General Gott, commander of the 7th Armoured Division, and relates to Operation *Crusader*. It reads like a tactical manual for the German Army and fits seamlessly with the picture outlined earlier:

> **Offensive actions**
> Before the offensive was launched, the Germans carefully reconnoitred the battle site early in the day. They used armoured cars, tanks and infantry for this. The intention was to entice the defence to enter into battle and thus reveal the positions of the artillery, etc. Artillery observers kept a close eye on everything, and every piece of artillery that opened fire was accurately located and then neutralized at the moment of the attack. Around noon, tanks, anti-tank guns and motorized infantry advanced to approximately 2,000 metres from the objective, and the troops were regrouped behind an anti-tank screen. The attack was launched at approximately 3 p.m.; tanks

attacked, supported by very accurate fire from mainly PzKpfw IVs, and artillery fire on artillery positions and on anti-tank gun positions.

All in all, this created a lot of dust on the battlefield, confusing the defenders, and the attack was launched by the Germans in front of a setting sun, which blinded the defenders. The Germans responded alertly to every action by the British defence by accurately deploying artillery. Groups of German tanks advanced from different sides in strong, compact formations. The tanks then attacked British artillery and tanks, and as the battle developed the Germans brought out their anti-tank guns and placed them between the tanks in inconspicuous positions. The anti-tank guns preferably nestled near destroyed vehicles to make them more difficult to locate. From there they caused many casualties among the British. The next phase began when a tank formation forced a breakthrough. Immediately afterwards, the motorized infantry advanced to a few hundred metres before the breakthrough and then disembarked. Anti-tank guns and MGs followed close behind. The breakthrough site was consolidated and shielded with anti-tank guns. By this time it was getting darker, making it difficult to counter-attack once the Germans had reached the objective.

The success of this method of attack was explained by the British as a result of deploying anti-tank guns, and the fact that the PzKpfws III and IV 'outgunned' and 'outranged' the British Cruiser tanks, as well as having superior viewing and aiming equipment. Moreover,

the Germans were equally skilled in coordinating all weapon systems both in defensive actions and in withdrawal. They fell back from one prepared defensive position to another without engaging the attackers. They offered stiff resistance as long as they were not in danger of being overrun, but were particularly sensitive to threats to their communications lines. The Germans' policy was aimed at saving people and equipment and conceding ground. If they had selected an easily defensible position to withstand an attack by tanks or mobile infantry, they stationed their reconnaissance units a lot closer to their anti-tank screen than the British would do. The basis for their defence was their anti-tank guns and their field artillery – the former as the first line security screen, and within that screen infantry units and behind that screen reserve infantry units and field guns. Within this defensive position there were two types of mobile reserve: firstly, a reserve of anti-tank guns to replace disabled artillery pieces, and secondly, tanks to be able to immediately counter-attack. Sometimes other tanks drove around the flanks of the anti-tank screen to entice British tanks to attack. The tanks were mainly active late in the afternoon. [This is a clear description of 'sword and shield tactics'.]

The falling back from one defensive position to a subsequent one took place in two phases. During the first phase, all trucks of the supporting units and some of the non-armoured vehicles were withdrawn. In the second phase the tanks advanced forward to form a protective cordon behind which the rest could withdraw. Vehicles formed compact columns and moved at high speed, while the rearguard of the tanks protected them. Ideally, the first phase took place at night or under cover of the afternoon heat. The second phase usually took place in the last daylight or at night. The tanks that formed the rearguard were extremely offensive and very effective.

In at least one case they charged British artillery to give their unarmoured vehicles room to withdraw.

The main conclusions based on this analysis were:

- In every phase of the battle, the DAK coordinated its anti-tank guns, field artillery, infantry and tanks, thus working as *Verbundene Waffen*.
- Manoeuvres were characterized by speed and compactness. Vehicle movements were shielded by an outer screen of anti-tank guns and an inner screen of tanks.
- Their convoys were vulnerable to air attacks and Jock Columns. To reduce their vulnerability, they often moved at night.
- British offensive actions were very expensive due to the above-described way of operating by the Germans. In addition, British offensive actions were not focussed on flexible manoeuvring. The withdrawal of German units was therefore difficult to control unless one was able to pursue them for a very long time, constantly threatening their flanks. (11: 107–9)

The Germans also learned a number of things from their *Erfahrungsberichte*:

- Not all units had reported the actual situation and their position (the agreement was to report once every two hours, even if nothing had changed).
- Not all units had carried out the necessary reconnaissance to map the position of enemy units when the situation changed.
- Not all commanders had a clear picture of the actual status of the key supplies of the units under their command at all times. Commanders and their staff officers needed to know exactly how much fuel and ammunition were available, when and what supplies could be expected over the next 24 hours and how many of the key weapon systems were operational.
- Fighting in the open desert posed great dangers to the higher staff units [for instance, the headquarters of the DAK was overrun]. The *Kampfstaffel* [headquarters protection unit] therefore had to be strengthened with tanks, anti-tank and anti-aircraft guns up to the strength of a battalion. These units also served as a tactical reserve.
- There was a constant danger of southern flanking movements from the enemy if a defensive position was taken up. The northern part of the front was always protected by a defence line up to the coast. The Germans were therefore forced always to station a strong mobile reserve with sufficient ammunition and fuel in the southern part of the front to counter this danger.
- Retreating movements almost always had to take place over existing roads, which had few natural defences. Units had to withdraw in a continuous column over a greater distance to avoid breaking into smaller, vulnerable groups. Therefore, good management and strict control of all traffic were essential; it might be necessary, for example, to halt transport convoys at regular intervals in order to keep them together and to prevent units from withdrawing faster than necessary [and turning a retreat into a flight].

- Because every movement was accompanied by a great deal of dust, it was difficult to distinguish friend from foe from the air. To add to the confusion, the British and especially the Germans often used captured vehicles. It was therefore necessary to indicate demarcation lines up to which the Luftwaffe could bomb. (45: 40)

It is also striking that overrunning the DAK headquarters did not lead to a paralysis of German activity, since it was possible to quickly build a parallel communications structure via the remaining C3I capacity.

One German attack stands out for its difference, namely that on the 1st South African Division on 23 November. This was carried out contrary to all the rules: head-on by units in largely unarmoured vehicles. The consequences were terrible for all involved and there were many casualties, especially among officers.

A closer look at tank tactics

Chapter 3 briefly described how the Germans deployed their tanks. Since *Crusader* was the largest confrontation to date in terms of the number of tanks involved, we will take a further look at the tactics used. A tank regiment could carry out an attack with both its Abteilungen one after the other in two waves, or next to each other. The Abteilungen were made up of three companies of between twenty and twenty-five tanks each, depending on how many were operational at a given moment. They were deployed in triangles, the so-called *Keil* with the point of the triangle forward, or the *Breitkeil* with the base of the triangle in front.

The companies within the triangle were positioned during the attack in such a way that all tanks had the maximum field of fire and could cover each other as fully as possible. When one tank failed, another took its place, so that the formation was maintained for as long as possible.

Attacking formation of a German Panzer Abteilung in *Keil*

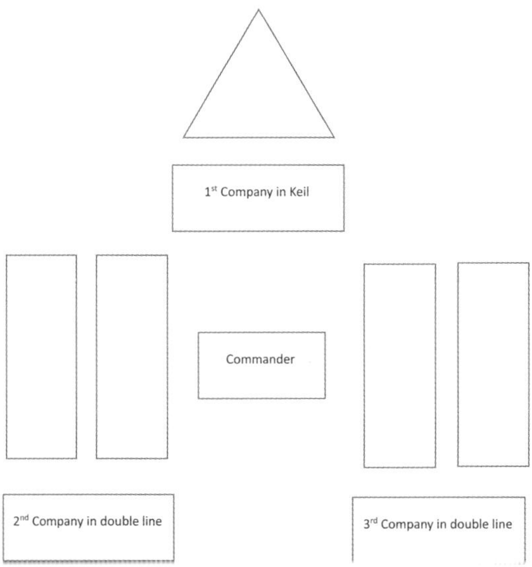

Logistics management

The importance of 'just in time' re-supply during the advance and after battle cannot be overemphasized. In German divisions the supply columns were responsible for this, and as we have previously seen, these were, together with the recovery units, an integral part of the combat formations.

The mobile nature of the Germans' preferred method of fighting placed high demands on these supply columns. Not only did communication have to be optimal, the columns also had to be able to find their way across the battlefield and operate in the vicinity of enemy units. In North Africa relative positions were often unclear, and the enemy could appear from behind every hill. Apart from this threat, enemy aircraft could wreak havoc among these columns. Their lack of armour and their high-explosive cargo could result in extremely short-lived confrontations. The result of not delivering fuel and ammunition on time quickly became apparent in the form of tanks that came to a standstill: for example, on 24 November the 5th Panzer Regiment was left without fuel for half a day because the supply columns and tanks had lost contact. This would have spelled the end of the regiment if British tank units had been able to launch an attack

According to Auchinleck, the performance of these supply columns was one of the reasons for the success of the Germans in this period. (29: 217), although it is estimated that approximately 50 per cent (!) of Germany's transport capacity was destroyed at this time, mainly by roving Jock Columns. The loss of transport, including that bringing supplies from the depots to the west, ultimately forced Rommel to break off the fighting and withdraw.

Improvised logistics

What the supply columns could not bring in, the tank crews carried with them. Many tanks had spare parts in or on the tank in the form of running wheels and track links. The latter also served as extra armour, especially in the later phases of the conflict, and were for that reason often mounted at the front. In addition, food supplies, cooking utensils (including folding kitchens captured from the British), tents and other practical items were carried on the quarterdeck. After and sometimes even during battle, brief stops often made it possible to examine stranded or disabled enemy vehicles in order to replenish supplies. Captured British food was considered so good that senior officers liked to eat with their troops: the standard rations given men and officers were extremely meagre, as we have seen. Other troops supplemented their supplies by foraging in camps abandoned by friendly or enemy troops. Understandably, the focus was often on luxury and highly marketable items such as drink and cigarettes. Particularly during retreats, many of these items changed hands.

Recovery system

The Germans had an excellent recovery system, with which they proved able to maintain the deployability of their Panzer divisions, despite sometimes considerable losses. These units operated in close cooperation with the tanks they supported. During the fighting, damaged tanks were often repaired under enemy fire, towed away or lifted onto low loaders and transported to workshops in quieter areas. The units were also active at night, recovering all useful friendly or enemy material left on the battlefield, as well as caring for the injured:

> Through the sharp cold of the night the recovery units crept forward on to the battlefield and they were not unkind to our wounded lying there. They handed

> hot drinks to the men who lay helpless beside the smoking wrecks of their tanks and threw blankets over some who would otherwise have died of exposure before morning. (29: 93)

By rendering many of the damaged tanks ready for combat again in a short time, these units and the workshops further behind the lines made it possible for the Germans to compensate to some extent for their opponents' superiority in materiel. This meant that the number of available tanks could vary from day to day. Unsurprisingly, this recovery system is often mentioned as one of the key success factors in North Africa, since it ensured that a high percentage of tanks were always deployable.

The British were much less skilled in night actions, and this gave the Germans a considerable tactical advantage, since they were often able to nullify at night any territorial gains the enemy had made during the day. (17: 121) As we have seen, British tank formations withdrew at nightfall and undertook no recovery activities.

Recovery of tanks during battle: roadside assistance on the battlefield

During the Polish campaign and the May 1940 campaign, towing and repairing stranded tanks was relatively simple. After a battle, the tanks were collected and transported by rail to workshops in Germany. In North Africa and the Soviet Union the situation was completely different, and it was necessary to maintain combat power on the ground. The ability to tow tanks away from the battlefield thus became a critical success factor and developed into a specialism.

The Germans had special *Abschlepabteilungen* (towing battalions) for this, using their SdKfz 9 FAMOs with low loaders and other vehicles. The SdKfz 9 FAMOs, weighing 18 tons, were the heaviest members of the SdKfz family and were developed for towing 21cm and 24cm howitzers.

A single SdKfz 9 FAMO could tow a tank of the PzKpfw III and IV type, but for heavier tanks such as the later Panther and Tiger, three FAMOs were needed. These were connected with 5m steel cables and then towed away by the lead vehicle under the supervision of the commander of the recovery unit.

It was only later that the British developed specialized recovery units.

Men

We have seen that both tank divisions were in almost constant combat during *Crusader*. This took its toll on the troops. When the Sidi Rezegh airfield was finally retaken by the Germans for the last time on 1 December, their men had been reduced to little more than zombies, and the captured British could hardly believe that these were their victors. It is also clear that during this period the stress among, for example, the tank crews of both sides must have been enormous. Every crew must have lived with a terrible daily rate of destruction. Nowhere, however, is it recorded that either side's crews refused to go into battle, although on 25 November the 3rd and 33rd *Aufklärungsabteilungen* responded very tepidly to Rommel's order to advance. And there must have been other units which put their own interpretation on orders in the chaos of battle.

Among the ordinary soldiers, the feeling was that their Italian allies could do nothing about the fact that their combat performance was substandard compared to that of the

Tank 215

One crew, that of tank number 215 of the 5th Panzer Regiment, had a particularly adventurous time. This PzKpfw III had a certain cultural-historical value in the eyes of its crew; it was one of the last remaining tanks from the first shipment from February. In fact, at the end of *Crusader* it would be the very last one of all.

While regrouping after one of the many battles, the inexperienced commander of the unit to which tank 215 belonged ordered them to join a group of tanks which, in the eyes of tank commander Sänger, were clearly British. The crew agreed with their commander, and when the order came, the driver quickly performed a manoeuvre that caused the fan belt to break and the engine to overheat. They reported the tank as out of action, and while the other tanks of the unit promptly encountered a squadron of British tanks in the distance, tank 215 waited for its engine to cool down before fitting a new belt.

This was just the beginning of a series of adventures. First of all, the now immobile tank found itself in danger of being harassed by British reconnaissance vehicles, but surprisingly, these were chased away by a German unit with a mechanized anti-tank gun that suddenly appeared and turned out to belong to the *Kampfstaffel* of the DAK. The crew were then ordered to move into cover, but pointed out that the engine was still too hot. When they had settled in their tent at nightfall they were visited by an officer. He ordered the now repaired tank to be started, whereupon Sänger declared that he had run out of fuel and was waiting for the supply vehicles. 'Besides,' he said, cutting off discussion, 'the engine has too little compression.' The officer then asked how many kilometres it had done. Sänger's answer of 3,000 was hardly satisfactory, since the officer said that in the Soviet Union engines still had sufficient compression after 5,000 kilometres. When Sänger replied that the officer apparently did not realize that he was in Africa, the latter responded that as commander of the DAK he certainly knew where he was and did not appreciate being addressed in such a way by one of his men. There was a deathly silence in the tent, and just as Sänger was about to apologize, one of the others remarked, 'This must be another jerk from the 8th Regiment.'

This was how the crew of tank 215 found themselves up before Crüwell, the commander-in-chief of the DAK. (14: 207–8) After this awkward introduction, however, both parties would get to know each other better in the following weeks: during the DAK's retreat, tank 215 served as the DAK's command vehicle, with Bayerlein and Crüwell alternating as passengers.

The story is illustrative of the way in which other tank crews (and other units!) will undoubtedly have made their own plans or put their own interpretation on orders.

Germans. It was clear to everyone that poor armament and training, and not always optimal leadership, were to blame. There seems to have been some agreement about this. Rommel himself indicated several times that Italians, if properly armed and led, were excellent soldiers. Some Italian units such as the Ariete Division particularly distinguished themselves during *Crusader*. His views on the leadership of the Italian troops were clear: he partly blamed them for the retreat.

That morale remained high was evident on New Year's Eve 1941. The German troops celebrated, fired tracer ammunition at midnight and sang the national anthem. The

22nd Armoured Brigade was impressed and reported to British headquarters in Cairo that these troops were far from defeated. (14: 221)

Rommel

Crusader showed both the strengths and weaknesses of Rommel as a commander. The weaknesses included his fixation on Tobruk, refusal to recognize that a major British offensive was actually underway, the doomed counter-offensive towards Egypt and his own inaccessibility during two crucial days of the battle. The strengths were the preparation of his troops, the way in which he ultimately intervened and the planning and execution of the retreat. Above all was his personal commitment. It is also interesting to examine how Rommel's leadership style related to the principles laid down in *Auftragstaktik* and its further elaborations. What it came down to was that Rommel continually intervened at lower levels in the organization, whereas the management concept of the German Army actually emphasized that each level should exercise its own responsibilities and powers. Rommel's methods did not fit this concept. His interventions could be effective, but sometimes they led to confusion at both high and low levels in the hierarchy. He made the same mistake as many British commanders, namely believing that fighting the enemy with your own unit is the most romantic and exciting way of waging war.

4.8 Evaluation of the British Army

Tactical dimensions

The entire design of *Crusader* along two axes, one with tank units, the other with infantry, shows that Cunningham continued to insist on the separation of tanks and infantry within the organizational structure. The experiences of the recent past had not changed his mind, and the separation of tanks and infantry would remain the basic concept for the British Army throughout the entire conflict in North Africa. The consequence of this was that although the tank units were able to capture certain objectives, such as Sidi Rezegh, they were subsequently unable to defend them, because infantry, anti-tank guns and artillery were lacking to repel German attacks and destroy their tanks.

In theory, the British employed tank formations the size of a brigade, comparable in size to a German division. However, battle reports show that brigades were not deployed as a whole, and they usually fell back on using individual squadrons in successive attack waves. The Germans could then use the firepower of seventy-five tanks (half a division) in *Keil* or *Breitkeil* formation against the fifteen tanks of an individual squadron. For unclear reasons, the British never used a regiment with its fifty-two tanks as a combat unit, but used regiments as a kind of pool to draw tanks from. Thus they always found themselves at a disadvantage.

Structure of a British tank formation (one squadron up)

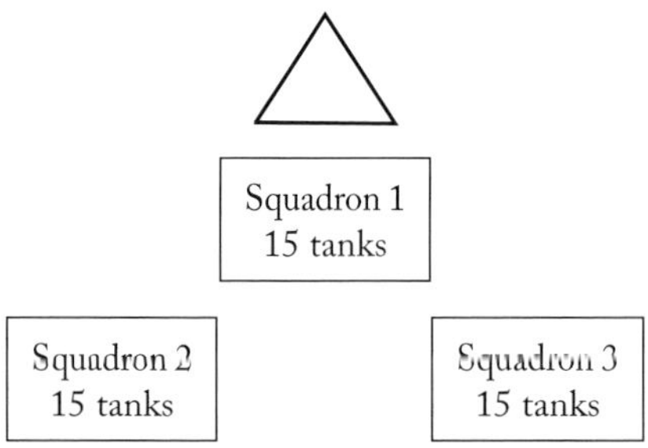

Structure of a British tank formation (two squadrons up)

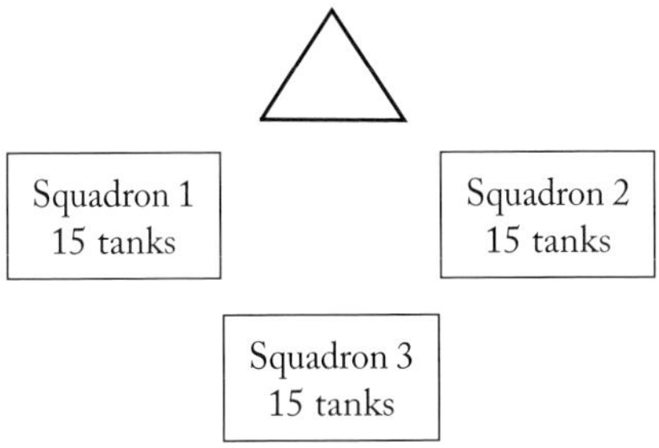

Gatehouse, the commander of the 4th Armoured Brigade, introduced three new tactics for his M3 Stuart tanks. The first was the charge, initially used on 19 November against the Panzer Regiment of the 15th Panzer Division. Used the next day, however, this proved useless, because the Panzer Regiment of the 21st Panzer Division, undoubtedly informed by its sister regiment, opened fire at a great distance, forcing the M3 Stuart tanks to zigzag closer to their target – the second new tactic, which also proved unsuccessful.

From the evaluation reports of these battles, a picture emerges that was described in February 1942 by Lieutenant Colonel de Guingand, Director of Military Intelligence of Auchinleck as follows:

> Our armoured brigades were commanded with great dash but not perhaps with comparable skill. Once they came into contact with Rommel's forces, very heavy casualties occurred. The tank returns that came into Army Headquarters were positively frightening. (46: 135)

In a third tactic used by Gatehouse later in *Crusader*, artillery in the form of a battery of 25-pounder howitzers from the Royal Horse Artillery, played an important role. In the meantime, Gatehouse had received 100 (!) new M3 Stuarts to replace his disabled tanks. He split the battery into two parts, one in the front, the other towards the rear. The leading artillery pieces bombarded the advancing German tanks until they got too close, at which point the guns were coupled to their tractors and quickly driven to the rear, while the rear artillery pieces took over, targeting the German tanks and covering the retreat of the returning guns. In this way the artillery was used to compensate for the relatively low firepower of the M3 Stuarts. (29: 104)

The above is a good example of combined weapons tactics by the British, although there are no other known instances of this tactic being used.

During this period British units often seemed hardly to move from their positions, something which can be explained by their orders and by the partial collapse of the British C3I capacity. The various tank units, such as the 4th and 22nd Armoured Brigades, operated almost continuously in the same area, often being mauled several times by active German armoured units during the course of *Crusader*. In the course of the fighting, it became increasingly clear that *Crusader* was primarily a battle of materiel, a harbinger of the battles that the Germans would have to wage in the following years.

C3I structure

During *Crusader*, as we have seen, the Armoured Divisions were never deployed as a whole, but were split into Armoured Brigades and Support Groups. The reason for this was that the British had problems coordinating the deployment of division-sized units. In addition, Operation *Crusader* was the largest offensive by the British up to that point in the Second World War, and they had little experience with directing and coordinating so many units on a rapidly changing battlefield. In other words, their C3I capacity was inadequate in many areas, and as a result the offensive broke up into a large number of smaller, isolated battles, which largely escaped central command and control.

Another important weakness was also present during *Crusader*: the British had no unified leadership, so that the various armed forces had to fight independently. Although the offensive was based on a jointly drawn up plan, as soon as events overtook this plan, coordination between the various forces collapsed and each fought its own war. This weak point in British organization cannot be overemphasized; against the Germans operating as a single combat unit, with their built-in flexibility and *Verbundene Waffen*, the British could deploy no more than poorly coordinated troops, split into tanks, infantry and artillery. It is a testament to the courage and commitment of these units that they were not overrun again and again. (14: 187)

This lack of unity in leadership and coordination occurred not only at an operational level, but also higher up in the organization. Orders from on high were often interpreted as instructions or suggestions, which lower-level commanders could interpret at their discretion. This led to ambiguity, miscommunication and coordination problems at all levels. Auchinleck would try to get a grip on this during the next phase, but only Montgomery managed to put an end to this free-spirited approach.

Under the pressure of combat, this weak point in British command structure became more prominent: in the crucial period of 28–30 November the British High Command was unable to provide clear and unambiguous leadership, and the entire C3I structure collapsed. Cunningham stayed far behind the front, while both corps commanders had great difficulty keeping abreast of developments and were unable to effectively coordinate the deployment of their troops. As a result, *Crusader* broke into a large number of small battles, without cohesion. The use of Jock Columns can be seen as an attempt to deal with this.

Even lower down in the organization, these poor communication options meant that units operated separately from each other, could not reach each other if they encountered the enemy and sometimes found themselves in uncoordinated battles with the same enemy units without knowing that others were involved. Other units roamed the battlefield in search of the enemy and took up the fight individually.

In addition, although the British had a relatively inexhaustible supply of tanks at their disposal, lost command tanks with their valuable communications equipment were difficult to replace. As the fighting continued, the C3I capacity of the various Armoured Brigades continued to decline.

Auchinleck's personal intervention, and his replacement of the demoralized Cunningham with Ritchie, are generally seen as appropriate and effective. He rescued units from the impasse and ensured that the battle of materiel was ultimately settled in favour of the British. Rommel respected him as an opponent and contrasted his ability with the weaknesses of the other commanders:

> Auchinleck was a very good commander, but he left most of his tactical operational command to his subordinates (General Cunningham and General Ritchie), who quickly gave me the opportunity to set the rules of the game by reacting rather than to take initiative. This was completely unnecessary ... When General Auchinleck himself took command at El Alamein, he led the operations expertly and courageously. (36: 78)

The Jock Columns were surprisingly effective, although the formation of these units was largely an emergency measure. It does not appear anywhere that their explicit assignment was to disrupt the German lines of communication behind the front, but this was where they caused the greatest damage, and approximately 50 per cent of the Germans' transport capacity was destroyed in a short period. (5: 190) This led to acute supply problems and was one of the most important reasons, if not the most important, for Rommel to withdraw to the west. Strangely enough, with one exception, in van Creveld's *Supplying War* no explicit mention of this is made. The British also gave no indication that they realized how decisive a blow had been dealt to Rommel by the Jock Columns.

Training and deployment of new troops

Two things stand out regarding the deployment of new troops on the British side.

In the first place, unlike the Germans, the British did not operate an *Ersatz Bataillon* system – battalions in which the newly trained troops acclimatized, were trained in the latest tactics and met their future commanders. Rather, it seems that fresh units were deployed directly to the front without additional training or acclimatization. This even happened to entire divisions. For example, in February 1941 the 2nd Armoured Division arrived at the front fresh from Britain without any experience in the North African theatre. There was no specific training programme for them. (28: 26) Other units such as the 22nd Armoured Brigade also came directly from home, had no experience in desert warfare and were not given the opportunity to practise this, because they were immediately deployed. Another unit, the 1st South African Division, had been so busy building reinforcements that training had been neglected. Other units with experience in desert warfare were in turn given little or no opportunity to practise with the new M3 Stuart tanks, which they had never seen before.

There were constant complaints at all levels about the low level of training, but this did not lead to fundamental changes. Apparently, just as in the First World War, it was accepted as an established fact, an excuse that could be used to explain the successes of German troops, who in the eyes of the British were much better trained.

Secondly, during the North African campaign, British troops were continually transferred, experienced units often being replaced by newly trained men. The reason for this was undoubtedly the shortage of manpower; on the other hand, units were regularly transferred without any clear plan. Thus, after *Crusader*, well trained and acclimatized troops were replaced by new units. And after being evacuated from Tobruk, the experienced Australian 9th Division was moved to Syria to build fortifications, and training was neglected during the six months of their deployment there. When it was deployed to the front again in July 1942, the division was 'not in suitable training for very mobile operations'.

Because of all these movements, it was not possible to record the practical experience of these divisions in tactical tips and recommendations or to share them with recruits in training in Britain or elsewhere in the Empire. In comparison, the German divisions were continually involved in the conflict. In Chapter 5 we will discuss the troop movements on the British side in more detail.

Rommel noted a number of other points of difference:

> The inherent weaknesses of the otherwise excellently motorized British units could not be remedied by short-term additional training of officers and men, without also reorganizing the entire command structure: this was extremely cumbersome …It is absolutely true that the British military leadership was characterized by a rigid, bureaucratic attitude …Neither Cunningham nor Ritchie had experience with tanks and they could not be expected to be able to train their men in modern mobile tactics. (36: 78)

Men

During this period a new problem emerged on the British side: the large number of different nationalities in their forces. While the Axis had only German and Italian troops, the British eventually had units from Britain itself, Australia, South Africa, India, New Zealand, Poland, Greece and France. All these nationalities were trained and led in different ways, had different strengths and weaknesses in terms of knowledge and skills, and different temperaments, political backgrounds, etc. Moreover, not all of them spoke English.

Furthermore, the deployment of their troops was closely watched by national politicians, and Australian, New Zealand and South African units were primarily responsible to their respective governments. These nations still vividly remembered the slaughter of Gallipoli, Messines and Passchendaele in the First World War. South African soldiers were allowed to fight only in Africa, because of the bitter experience of Delville Wood in 1916. In addition, the Free French under de Gaulle often followed their own course. In other words, no commander-in-chief had a completely free hand; every decision had a political dimension. (46: 116)

Australian Prime Minister Fadden, like his successor Curtin, demanded that the Australian units from Tobruk be relieved, saying, 'It is vital to the Australian people to have concentrated control and direction of the Expeditionary Force.' This was not an unreasonable demand: Australia had sent its best troops to the Middle East, and they were now stuck in a theatre of questionable strategic value while the Japanese were advancing towards Australia. Despite resistance from Churchill, these troops were evacuated from Tobruk at great expense during the moonless periods of 19–27 September and 12–25 October. (46: 118)

Tanks

One of the striking things about British tanks in this period is their poor mechanical condition. Some tanks were technically 'used up', while others had yet to be adapted to conditions in the desert. Sometimes the problems were more serious. For example, Smith, Auchinleck's superior, noted in a letter in early December: 'I have just seen Lumsden [commander of the 1st Armoured Division] who tells me that not a single tank arrived from England complete with equipment and one was quite empty except for a tow rope.' (46: 143)

In addition, the new Crusader tanks had a number of construction weaknesses. Firstly, just before the offensive began, it was discovered that, due to a manufacturing error, the suspension arms of the wheels broke off very easily. The problem with these otherwise very heavy arms (each tank had ten) could be solved by welding a plate at the back, but this task created an additional burden for the already overloaded field workshops. Secondly, the tank was powered by a 12-cylinder 400hp aircraft engine from the First World War. As an aircraft engine this was very reliable, but cooling it in a tank posed a major problem, which could only be dealt with by two fans and two water pumps. However, sand then caused the ventilation chains to come loose, and it took three days to reassemble them. Sand and heat also caused the water pumps to leak, and they had to be completely redesigned. All together, in January 1942, 200 Crusaders (!) were under repair in the workshops of the 13th Corps; a request for 400 water pumps to be flown in from Great Britain was answered with 'Regret not available in UK'. (46: 147) This was partly the reason why Rommel was able to advance east again during this period (see next chapter).

Armoured infantry vehicles

Another weak point for the British was the lack of a good armoured vehicle to transport infantry to the spot from which an attack on foot could be launched. They did have access to so-called Bren carriers: light tracked vehicles in which a limited number of troops and a machine gun (of the Bren type) could be transported. But with no armoured half-tracks, the British found it very difficult to organize, equip and deploy infantry in the desert. Meanwhile, it had become clear that men on foot or in unarmoured vehicles, and without the ability to hide behind natural obstacles or buildings, were extremely vulnerable, especially to artillery and tank guns. (3: 53)

The 2-pounder gun (again)

At this stage of the conflict, the British still assumed that the German tanks had superior guns. They did not realize that many of their tanks were falling victim to the anti-tank guns that worked closely with the tanks. As a result, their own 2-pounder (37mm) artillery was considered inferior. That was not entirely correct, however. For example, the 2-pounder gun had slightly better armour-piercing properties than the 50mm gun of the PzKpfw III with AP ammunition or the 75mm gun of the PzKpfw IV with HE ammunition. At a range of 1,000m this gun could penetrate the armour of all German tanks, except those equipped with extra armour plates. The German 50mm gun could also pierce the armour of the Cruiser VIs and the M3 at that distance. In other words, there was little difference in the effectiveness of the guns used by each side. (3: 52) What may have played an important role was the tendency of the British to shoot while on the move. This cavalry-style method of operation was spectacular, but significantly reduced the chance of hitting the target. The Germans, on the other hand, always fired from stationary positions.

The lack of confidence in the 2-pounder gun led to the 25-pounder howitzers being distributed among the units to fulfil the role of anti-tank guns. In this way the most effective weapon of the British, their field artillery, was stripped of its power. Montgomery was aware of this and cancelled the transfer.

The British were also confronted with an interesting, albeit rare, innovation on the German side, namely British 3-inch anti-aircraft guns being used as anti-tank guns. After *Crusader*, Colonel Berry was asked to look at a captured cannon:

> I could not believe my eyes. It was a British three-inch AA gun manufactured by Vickers and fitted to a Russian carriage. It was a very effective and powerful weapon. Clearly it had been sent to Russia, captured by the Germans, serviced and sent to the Middle East.

The gun turned out to have come from a batch of several hundred that had become redundant with the introduction of the 3.7-inch gun and had been supplied to the Soviet Union. (46: 148)

Logistics on site

An important practice in the British Armoured Brigades was the use of so-called laagers, defensive positions which were a legacy of the Boer Wars at the end of the nineteenth century. During the day a division's vehicles were spread over a large area, but in the evening the British tank units literally set up camp: trucks, command vehicles, etc., were buried up to their axles in a large circle in the sand, protected by a cordon of anti-tank guns. From the various laagers the tanks travelled to the battlefield at dawn and returned at the end of the day (or earlier) to load fuel and ammunition and rest. British tanks, unlike German ones, did not operate in combination with supply or recovery units and were therefore dependent on their laager. They had to remain near these fixed positions to be supplied with fuel and ammunition, although supply columns were sometimes used.

German tanks were active at night, while British ones withdrew to the laager at the end of the day and were sometimes surprised by roving German tank units. For example, the 4th Armoured Brigade was first attacked by *Kampfgruppe Stephan* on 19 November, then by the 15th Panzer Division on 20 November, and the same units followed it on the night of 22/23 November to one of the laagers, where it was partly neutralized. The same 15th Panzer Division escaped punishment by the 4th and 22nd Armoured Brigades during the retreat to Tobruk because the British broke off the fighting at the end of the day (perhaps forced to by fuel and ammunition shortages) to withdraw to their respective laagers.

Coordination with the RAF

Crusader was characterized by the superiority of the RAF, which in this phase of the conflict waged its own war without much coordination with ground troops. Nor was it prepared to subordinate itself to operations on the ground. The units on the ground, on the other hand, were of the opinion that the deployment of the air force should be an integral part of the battle. Only later would the RAF recognize the need to support ground forces, and methods and techniques would take time to be developed for air-ground communication, target recognition and communication between the Army and the RAF.

Chapter 5

Operation *Theseus*: on the Road to the Nile Delta

5.1 A first step back

Despite retreating, Rommel's position had not deteriorated. Under Kesselring, the *Zweite Luftflotte* had been quickly built up in the Mediterranean in recent months. Luftwaffe squadrons, operating from Sicily, put increasing pressure on British forces on Malta, and U-boats posed a threat to British shipping. On 5 January Rommel received a shipment of fifty-four tanks, twenty reconnaissance vehicles and large quantities of ammunition and fuel. New faces also arrived on the German side: Major General von Bismarck became the new commander of the 21st Panzer Division and General von Värst took over the 15th Panzer Division. Rommel was as active as in the preceding months, constantly with his troops, inspecting reinforcements, people and equipment and studying the terrain from his Fieseler Storch reconnaissance aircraft. The logistical picture had also changed: it was now the British who had to send supplies over 1,500km and were experiencing shortages in all kinds of areas. Rommel could now plan a new offensive, despite the differences in strength of armament – 89 relatively weak Italian tanks and 150 German ones, including some new Panzer IIIs with reinforced frontal armour and 50mm guns, against the 360 tanks the British could deploy.

However, British grand strategy had undergone a reorientation in the past month: the Japanese attack on Pearl Harbor and their subsequent advances in the Far East had placed British interests in the region in acute danger. The 70th British Division and some experienced tank units were transferred to this theatre, the remnants of the 7th Armoured Division were withdrawn to the Nile Delta and the inexperienced 1st Armoured Division with Cruiser tanks took its place. Part of this division was the 22nd Armoured Brigade, which we have already met and which arrived in theatre in July 1941, during *Crusader*. This 1st Armoured Division, together with the 4th Indian Division, both led by Godwin-Austen, had to hold the front against Rommel. However, there were major logistical problems that prevented the newly arrived units from being able to train sufficiently. The recently arrived brigade of the 1st Armoured Division had not been able to practise since August because it was en route to North Africa. The British wanted to continue Operation *Acrobat*, but their estimate of Axis losses was too high and their estimate of the enemy's number of operational tanks was too low. They believed that Rommel had forty-two German and forty to fifty Italian tanks at his disposal; in reality he had twice as many. They also assumed that the logistical problems on the German side were greater than their own and that Rommel would be unable to launch an eastward offensive in the near future.

The logistical problems and the weak troop build-up on the British side had not gone unnoticed by *Panzergruppe Afrika*. On 18 January, Rommel discussed with Crüwell and

Bayerlein new plans for a three-axis attack towards the east. To preserve the element of surprise, only a limited number of commanders were informed, all freight traffic towards the front was prohibited during the day (the trucks drove west at daytime, returning by the same route at night), and tanks and guns were well camouflaged. In addition, neither the Italian *Commando Supremo* nor the OKW were informed of the plan, so no Enigma messages were sent. A rumour was spread that *Panzergruppe Afrika* was going to withdraw to Tripoli.

On 21 January, the attack along the three axes began. *Kampfgruppe Marcks* advanced along the Via Balbia, the XX Corps under General Gambara was in the centre, and the rest of the DAK under Crüwell advanced 30km south of the Via Balbia. Rommel himself accompanied the attack along the Via Balbia with his *Gefechtsstaffel. Kampfgruppe Marcks* consisted of the 155th MG Regiment of the 90th Leichte Division, tanks of the Ariete Division and some units of the 21st Panzer Division. They had to force a gap in the front of the 22nd Armoured Brigade, so that the rest of the 90th Leichte Division could advance through it. The British withdrew without resistance. A first attempt at encirclement by the Germans failed because of the speed of the British withdrawal, but a second attack was successful: 299 armoured vehicles and 147 artillery pieces were captured, and 935 soldiers were marched off into captivity. Losses on the German side were negligible, and on 22 January German troops re-entered Agedabia. The Italian supreme command was furious at this unannounced attack, and General Cavallero flew to Rommel with a directive from Mussolini to immediately withdraw to the Mersa el Brega Line. Rommel's response was that only German troops were involved in the fighting, and so only Hitler could stop him. However, he realized that Mussolini was ultimately pulling the logistical strings and decided not to advance any further, limiting himself to bringing in the equipment left behind on the battlefield.

However, radio reports showed that panic on the British side was total, and Rommel found the temptation too great not to continue the offensive. On 26 January, Bayerlein flew to the headquarters of *Panzergruppe Afrika* to discuss follow-up plans. The next objective was to occupy Benghazi and capture all British supplies there. A diversionary manoeuvre would focus on Mechili. On 27 January, the next phase of the offensive began and was immediately successful. The British thought that the main force was focusing on Mechili, and on 28 January Rommel managed to attack the 4th Indian Division in the rear, on its retreat to Benghazi via the Via Balbia, with an outflanking movement through swampy areas and the difficult Cyrenaica mountains. Within an hour this division, which had fought so bravely over the past year, had been scattered, and on 29 January Benghazi was back in German hands. The loot was enormous, 1,300 trucks alone being captured. Godwin-Austen's proposal to evacuate Benghazi led to his resignation at the hands of Auchinleck.

Rommel, meanwhile, drove the British forces back further east until the Eighth Army reached the Gazala Line. There the retreat came to a halt and the British began to entrench themselves. By 6 February all of Cyrenaica had been cleared of British forces, and on 9 February the airfields of Martuba, Derna and Tmimi were put to use by Luftwaffe squadrons. In the meantime, the *Panzergruppe Afrika* had been renamed *Panzerarmee Afrika* on 30 January and Rommel had been promoted to colonel general. Once again, Rommel – the 'Soldiers' General' – had proved that his presence rendered his men capable of unprecedented achievements.

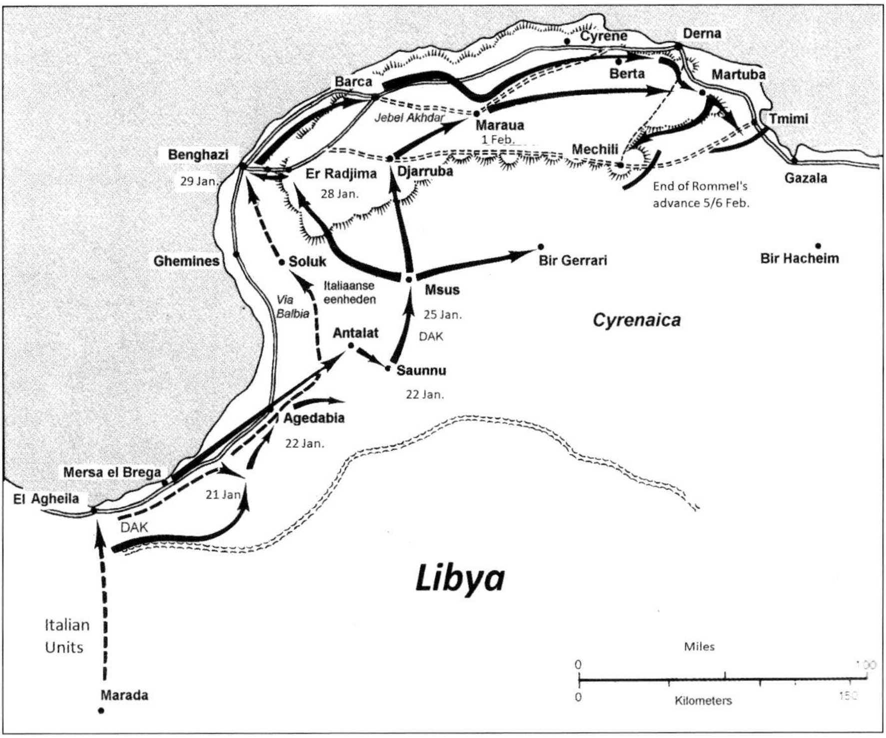

Big steps to the east.

Their commander's appearance had a magical effect on everyone. His soldiers addressed him as 'Erwin', he slept beside them during breaks in combat, he ate the same rations and he explained complicated matters to them clearly. On the other hand, this rapid recapture of territory was devastating to the Eighth Army. Rommel, described by Churchill in the Commons as 'a great general', was threatening to become a legend, undermining the morale of British troops. His style of leadership, the Germans' equipment and their tactics seemed to outclass anything the British could offer. In response, Auchinleck issued a ban on mentioning the name 'Rommel' when talking about the enemy, to prevent further glorification of his opponent.

Rommel and Westphal left for Rome on 15 February to inform Mussolini of the latest state of affairs. Rommel then flew to Germany for discussions with Hitler. The Führer was not really interested in the situation in North Africa; although he appreciated the results of Rommel's final offensive, his attention was focused on the Eastern Front. Rommel's request for six additional divisions to drive the British permanently out of Africa was therefore not honoured. Consultations between Westphal and Jodl also led to nothing because the OKW was also completely preoccupied with the battle in the east.

Back in Rome, Rommel tried to warm Mussolini to the idea of first taking Malta, then Tobruk – or if an invasion of Malta was not possible in the short term, to tackle Tobruk first. Although Il Duce gave evasive answers, Rommel assumed that he had effectively agreed to a new offensive. Hitler also had doubts about an invasion of Malta: despite the preparations by General Student of the *Fallschirmjäger* (paratroops) for this invasion, the

Structure of the Panzerarmee Afrika

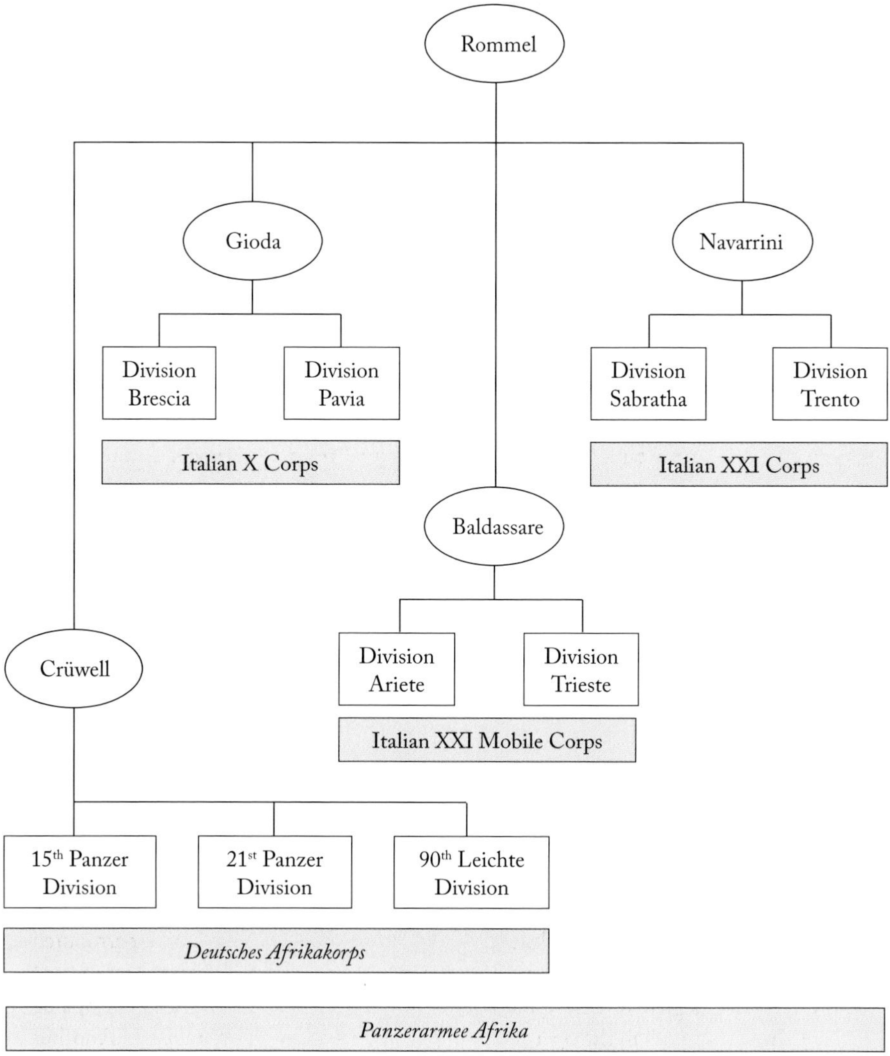

Führer had no confidence in the units that the Italians wanted to deploy. The end result was that Romel received a mandate from Hitler to launch a new attack in May to break through the Gazala Line and take Tobruk. He then had to move into defensive positions. After more than a month's leave, Rommel returned to North Africa on 29 March to prepare his troops with renewed energy for the coming offensive.

Rommel spent his time training the newly arrived infantry units in how to work with tanks. Tank officers had to learn to function as artillery observers for the guns operating further to the rear. The anti-tank gun crews had to learn to use machine guns, and the infantry units had to learn to operate the anti-tank guns. Such 'cross training' had been common in the *Reichswehr* since the 1920s and led to great flexibility. Dummies and decoys were built, the most imaginative being ten trucks with aircraft engines mounted on the back to throw up large clouds of dust and simulate troop movements. There were still major logistical problems, but Rommel assumed that he would be able to take several supply dumps which the British were building for their own offensive.

The 15th Panzer Division was led by von Värst, the 21st Panzer Division by von Bismarck and the 90th Leichte Division by Kleeman.

German tanks and anti-tank guns

The strength of the *Panzerarmee Afrika* grew steadily. Between January and May 1942, Rommel received a total of twenty PzKpfw IIs, 211 PzKpfw IIIs, forty-nine PzKpfw IVs and some Panzer *Befehlswagen* (command tanks). The PzKpfw IIIs and IVs also included nineteen III Js and nine PzKpfw IV F2s. These two tank types had a new gun with a longer barrel and could penetrate armour at longer ranges. The PzKpfw III J had a long 50mm gun, similar to the Pak 38, and an extra plate at the front with a space of 6cm between it and the hull. Its weight had increased to 22 tons and its speed was 42kph. The PzKpfw IV F2 had a 75mm gun with high muzzle velocity, excellent for piercing armour at greater ranges. Both tank types were highly valued by the Germans as a response to the increasingly heavily armed and armoured British tanks. In addition, numbers of the PzKpfw III H were also introduced, with the 'old' 50mm gun, but with heavier armour at the front.

During this period, the Germans also received the first 76.2mm anti-tank guns captured from the Soviets and converted for German ammunition. These were a welcome addition to the existing anti-tank guns and in many respects comparable in performance to the 88mm Flak gun.

Time for evaluation

At the end of January, after Rommel's lightning offensive, Auchinleck had already indicated where he believed the weak areas in the British Army were: equipment, organization and training. In a letter to Smith on 30 January, he wrote:

> We have got to face the fact that, unless we can achieve superiority on the battlefield by better co-operation between the army and more original leadership of our armoured forces than is apparently being exercised at present, we have to forget any idea of mounting a strategical offensive, because our armoured forces are tactically incapable of meeting the enemy in the open, even when superior to him in numbers …Another serious aspect …is the growth of an inferiority complex among our armoured forces, due to their failure to compete with enemy tanks, which they consider …superior to their own in certain aspects …Before we can really do anything against the Germans on land, they have got to be made as good and better both in equipment, organization and training.

In a telegram to Churchill that same day he made the following points:

> I am not sure that the tactical leadership of our armoured units is of sufficiently high standard to offset German material advantage …To meet German armoured forces with any hope of decisive success, our armoured forces as at present equipped, organized and led, must have at least two to one superiority. Even then they must rely

The PzKpfw IV F2 with its long 75mm gun was highly valued by the Germans as the answer to the increasingly heavily armoured and armed British tanks.

> for success on working in the very closest co-operation with infantry and artillery, which except for their weakness in anti-tank guns are fully competent to take on their German opposite numbers. (46: 155–6)

In the same telegram, Auchinleck once again mentioned the weakness of the 2-pounder gun and the technical unreliability of the Cruiser tanks. Based on this analysis, he used the period from February to May to improve organizational structure and level of training. First, he reorganized the Armoured Divisions so that tanks, infantry and artillery could work together more effectively. Secondly, he emphasized that divisions had to learn to operate as one. In other words, the various units within brigades, or individual brigades, were no longer to fight separately from the rest of the division, but had to subordinate themselves to the larger whole. (44: 104)

Structure of the Eighth Army

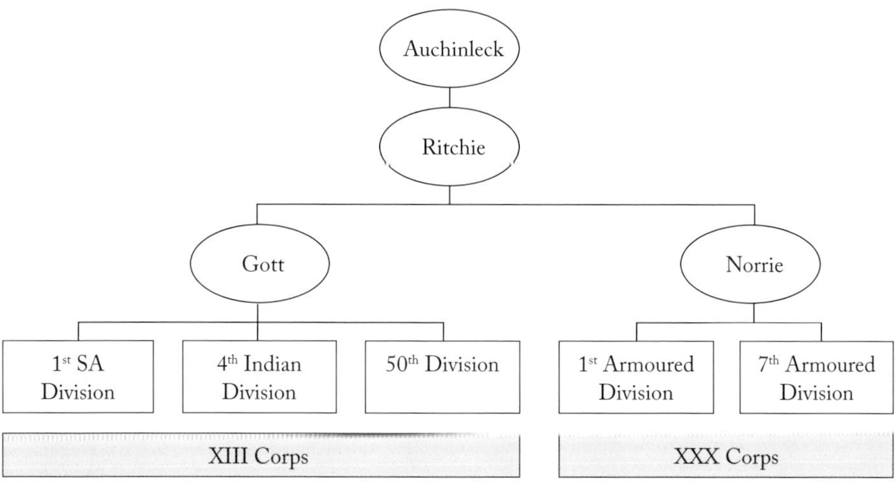

However, the separation between infantry and tanks was broadly maintained, and the Eighth Army was split into an infantry corps and a tank corps. Clear agreements were also made between the RAF and the Army to improve coordination: the RAF should focus primarily on disrupting ground support by German aircraft, and pilots should not seek individual duels with German fighters.

The 7th Armoured Division was led by Messervy, the 1st Armoured Division by Lumsden. In addition to these units, there were the 1st and 32nd Army Tank Brigades, equipped with Mathilda and Valentine infantry tanks. These units served in support of the infantry units of the XIII Corps and did not belong to the tank units in the narrower sense, under Norrie. The 2nd South African Division was in Tobruk, while the rearguard was covered by the 5th and 10th Indian Divisions. (38: 104)

British tanks and anti-tank guns

Here there was good news for the British; they could look forward to the arrival of a new tank, the American Lee/Grant.* This tank weighed 29 tons, was well armoured and had a maximum speed of 40kph. The armament consisted of a 37mm gun in the turret and a 75mm gun placed low in the hull. The advantage of this second gun was that it could fire both HE and AP ammunition, although it was mounted in a 'Cambrai' manner: low in the hull and only able to move by a few degrees, which could be a fatally weak point in a mobile battle of tank against tank. The armour was a maximum of 88mm thick.

In total, 144 of these tanks were available and would deliver an unwelcome surprise to the Germans during the next offensive. The 2nd, 4th and 22nd Armoured Brigades were the first to be equipped with them: each of their regiments received one squadron's worth.

The Lee/Grant tank, with a good combination of armour, armament and speed, was a welcome addition to the British arsenal. The tank and crew in the photo are well protected from the dust. (*Photo BTM*)

* The Germans initially called them M III 'Pilot', after a photo they found with this designation. (3: 145)

Another important addition was the new 6-pounder anti-tank gun, which replaced the outdated 2-pounder. The British received 112 of these, which were assigned to XXX Corps.

5.2 Operation *Theseus*

In the weeks after his return, Rommel planned Operation *Theseus*, with the aim of breaking through the British positions at the Gazala Line and taking Tobruk. The positions at Gazala consisted of two parts: a static defence line, and in the area behind it half a dozen defensive 'boxes' containing infantry, as well as a mobile tank reserve.

The boxes were connected to each other and surrounded by extensive minefields holding 500,000 mines. They were square in order to be able to resist attacks from any direction, and surrounded by barbed wire, mines, trenches, foxholes and fortifications; the units in the boxes had sufficient supplies for seven days of combat. The Line was 60km long, from Gazala in the north to Bir Hacheim in the desert in the south. The British assumed that the German tanks would be able to break through the defence line but would ignore the boxes during their advance and simply occupy empty desert. British units from the boxes would then attack the Germans in the flank and from the rear, while the mobile tank reserve would tackle them frontally. The German units would thus be caught between two fighting forces.

The XIII Corps was stationed in these boxes, South African troops in the north near the sea, and British units south of this and in the centre, christened 'Knightsbridge' after the fashionable London street. French troops were also stationed in the southern part near Bir Hacheim. Tobruk itself formed its own box, manned by British and Australian units, as did El Adem with Indians.

The tanks of XXX Corps were stationed by Ritchie as a strategic reserve in the rear, divided as usual into different brigades, namely the 2nd, 22nd and 4th Armoured Brigades. This division was not positioned in line with the views of Auchinleck, who wanted to deploy the tanks as one concentrated force. The 4th Armoured Brigade was stationed in the southernmost corner, partly equipped with new American Lee/Grant tanks in place of the M3 Stuarts.

Theseus would be Rommel's boldest offensive yet: instead of an obvious frontal attack, it would be built around a frontal assault as a diversionary manoeuvre, followed by a broad southward flanking movement. The frontal attack would be carried out by:

- The Italian X Corps consisting of the Brescia and Pavia divisions
- The Italian XXI Corps consisting of the Sabratha and Trento divisions
- The 15th Infantry Regiment of the 90th Light Division
- Artillery of the Panzerarmee

The southward flanking movement would be carried out by:

- The 15th Panzer Division
- The 21st Panzer Division
- The 90th Leichte Division (without infantry, which would be deployed in the frontal attack)
- The Ariete Division
- The Trieste Division

In short, the plan was as follows. At 2.00 am on Day X it would seem to the British that a major tank attack was about to be launched: a German Panzer Abteilung and an Abteilung with captured British tanks would carry out several attacks. Rommel assumed that in response the British would have their own tank units, spread in the hinterland as a strategic reserve, advance to the Gazala Line to confront the German armour.

After darkness fell, the Panzer Abteilung would withdraw and advance south together with the other tank units at 9.00 pm on Day X. In the meantime, the build-up of a large tank force at the Gazala Line would be simulated by, among other things, the trucks with aircraft engines.

At 4.30 am on Day X+1 the entire tank force of the *Panzerarmee Afrika*, including the supply columns, would make a southward flanking movement around Bir Hacheim, the southernmost point of the Gazala Line. From Bir Hacheim the troops would advance in four Kampfgruppen to the coast in the north and thereby encircle the British troops at the Gazala Line. This attack along four axes would resemble the fingers of a hand emerging from the south:

- a left Kampfgruppe would advance northwards within the Gazala Line and be supplied on the coast
- a Kampfgruppe operating on the extreme right flank would advance to El Gobi
- a third, the 90th Leichte under Colonel Marcks, would advance past El Adem to El Duda and Sidi Rezegh near Tobruk
- the greater part of the two German tank divisions and the Italian tank divisions would await the British tank attack at Knightsbridge

The British tanks advancing towards the Gazala Line would be attacked in the flank. In order to prevent a possible fall back on Tobruk, the German armoured troops had to cut off the route of the retreating British. This was also the force which was to take the city. On Day X+2 the British would be surrounded, and on Day X+3 Tobruk would be captured.

An important element of these plans was the agreement that Rommel struck with Kesselring, supreme commander of the Mediterranean area, about deployment of the Luftwaffe. Rommel could count on their considerable help until mid-June, but from the end of the month Luftwaffe units had to be deployed for the planned invasion of Malta, Operation *Hercules*.

Although Rommel attached great importance to secrecy in the preparation of this offensive, this time detailed plans were sent via Enigma to the *Commando Supremo* and the OKW. Thanks to Ultra, the British were therefore aware of Rommel's intentions at an early stage, but for inexplicable reasons they did not take advantage of this knowledge. Through the hierarchical British command structure, the only information that ultimately reached the commanders in the field was that an attack might take place at the end of May, probably in the form of a southward flanking movement. This was scarcely a surprise to anyone, since all of Rommel's offensives so far had been more or less along these lines. (14: 231)

At the time of this new offensive, the balance of forces was approximately as follows:

Balance of forces prior to Theseus

	German/Italian	**British**
Tanks	German tanks 20 PzKpfw IIs 242 PzKpfw IIIs* 40 PzKpfw IVs**	167 Grants 149 M3 Stuarts/Honeys 257 Crusaders 166 Valentines 110 Matilda IIs
Subtotal	*302 tanks*	*849 tanks*
	Italian tanks 228 M-13/40's and M-14/41's	
Tanks in reserve	40 PzKpfw II's 38 PzKpfw III's 1 PzKpfw IV	75 Grants 70 M3 Stuarts/Honeys
Total tanks	609	994
Planes	497	190
Planes in reserve	1,000	749
Total planes	1.497	939

* including nineteen PzKpfw III Js with 50mm anti-tank guns
** including nine PzKpfw IV F2 'Specials' with 75mm anti-tank guns (11: 145)

The Italians' M-13/40s and M-14/41s had known limitations in terms of armour, artillery and speed, but they could also deploy good mechanized artillery in the form of the 75/18 Semovente. The above figures are of course relative and say little about the quality of the equipment and the way in which it was deployed. The totals show that the Germans enjoyed clear superiority in the air and the British had more tanks on paper. Rommel could also deploy forty-eight 88mm Flak guns and a number of captured Soviet 76.2mm guns converted to use German ammunition.

German units line up to drive south at the beginning of *Theseus*. 88mm Flak guns, a PzKpfw III and several PzKpfw IVs can be seen. (*Photo S. Klein*)

27 May

At 9.30 pm, 10,000 vehicles from the various units, with Rommel in a leading one, started their journey south. To his left, the Italian XX Corps led by General Baldassare advanced with 228 tanks; on the right was the DAK with the 21st and 15th Panzer Division. At 3.00 am they reached Bir Hacheim, 60km south of Tobruk, without being spotted by the British. The troops were in formation: tanks at the front, with engineer units, artillery and communications units behind them, infantry and anti-tank units on the flanks, and the thousands of supply trucks in the centre. After taking on supplies, the entire force advanced north at 4.30 am and was eventually seen by the British.

Early on the morning of the 27th, a British commander saw through his binoculars an unusual cloud of dust coming towards him from the south near Bir Hacheim. Peering through the glasses he saw the dust cloud growing wider and deeper, and small dots could be seen at the bottom of it. 'Looks like a brigade of Jerry tanks coming', he reported over the field telephone to headquarters, then looked again and hastily added, 'It's more than a brigade. It's the whole bloody *Afrika Korps*!' (29: 133)

However, the Germans were in for an unpleasant surprise. After a rapid advance in the first hours, they encountered unexpected British resistance in the form of the new Grant tanks of the 4th Armoured Brigade positioned in the south. The British had not fully adhered to Rommel's scenario and had not been seduced by the diversionary frontal manoeuvre. Based on the information available to them, they had carefully oriented themselves to the terrain that the German units would have to cross during a southern outflanking movement. They had prepared positions there, reconnoitered the area and adjusted their targeting equipment with unusual accuracy. And with a screen of zigzagging M3 Stuart tanks in front of them, on the afternoon of the 27th the 4th Armoured Brigade carried out a frontal attack on the advancing Germans with sixty tanks, followed by an unexpected flank attack across a broad front. These attacks threw the DAK units off balance, and almost immediately there was a tremendous chaos of tanks, artillery, infantry, staff units and supply trucks driving through each other. The entire force was in danger of being scattered, but the tide was turned in time when two batteries of 88mm Flak guns were halted by Rommel and other officers in the fleeing columns and deployed against the advancing Grants.

Colonel Wolz, the commander of one of the Flak regiments, was talking to Nehring when all hell broke loose:

> In the middle of the chaos I discovered a pair of Flak 88s. We raced there and were surprised to find Rommel completely surrounded by panicked troops. He angrily accused me, saying that my Flak was to blame for all this, because we had not returned fire. I managed to stop three Flak 88s and bring the Flak 88s of the *Kampfstaffel* into position. The armada of enemy tanks was closing in fast and was only 500 metres away from us – twenty, thirty tanks – driving all kinds of trucks from the supply units in front of them, all extremely vulnerable to tank guns. In the middle of this tangle of vehicles were Rommel, the headquarters of the Afrika Korps, communications units; in short, the entire nervous system of a fighting division at the front. (17: 157)

Thanks to other batteries that came to the rescue, an anti-tank screen 3,000m long was eventually created by a total of sixteen 88 mm Flak guns. By evening, the attack of the British tanks was finally thrown back. (19: 136)

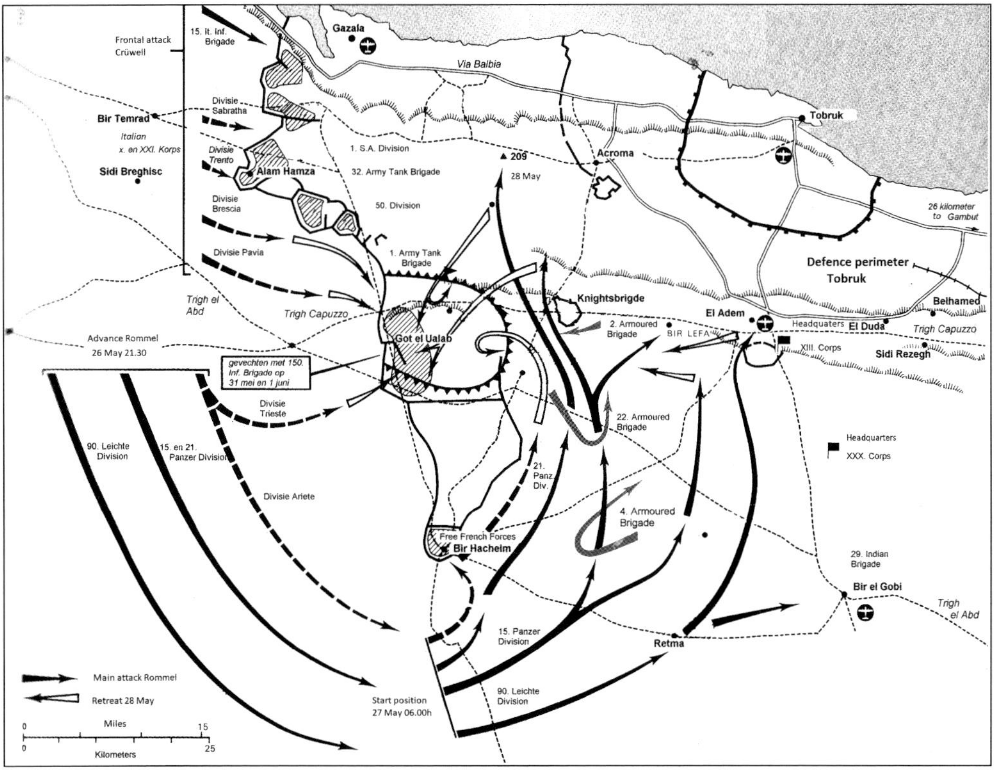

Operation *Theseus*: first phase.

Rommel also turned up elsewhere that day. Von Värst, the commander of the tank regiment of the 15th Panzer Division, had himself been involved with one of his Abteilungen in a fierce battle with British tanks which had led to heavy losses on both sides. The British eventually withdrew.

> The company commander of the leading tank called to von Värst through the megaphone, 'Which way should we go now?' Before von Värst could respond, his adjutant shouted back, 'That way! There's Rommel! Follow him!' And there indeed was Rommel, standing upright in his car, driving through the smoking, wreck-strewn battlefield, at the head of his armoured troops. (17: 157)

This first day cost Rommel a third of his tanks, and he had only been able to advance as far as Bir Lefa. The remaining tanks lacked fuel and ammunition and had lost contact with their supply units. In addition, Rommel's headquarters had been scattered by the advancing British. What worried Rommel was the fact that the Italians had carried out their frontal attack on the Gazala Line with such little enthusiasm that the British had been able to move their reserve units east to counter the Germans. In addition, during the southward flanking movement, contact with the Ariete and Trieste divisions was lost (despite the fact that German liaison units had been added to these divisions), indicating that the Italians were trying to hold back from the fighting.

28 May

Because Rommel had lost control of the fighting he ordered all tanks to withdraw to the west. The remaining infantry were ordered to dig in. The result was that the troops were spread over a large area and coordinated actions were thus no longer possible. Due to the loss of contact with the headquarters of the Panzerarmee, the Luftwaffe under General von Waldau was unable to provide ground support to the troops. Local battles raged here and there, and dark clouds from burning tanks and trucks hung over the battlefield. Because the German troops did not know where they stood, the wildest rumours began to circulate.

Towards the evening of the 28th, Rommel tried to gain a picture of the state of affairs from a hill. The route around Bir Hacheim, where the Free French Forces under General Koenig refused to surrender, proved too dangerous, and the supply units were coming constantly under fire from roving British groups. Marcks and his Kampfgruppe had had to withdraw from the region near El Duda and had fallen back on German positions at Knightsbridge. The same applied to the left Kampfgruppe; its supply columns had been destroyed, and it had also had to withdraw. In other words, a large part of the *Panzerarmee Afrika* was in danger of being trapped in the centre of the Gazala Line and running out of supplies. Taking stock of the situation, Rommel decided to withdraw his troops further west to try to achieve supply from the south, where large columns stood ready.

29 May

On the 29th, a supply convoy with a total of 1,500 trucks (!) managed to reach both divisions and provide them with the necessary fuel and ammunition. This took place in the early morning hours under the personal leadership of Rommel; it was an adventurous journey, during which the convoy was attacked constantly by the British. Miraculously, however, it managed to arrive without suffering many losses. Now re-supplied, the DAK was once again able to go on the attack. Rommel, together with Gause, Westphal and Bayerlein, set up a new headquarters for the Panzerarmee. A plan was drawn up for the 30th, by which Rommel would try to create a corridor to the west through the minefield in the British Gazala Line to bring in new supplies. British tanks from the east would be stopped by a screen of anti-tank guns.

Apparently, not everyone knew how to operate the new Soviet 76.2mm guns. South of Bir Hacheim, Günther Halm and his gun crew were stranded in a truck with one of the new artillery pieces behind it. The truck's fuel pump turned out to be defective, and while they were trying to solve the problem, a British column of 150 trucks, guarded by armoured cars, was seen in the distance:

> Instead of taking cover, they threw themselves at the gun and somehow managed to open the chamber and shove a shell down the barrel. But the brute would not fire. Finally they found the safety catch. The gun went off with a thunderous bang, but after the third shot the recoil had pushed it under the truck. The recoil was so great that they had to re-embed it in the hard, stony desert ground after each shot.

Meanwhile, the armoured cars began to show an unhealthy interest in the stranded group, but when Halm and his party aimed the cannon at them, they withdrew, although 'They needn't have worried; the gun's recoil mechanism had become so full of sand that the barrel had become stuck in the recoil position.' (14: 241)

During the day, Von Waldau decided to wait no longer for further instructions, but to deploy his planes. However, due to a lack of coordination, German units often fell victim to 'friendly fire'. This was also the day that Crüwell fell into British hands. He had wanted to discuss with Rommel the current situation of his troops on the other side of the Gazala Line, but due to a misunderstanding, the agreed flares were not fired; consequently, his Fieseler Storch flew over British territory, where it was shot at and had to make an emergency landing in a British box. After being given a meal by the British commander, Crüwell was taken to Cairo and lodged in the famous Shepheard's Hotel. Observing the hotel's luxurious accommodation, he remarked, 'It will be a great headquarters for Rommel' – words that were heard around the world, much to Hitler's delight.

30 May

The 30th started badly for Rommel. First, his headquarter was bombed, then it came under artillery fire. To make matters worse, the planned breakthrough route to the west turned out to be blocked by one of the boxes, Got el Ualab: due to navigational errors, the engineers had created a corridor that ended on the eastern side of this box. Another player also entered the scene, namely Kesselring, the Commander-in-Chief of the Mediterranean. The previous day, he had taken command of the units west of the Gazala Line from Crüwell, now a prisoner of war, and was surprised at the way in which Rommel had lost control of the fighting. He wanted to speak to Rommel personally and flew south himself (!) in his own Fieseler Storch, meeting Rommel at the headquarters of the Italian XX Corps. Kesselring, a field marshal and six years older, tactfully placed himself under Rommel's command in order to avoid conflict. He then emphasized the importance of regaining control and coordination of the units, and together they discussed Rommel's plan. Kesselring agreed with the plan drawn up by Rommel: the British would be confronted with the screen of anti-tank guns, with the tank divisions behind them which could then launch a counter-attack.

On this day, contact was also restored between the Panzerarmee and von Waldau, so the Luftwaffe's more than 300 aircraft were able to provide effective support to the German units.

During the night the DAK began to move westward. In the early morning, Generals Nehring and Bayerlein looked out from one of the leading armoured cars at the busy British activities in Got el Ualab. The British, as yet unaware of what was to come, were engaged in a fierce artillery duel with Italian units on the west side of the Gazala Line. While German tanks rolled forward, fierce fighting broke out with the 2,000 men of the 150th Infantry Brigade who occupied the box and could count on the support of eighty Matildas.

31 May

The German attempts to break through the box to the west continued on this day. The Luftwaffe were now providing concentrated support, and Rommel was at the front with the infantry units. However, the British continued to resist successfully and did not surrender until 1 June, whereupon Rommel now had a corridor to the west with a width of 7.5km. The British artillery continuously shelled the German positions and units in the corridor, but it was clear to Rommel that supply through it would give him the opportunity to continue his offensive eastwards; the British had lost the chance to deliver a decisive blow. Ritchie was convinced that Rommel wanted to withdraw westward and did not consider the possibility that he would continue the offensive to the east with renewed vigour. He and Auchinleck assumed they had won a victory, and Auchinleck complimented the Eighth Army from Cairo: 'Well done, Eighth Army. Keep it up!' The British did not yet know what awaited them. On the German side, the number of wounded senior officers had mounted: Westphal was injured by mortar fire early in the day, and Gause was suffering from concussion.

Westphal had gone out with Rommel in a *Panzerspähwagen* to check coordination with the Luftwaffe at the Got el Ualab box, since Luftwaffe aircraft had recently accidentally bombed a battery of 88mm Flak guns. The pair soon came under artillery and mortar fire, and Rommel ducked down under the vehicle's armour, but Westphal stubbornly remained where he stood, because he had been having a heated argument with Rommel moments before.

> Shortly afterwards he felt something hit his leg and he was thrown out of the car. The large eight-wheeled armoured vehicle immediately moved to take cover. Westphal was fortunate to have two officers who had followed the armoured car in a *Kübelwagen*, saw him, pulled him out of the line of fire and transported him to headquarters. In the meantime, Rommel had told everyone there that Westphal had probably been killed.

Westphal refused to be transported by Fieseler Storch and was delivered to the hospital in Derna as dead, after a terrible journey over a desert track. Because everyone assumed he had expired, he was taken to the morgue, where he recovered just in time to discharge himself. (14: 252) By evening, the British at Got el Ualab had ceased to resist, and Rommel had his corridor between west and east.

1–11 June

After the surrender of the units at Got el Ualab, Rommel could now fully focus on Bir Hacheim, the fortification in the far south-east of the Gazala Line. Bir Hacheim was defended by 4,000 Free French with anti-tank guns, 25-pounder howitzers and Bren guns, led by Colonel Koenig. The defence line consisted of a complex system of bunkers, trenches and foxholes, and the defenders had substantial supplies of water, food and ammunition. Reluctant to use tanks, because the area was littered with mines, Rommel decided that two infantry divisions supported by the Luftwaffe should be sufficient to take the fortification. However, this turned out to have been optimistic: the French troops heroically resisted all attacks in the following days. And now Rommel, the expert in the field of infantry attack, found himself unable to deal with an enemy who had entrenched himself in a fortified position – as we saw earlier, at Tobruk. Von Waldau, meanwhile, was furious: he accused Rommel of poor coordination between the Luftwaffe and the units on the ground, resulting in the loss of valuable time and materiel. Heavy losses had been incurred, especially among the Ju 87 Stukas. Kesselring also expressed his concern and more or less issued an ultimatum: Bir Hacheim had to be captured on 10 June after new air raids. The position finally fell a day later, on 11 June, after which General Koenig fought his way south with 2,000 men and escaped.

A battery of 105mm light howitzers (*Leichte Feld Haubitze* – LeFH) shells Bir Hacheim.

Krieg ohne Hass

We have already seen that the fighting in North Africa was characterized by a high degree of honourable behaviour on both sides. It is not surprising that the book which Rommel wrote about this period was entitled *Krieg ohne Hass* (War without Hate). During one of the battles, a unit of the 8th MG Battalion took a large number of seriously wounded British prisoners. They did not have the medical facilities to care for them properly, so after consultation they sent a message under a white flag to the British lines, where there were good facilities in the rear area. The wounded were duly taken there, and their transport returned loaded with food and drink as a thank-you!

However, British documents captured in Bir Hacheim threatened to disrupt this idyll: they stated that captured Axis soldiers were not to be allowed water, food, sleep or other rest. Rommel and his staff were dismayed to read this, as the conflict had until then been fought with great mutual respect. On 5 June, Rommel's staff sent this material to Berlin, and Hitler decided immediately that British prisoners of war would also receive no water, food, sleep or rest until the British High Command revoked their instructions. The British immediately agreed to this. (17: 165)

The British had not been idle during the battle for Bir Hacheim and on 5 and 6 June they tried to close the gap in the Gazala Line with two poorly coordinated tank attacks. On 5 June, the 22nd Armoured Brigade and a regiment of Matilda tanks were deployed, along with infantry and artillery. Coordination between the various units was very poor, however, and the tanks got stuck within range of 88mm Flak guns and anti-tank guns. Without the support of their infantry and artillery, sixty British tanks were knocked out and left on the battlefield. On 6 June, two regiments of Matildas supported by a squadron of Valentines, a total of eighty-two tanks, attacked German positions under cover of a smokescreen. While they were engaged they were attacked in the flank by a previously unseen battery of 88mm Flak guns. Both regiments went down fighting, and a total of only twelve tanks returned from the battlefield. This battle also marked the definitive end of the operational life of the Matilda, production of which was halted the same year.

> Amid the touching mixture of bravery and ineptitude which still characterized British actions, the two regiments went under. Colonel Foot's* [the commander's] tank was knocked out, and as he was transferring to another tank he was wounded in the neck. He lost his tank, too, and wandered around the battlefield on foot – one solitary defenceless man among the metal monsters and flying steel. He directed his rapidly diminishing force with hand signals, travelled standing on top of tanks, and then had to retreat, nevertheless, with the twelve tanks remaining to him of the eighty-two which had gone into battle. (14: 260)

The British lost 130 tanks during these two days. The Germans also managed to neutralize more and more boxes and slowly but surely started to roll up the Gazala Line.

11–16 June

After the fall of Bir Hacheim, Rommel was able to continue his advance to the east. He still had 125 operational tanks at his disposal, in addition to approximately sixty Italian ones and twenty-five PzKpfw IIs. Among the tanks were PzKpfw III Js and IV F2s. The British had a varied assortment of tanks left, approximately 210 in total.

For Ritchie the situation was confusing: half a dozen infantry units were requesting tank support, while Ritchie wanted to prevent his tank force from being spread over too large an area. For this reason he concentrated the 4th and 22nd Armoured Brigades at the 'Knightbridge' box. On 12 and 13 June, a third major tank battle was fought in this region, costing the British another 140 of their tanks. The DAK tank units advanced on the 12th and accidentally positioned themselves between the two brigades during the night. The next morning, the German units first encountered the 4th Armoured Brigade, which requested help from the 22nd Armoured Brigade, advancing further south, through an open channel. When the latter came to the aid of the 4th they ran into a screen of anti-tank guns erected by the Germans. A real slaughter of British tanks ensued, and since the battlefield was left in Rommel's hands the British were unable to recover their damaged tanks, which could be considered lost.**

Günther Halm and his crew had gained a lot of experience with the new Soviet gun in recent weeks:

> As the great silhouettes of the tanks appeared in the heat-quivering air, Rommel emerged from behind the line in his half-track and drove some distance towards them, his binoculars pressed to his eyes. An HE shell, probably from a Grant, exploded right in front of his vehicle. He pulled over a little more and stopped, then continued to peer through the binoculars. Only when the tanks came uncomfortably

* On 12 and 13 June, Colonel Foot would give orders to his tanks on foot. For his bravery during this period he was awarded the Victoria Cross.

** Ritchie eventually had fifty Grants, Stuarts and Cruisers and twenty Infantry tanks at his disposal.

> close did Rommel tear back and stop at the guns, saying, 'Be careful, men. Don't let them pass.' Rommel parked his vehicle fifty metres behind them in a fold of the hill. Halm* and his crew managed to eliminate two Grants, and the British turned around. Rommel drove past them and shouted, 'Good work, boys!' And he was off, chasing the tanks. (14: 247)

This tank battle broke the last British resistance and they were ordered to withdraw from the Gazala Line to the Acroma–El Adem Line. While the Germans were in control on the ground, air superiority was moving to the British. In accordance with previous agreements, the Luftwaffe had shifted its attention to Malta in preparation for the invasion of the island. Meanwhile, RAF aircraft bombed advancing German units and supply columns with great success.

> During the advance north [towards Tobruk] battery commander Dammann walked along his column like an alert sheepdog to keep his vehicles at a sufficient distance from each other ...A formation of 'Stubborn Eighteens' (US-made Boston bombers operating in a formation of eighteen), which owed their nickname to the complete lack of respect for anti-aircraft guns, attacked them, and everyone ran from the vehicles into the desert. Just when it was about to release its bombs, the formation soared upward, and Dammann saw to his horror that in the direction in which they were flying, another battery of 88mm Flak guns was driving close together in a column, and that its 'Luki-Luki' men (plane spotters) had clearly not noticed the Bostons. A large number of bombs hit the column just as it started moving again, and it disappeared in a great cloud of dust, from which wreckage, men and entire *Kübelwagens* flew into the air. As a combat unit, the battery was written off. (14: 269)

Despite the presence of German units in the area, Air Marshal Coningham refused to give up the airfields in the Gambut region. Pilots and ground crews worked around the clock, and airfields were only evacuated when clouds of dust heralded the arrival of German tanks. Pilots and crews then flew their planes to other airfields that had been prepared further east, while ground crews jumped into their trucks and took off, often just before the airfields were overrun, then regrouped further behind the front on the way to their new airfields. In this way the British could continue to exploit their air superiority.

Meanwhile, a fierce debate raged within the British command structure about whether or not to withdraw and leave Tobruk to its fate. Churchill, who participated in the discussions from a distance, was of the opinion that retreat was out of the question, but Gott and Ritchie disagreed, because their units were in danger of being surrounded. Auchinleck hesitated between the two options. Ultimately, Auchinleck formulated the following principles for Ritchie:

- The Germans should not be allowed to cross the line Acroma–El Adem–Bir el Gabi
- The Eighth Army should not allow itself to be confined in Tobruk
- Life must be made as difficult as possible for the enemy

* Halm received the Ritter Kreuz for these and other actions.

Ju 87 Stuka bombers provided particularly effective support to ground forces in the early years of the war. However, their relatively low speed made them vulnerable, as was also demonstrated at Bir Hacheim and Tobruk. (*Photo LKK*)

In addition, Auchinleck began massing reserve units at Sollum–Fort Maddalena for a future counter-offensive. However, at the time that Auchinleck formulated these principles, units of the 50th Division from the boxes in the south and units of the 1st South African Division from the boxes in the north of the Gazala Line were rapidly moving to positions east of Tobruk, beyond the line that Auchinleck had in mind. Ritchie, in turn, simply refused to follow Auchinleck's orders, saying that in his view they had been overtaken by events. El Adem finally fell on 16 June, allowing the net to be tightened around Tobruk.

17–19 June

At 3.00 pm on 17 June, the tanks of the DAK and the Ariete Division headed east, then turned north to completely encircle Tobruk. To keep up the momentum, Rommel rode ahead of the tanks with his own *Gefechtsstaffel*, passing surprised British units to his left and right on the way to Tobruk. The advance was halted by a minefield in the early evening, and it was only the next morning that the encirclement of Tobruk was complete. Rommel set up his HQ in Hatian, until recently the headquarters of the British. There were still occasional clashes between German and British tank units, but without the intensity of recent weeks. The British lost another twenty-five tanks during these days to mechanical defects, in addition to seven knocked out by the Germans. Tobruk itself had changed in the past six months. The minefields around the city had been partly reduced to strengthen the Gazala Line, the anti-tank ditches were covered with desert sand and the Australian troops had been replaced by others. The city itself was full of thousands of troops from retreating units, tired, hungry, thirsty and often without equipment or artillery. The roads were clogged with cars, the communications system was under great pressure and units had often fallen apart. The morale of the Tobruk garrison suffered a serious blow when the arrival of rows of trucks carrying demoralized soldiers indicated that the Germans were closing in. Valuable time was lost regrouping the units before the building of fortifications could begin.

In the following days, Rommel, together with von Waldau, planned the attack on the surrounded city. The Luftwaffe would bomb the main fortifications in the defence line in the early hours of 20 June. Maps and radio channels were coordinated, and a test bombardment was carried out on the 19th. That same day, Kesselring visited Rommel and approved his plans. Meanwhile, more and more German and Italian units arrived at Tobruk. Although the infantry took up positions near the city, Rommel had not yet given up the idea of an advance into Egypt: in the afternoon of the 19th, German and Italian tank units, with Rommel and his *Gefechtsstaffel* again in the lead, raced towards Bardia. They met no resistance, and at the end of the afternoon some of the tank units were ordered to return to the Tobruk area. Units of the 90th Division continued the advance east towards Bardia and were surprised to discover their old artillery positions, including ammunition, still intact south and east of Tobruk.

20 June and beyond

In accordance with the plan, the German and Italian artillery opened fire at 5.20 am, followed half an hour later by Luftwaffe bombing. The infantry and engineers built a bridge over the anti-tank ditch under heavy fire and at 8.00 am the first tanks rolled towards Tobruk. The British defence was poorly coordinated, and at 7.00 pm German tank units reached the port of Tobruk. The city had finally fallen, and at 8.00 am on the 21st Major General Klopper of the South African garrison surrendered. Now Rommel could turn all his attention to Egypt. The fall of Tobruk and Rommel's victories dominated the news in Germany in the following days. The Germans had lost 3,500 men up to that point, compared to 50,000 British taken prisoner and killed in action, and the loss of a large part of their tanks. On 22 June, the publicity surrounding Rommel culminated in a special radio address by Hitler, in which he promoted Rommel to field marshal, the ultimate honour for a soldier. Rommel had already taken his next step: at 8.30 pm he ordered his tank divisions to advance to the barbed-wire fence in the south which marked the border with Egypt. He proposed to Mussolini that the previous agreement on a relatively limited offensive be revised, and asked that all troops be brought under his command and allowed to advance to the Nile Delta. Conquering the Delta would also solve the supply problem, given the large reserves the British had built up there. The capture of Tobruk, and the enormous quantity of supplies the British had held there in view of a possible siege, had already eased the Germans' logistic problems.

Before war reporter Moorehead had to leave Tobruk he visited the supply dumps:

Finally – Rommel in his Mercedes Benz 240 staff car looks out over the harbour of Tobruk. (*Photo IHC*)

> In the narrow sea plain between the coast and the cliffs, thousands of sand coloured vehicles were dispersed about. We were in the midst of an immense car park. Crudely painted notices were posted along the road at every side-track. These led to ammunition and food dumps, petrol and water points, engineers' and tank stores, hospitals, unit headquarters, ack ack batteries, rest camps. We collected sacks of tea and sugar, big tins of cheese, jam and fish. We even got fresh onions and dates. There were enough of these stores to have maintained twenty to thirty thousand men for three months. (29: 156)

The Germans happily took possession of these items,* which allowed them to replenish their fuel and ammunition and continue the pursuit. Mussolini was delighted by Rommel's plan, envisaging a triumphal personal entry into Alexandria. It also appealed to Hitler, since Rommel's advance to the Delta would eliminate the need to conquer Malta. Considering the great German losses incurred in the conquest of Crete, this seemed to Hitler a welcome solution to a thorny problem, and plans for the invasion of Malta were put on hold for the time being, never to be revived. In fact, this decision sealed the fate of the Panzerarmee in the long run, for in the coming months British strength on Malta would recover and put the supply route of the Axis troops under increasing pressure, despite the capture of Tobruk and its port facilities.

The balance of power in the Mediterranean would once again swing towards the British in the coming months. The threat of Rommel's advance deep into Egypt had

* The fall of Tobruk yielded the Germans 33,000 prisoners of war, 2,000 vehicles, 5,000 tons of food and 1,400 tons of fuel.

The pressure on Malta would decrease in the coming period. Here British anti-aircraft guns are seen at the harbour. Their ammunition is stored between the protective sandbags.

caused Roosevelt great concern and, after insistence from Churchill, he agreed to supply at short notice 300 tanks of the new Sherman type and 100 105mm guns, weapons that would be the mainstay of the American Army in the coming years. In Roosevelt's view the coming months would be of decisive importance. In the coming weeks, however, all attention would turn to Rommel's advance. With the permission of Hitler and Mussolini, German and Italian tanks rolled eastward.

Because the Germans used some of the same vehicles as the British, and there was little difference in clothing, they could easily infiltrate retreating British units; it was thus a diverse body of troops that started to travel east. However, despite Rommel's constant encouragement, a large number of German units had reached the limit of their physical capabilities.

Because of the acute threat posed by Rommel to the British position in the Middle East, units were transferred from all over the world; for example, X Corps under Holmes, consisting of the New Zealand Division from Syria, the 5th Indian Division and the 50th Division, moved to the Nile Delta. The headquarters of Norrie's XXX Corps had already been sent back to build up the defence lines at El Alamein and to receive and regroup the retreating troops. In the meantime, Gott's tank formations were ordered to make the area between El Alamein and the Libyan-Egyptian border unsafe for the enemy. Gott had the 7th Armoured Division with approximately 100 operational tanks at his disposal, against Rommel's forty-four German and fourteen Italian tanks. Just as Gott's units got into position, however, Ritchie ordered them to withdraw further east and regroup at Mersa Matruh, the next line of defence.

During the 23rd the main German fighting force advanced south before gradually veering east. In the following days, Gott tried to keep his retreating units as intact as possible and prevent them from being tempted into a heroic final battle. Rommel, in turn, wanted at all times to deny the British the chance to dig in defensively. Finally, units of the exhausted 90th Leichte Division reached the line El Alamein–Ruweisat Ridge–Dier el Munasib near El Alamein in the early evening of 2 July.

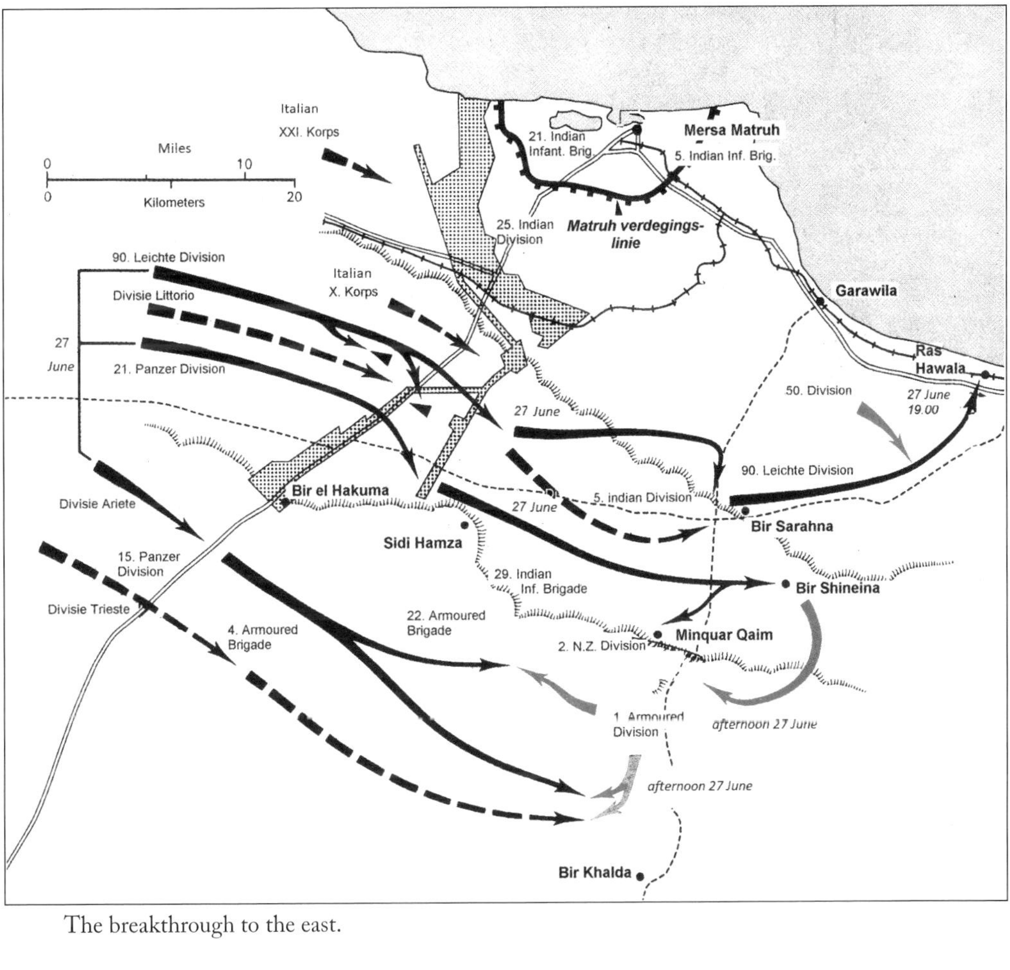

The breakthrough to the east.

A 150mm howitzer (*schwere Feld Haubitze* – sFH) races east. (*Photo BTM/von Esebeck*)

The advance came to a standstill under a rain of shells, and Rommel with his *Gefechtsstaffel* was unable to break the British resistance. The troops dug in under constant air attacks to wait for better times. The next morning, the attack was resumed, only to stall again after about 2,000 metres. A third attack, now supported by the twenty-seven still operational tanks of both Panzer Divisions, was also unsuccessful and cost eleven tanks.

In the meantime, Rommel's advance towards Cairo had caused great panic among the British in the city. The evacuation of women, children and non-essential personnel began; secret diplomatic and military documents were burned; and plans were activated to blow up strategic sites such as radio stations, the telegraph and telephone system and oil installations. British troops took over police duties to quell any civil unrest. The first ships of the British fleet in the port of Alexandria had already weighed anchor to flee to safety via the Suez Canal. Auchinleck prepared a phased retreat from Egypt as well as the setting up of a new headquarters in Palestine. His goal was to keep his Eighth Army together as a unit, even if it came at the cost of abandoning Egypt. He himself estimated Rommel's combat power at 120 German and 110 Italian tanks; however, Ultra, as always well informed, gave the correct numbers as thirty-seven tanks for the 21st and seventeen for the 15th Panzer Division. On the 25th Auchinleck took over Ritchie's command and, to the surprise of the various commanders, ordered that from now on units were to be grouped into 'battle groups' and wage a mobile and fluid war: a structure and style that was completely new for all involved. It was concluded that the situation was hopeless and that these new orders heralded a retreat further east. (3: 127)

However, in the following days, Rommel tried in vain to break the British defensive lines, suffering significant losses. The past few weeks had placed the utmost demands on his troops, and he only had a very limited number of German and Italian tanks at his disposal. His men were exhausted after the physical and mental exertions of the past month, the constant fighting, the heat and other hardships. When it finally dawned on Rommel that there was no point in further attacks, he regrouped his troops: the infantry divisions were placed at the front and the tank units reorganized behind these lines.

However, his exhausted troops were granted no rest. On 4 July, the newly arrived New Zealanders managed to disperse the Ariete Division and capture many of their guns. On the night of 10/11 July, the newly arrived 9th Australian Division, together with the 1st South African Division, attacked positions of the Italian XXI Corps north of El Alamein and completely overran the Sabratha Division. If they had managed to break through the lines, the Germans' supply route would have been severed. Disaster was avoided by the rapid deployment of all kinds of German support troops, ranging from Flak, communications and kitchen units to two Kampfgruppen personally led by Rommel. The following day, the Trento Division suffered a similar attack and was only saved by units of the 164th Leichte Division, which had just flown in from Crete. Rommel was very disturbed by these attacks; it seemed as if the British were deliberately attacking only Italian units, which in his opinion surrendered too easily.

Preventing the collapse of the front as a result of these relatively limited British attacks was very demanding on the Germans, unbalanced the Panzerarmee and cost a great deal of fuel and ammunition. The Panzerarmee paid a high price when the special eavesdropping unit, the 161st Nachrichten Abteilung under Captain Seebohm, had to be deployed to assist Italian units. A large number of the men from this specialized unit were killed or taken prisoner, and their loss deprived Rommel of his eyes and ears in the coming period.

Tensions in the coalition

Under pressure from the success of the Axis forces, political considerations began to play an increasingly important role. For this reason, the achievements of the Italian troops were widely reported in the German press, to the disgust of their German colleagues. Furthermore, there was bickering between Rome and Berlin about the appointment of an Italian governor for Egypt and his relationship to Rommel and to a future occupying army. To top it all, Mussolini, with an entourage including a white horse, was waiting in Libya for his celebratory entry into Cairo. And rumours that only German troops were entitled to the 'treasures of Egypt' had caused unrest among the Italians. (17: 179)

On 13 July, Rommel made another attempt to isolate the fortifications at El Alamein through an outflanking movement with his Panzer Divisions and infantry, but the attack stalled, and the tanks abandoned the infantry on the battlefield at nightfall, although they successfully retreated under cover of darkness. The British launched limited attacks along the Ruweisat Ridge on 14 and 15 July, again mainly aimed at Italian divisions such as Pavia and Brescia. Although they yielded limited territorial gains, they did demonstrate that Italian formations would disintegrate under pressure and their men surrender en masse.

On 21 July, the British launched their last offensive for the time being. Rommel now had forty-two German and fifty Italian tanks at his disposal, a fighting force that Auchinleck wanted to eliminate. A New Zealand infantry brigade infiltrated the El Mreir depression on the night of the 21st with the aim of attacking the German positions in combination with tanks the next morning. What the British did not know, however, was that Nehring and his troops were on the edge of the depression and ready to strike. At 4.00 am the Germans opened fire and their tanks rolled down, taking the New Zealanders completely by surprise. The tanks that were to support the infantry had only arrived from Britain two weeks earlier and were nowhere to be seen. However, sometime later they appeared to have broken through a minefield at another location and threatened to turn and attack Rommel's troops from the rear. The hastily retreating German infantry and artillery units were stopped by Colonel Bruer, who commanded the 21st Panzer Division in place of the wounded von Bismarck, and deployed against the advancing British tanks. Due to heroic intervention by the gun crews of two 76.2mm guns, the British tanks were halted before being attacked in the flank by the tanks of the 21st Panzer Division. In the ensuing fighting the British lost 146 tanks and 1,200 men. The severity of the situation was evident from the fact that the furthest British tanks had been stopped just 2,000m from the headquarters of the 21st Panzer Division.

Throughout this period the strength of the RAF, now supported for the first time by American units, grew. Not only were the German supply lines constantly bombarded, the units at the front also came increasingly under fire. The combat strength of the Luftwaffe, on the other hand, continued to decline in accordance with previous agreements, partly due to the transfer of Gruppen needed at the Eastern Front for the planned summer offensive in the Soviet Union. Slowly but surely the front calmed down in the following days. The events of the past few weeks convinced Rommel that a stalemate had been reached and a new phase in the battle had begun. Auchinleck had, meanwhile, recovered and was preparing plans that were very similar to those of Gazala – a collection of boxes built around artillery, with the surplus infantry being positioned in the Nile Delta, where a mobile tank force would have to deal with any German breakthrough. However, he was not given the opportunity to put his ideas into practice, but was relieved of his position by Churchill in early August.

Theseus' balance sheet in the period from 26 May to 20 July 1942 was as follows:

- On the British side: 60,000 taken prisoner, 2,000 tanks and armoured vehicles destroyed
- For the Axis:* 2,300 killed, 7,500 wounded and 2,700 taken prisoner (Germans); 1,000 killed, 10,000 wounded and 5,000 taken prisoner (Italians). (11: 148)

5.2 Evaluation of the German Army

The strategic dimension

Hitler's and Mussolini's permission for Rommel to advance to the Nile Delta had great strategic significance. Hitler assumed that Rommel would find sufficient supplies there and that the conquest of Egypt would make the position of the British on Malta untenable. The need for the planned invasion of Malta, Operation *Hercules*, would thus be eliminated, to his relief. Given the experience of the landings on Crete by airborne troops, this invasion could have led to great losses in men and materiel. Moreover, Kesselring believed on 10 May that Malta had already been neutralized and he had therefore moved bombers and fighter planes to other fronts. This gave the British on Malta so much breathing space that they were able to disrupt the supply lines of the Axis troops with renewed energy in

[1] Other sources give 845 Germans killed and 3,318 wounded. (17: 179)

the coming months, with fatal consequences for the Panzerarmee. Moreover, Roosevelt decided to deliver substantial supplies of tanks and artillery to restore the balance of power, partly in view of the planned Anglo-American landings in Tunisia later that year.

Both these decisions would ultimately lead to a completely different position for Rommel when the battle for El Alamein broke out later in the year.

Tactical dimensions

Operation *Theseus* is rightly judged one of Rommel's most convincing actions: a frontal attack as a distraction and a particularly daring southward flanking movement to encircle the enemy with two German and two Italian tank divisions. The large number of tanks, vehicles (10,000), anti-tank guns, supply units and staff units combined into one large Kampfgruppe gives an indication of the scale of this operation. Placed one behind the other, these vehicles would have formed a column 200km long. On paper it was a coordinated action, but in practice Rommel lost control and coordination over a crucial period of time, with his troops spread over a large area. Typically, he could be found everywhere except at the headquarters of the Panzerarmee. An impasse of several days followed, which rightly was of great concern to Kesselring, who flew over to discuss the situation with Rommel personally. The injured Gause and Westphal also expressed themselves in no uncertain terms about Rommel's leadership. We can only guess at what they said, since the comments they made against von Waldau were, in his opinion, not suitable to entrust to paper (17: 159). Once again, an atmosphere of crisis characterized this period of fighting. On the other hand, Rommel was always where he was expected to be: for example, at the head of a long column of trucks going to supply his hard-pressed tank divisions. He set an example to all his troops, and his presence always had an immediate effect on morale.

The last phase of Theseus shows us a characteristic picture of Rommel: '*an der Spitze*' (at the head) of a severely depleted and fatally tired fighting force, he raced to the Egyptian border to cross it almost alone, as he had a year earlier. He wanted to push on to the Nile Delta, but once again, after weeks of intense fighting, his troops no longer had the stamina to follow him.

An important question is why Rommel spent so much time cleaning up the various boxes. Without (armoured) transport, the infantry units in these boxes were particularly vulnerable during movement, so they had to remain where they were. These positions were thus not very dangerous to the advancing Germans, since they were only able to influence battles that took place within the range of their guns. (3: 99) Perhaps Rommel wanted to control the entire battlefield before taking advancing further, a lesson learned from *Crusader*.

The Germans also employed a new tactical combination of tanks and anti-tank guns in response to the better armour of the British tanks. The anti-tank guns advanced forward, while the tanks, stationary and dug-in as much as possible, gave them covering them fire. When the anti-tank guns had taken up new positions, the tanks in turn advanced under covering fire, then the process repeated itself. Attacks like this proved to be extremely difficult for the British to stop, especially due to the intensity of the fire. (43: 96)

The *Erfahrungsberichte* provide a clear picture of the vicissitudes of the Germans. Until May 1942 the following findings were noted:

- In pursuits, it was not so much strength that played a role, but speed and surprise. This depended on the person of the commander, with experience showing that relatively small units under young and energetic commanders were the most successful.
- It was considered of great importance to link liaison officers to rapidly advancing units. These officers had to stay in touch with the Luftwaffe via radio, in order not only to call in ground support, but above all to communicate the position of constantly changing battle lines and avoid the risk of friendly fire.
- Outflanking movements were difficult to carry out in the desert without the chance of being discovered, because advancing troops could not hide behind natural obstacles and therefore remained clearly visible at all times through the clouds of dust they generated.
- It was not expected that surprise actions which had proved successful in the past would be equally effective a second time.
- Terrain had to be carefully explored before any action. (45: 43)

The fighting in the subsequent period led to the following lessons:

- Once again, some tactical surprise actions appear to have paid off, especially because their design was constantly changed. However, using truck-mounted aircraft engines to create large clouds of dust appeared to have had no effect.
- It was dangerous to leave the rear areas unattended. If there was insufficient manpower to set up fortifications, it was a good idea to have strong *Aufklärungsbteilungen* guard the area and defend it, especially against Jock Columns.
- British minefields functioned more or less as natural obstacles and regularly forced German commanders to radically revise their tactical plans.

A wounded man is lifted into the Fieseler Storch. (*Photo LKK*)

- Attack columns had to stay close together. Only in emergencies were units allowed to be deployed separately against specific targets.
- Commanders of higher rank had to move their command post as little as possible and indicate a fixed location where they could be found, even in unclear combat situations (a clear reminder to Rommel).
- During air raids on enemy fortifications, the targets to be bombed must be indicated as accurately as possible to prevent friendly fire incidents.
- Supply units could not defend themselves and must be protected in convoys, especially in unclear and confusing combat situations. Otherwise they were easy prey for enemy reconnaissance units and Jock Columns.
- Tanks must be dug in immediately in defensive positions. They must be able to move away from these positions quickly if necessary.

Rommel

The North African campaign was a demonstration of the leadership style, bravado and personal courage that Rommel seemed to have a patent on. These were completely in line with his views on management:

> There is always a moment when the commander should not be with his staff, but at the front with his men. It is incorrect to assume that troop morale is the sole responsibility of the battalion commander. The higher the rank, the better the example. The troops generally do not care about a commander who they know is safe in his headquarters behind the front. They need his physical presence. In times of panic, fatigue, disorganization or when extra efforts are required, the personal example of

Fighting in the desert under Rommel demanded the utmost from man and materiel. Here the exhausted crew of an 88mm Flak gun are sleeping in the shade of the tractor. (*Photo S. Klein*)

> the commander can do wonders, especially when myths have already been created around his person. (36: 117)

These are some striking examples of how Rommel put this vision into practice.

- During Operation *Crusader*, Rommel visited a New Zealand field hospital that had been 'captured' by the Germans and talked to various German and British wounded about their experiences. Many British troops had never seen a general up close, and this encounter contributed greatly to his charisma and image. In another unconfirmed incident, when British prisoners in a PoW camp all started running towards the fence, the guards thought they were trying to break out. However, it turned out that what they wanted was to catch a glimpse of Rommel, who happened to be passing by.
- On the way back west after Operation *Crusader*, Rommel, Crüwell and Bayerlein met in the bus which served as headquarters for the DAK. British fighter planes suddenly appeared and bombed targets in the area. Crüwell and Bayerlein took cover in and under a tank parked nearby. Rommel, however, jumped on his half-track 'Greif' and opened fired at the planes with the machine gun. When Crüwell crawled out from under the tank, covered in dust, he looked up to see Rommel's smiling face. Crüwell and Bayerlein later shook their heads; they had no answer to such behaviour by their commander. (30: 212)
- During *Theseus*, while Rommel patrolled up and down the columns keeping a close eye on things, a PzKpfw IV F2 parked on the side of the road with a damaged track caught his attention. The crew, who were carrying out an emergency repair, informed him that an officer of the Panzer Werkstatt Kompagnie had told them the tank had to be repaired in a workshop behind the front. Rommel replied that in his opinion this officer was a jerk and that they should get the tank ready to carry on the fight. Not long after, the story went round that Rommel had spotted a sergeant major who was on his way to the rear with a slightly damaged tank. Rommel was said to have kicked him in the behind and directed him back to the front at pistol-point. (14: 249)
- Later, Rommel was to be found on his knees in the dust on the front line near Tobruk, working with his men to clear mines. A little earlier, he and his *Gefechtsstaffel* had just driven various British units retreating to Tobruk off the road, leaving them amazed on the roadside, wondering whether they had really just seen the great man in person.

This all reads like an adventure story (and perhaps Rommel saw it as such), but it illustrates the impact his charismatic personality had on both Germans and British.

5.4 Italian units

In the final phase of Operation *Theseus*, the Italian units appear to have been weakened to such an extent that they were no longer able to defend themselves. Rommel, who until now had always defended the Italians, became increasingly critical of their performance. The structural flaws in the organization of the Italian Army became more obvious during this phase, as did other issues. The officers considered themselves a caste apart, entitled to a personal servant, special clothing and weapons, and more and better food. Kesselring* brought this last point up several times with Cavallero, but without result. A survey at the beginning of the war had shown that both the men and the high command, the latter for logistical reasons, believed that officers and men should be given the same rations. The officer corps was overwhelmingly against this, sometimes arguing that officers simply could not function on the simple rations given to their men. Then there was the threat of closing the separate canteens for officers. For some this raised the spectre of having to fraternize with their men, with a consequent loss of prestige and authority which, in their view, could be fatal, especially for junior officers. In an evaluation of the officer corps after the defeats of the winter of 1941/42, the following shortcomings were noted:

- Inadequate leadership qualifications (lack of authority, hesitation in giving commands, uncertainty about how to address units)
- Insufficient knowledge of the technical side of weapons
- Limited knowledge of small unit tactics
- Rudimentary knowledge of communications equipment and organization
- Insufficient knowledge of map reading and compasses
- Insufficient knowledge of how to construct field reinforcements
- Insufficient fitness for long marches
- Total lack of interest in the administrative organization

Non-commissioned officers displayed the same weaknesses and frequently showed a complete lack of initiative. The men themselves responded only to direct orders, were insufficiently familiar with their weapons, or with the digging and use of foxholes, and showed 'extreme emotional reactions' to suspected or real enemy actions from the flank or rear. In response, greater emphasis was placed on training, particularly in the areas of platoon and company tactics. The training sessions were supposed to be as realistic as possible, but their effect in subsequent periods is difficult to determine.

At El Alamein the average infantry battalion had only one or two professional officers and too few NCOs. The reserve officers were willing, but insufficiently prepared. The result was that units readily disintegrated under the pressure of combat, something which happened regularly in the run-up to El Alamein. Sometimes, Italian combat units even had to be relieved by German support and kitchen staff. Support units in the Italian Army were not trained for combat actions and were unable to build defensive positions. This meant that when the front was broken, the rearguard was at the mercy of the enemy, and the *Intendenza* (administration) was easy prey to rapidly advancing enemy units. (25: 148–52)

Italian infantry divisions usually limited themselves to a static defence line, and carried out any offensive actions frontally. When these were halted, more men were simply deployed in the same place in an attempt force a breakthrough. In other words, Italian attacks were characterized by tactical rigidity, although the units generally performing remarkably well given their limitations.

An exception to this was the Ariete Division (tanks), which eventually developed a number of new tactics, such as carrying out night manoeuvres, locating and attacking the

---

* Kesselring was particularly dismayed when he heard that Italian units had to beg for food from the Germans.

flanks and rearguards of British units, and deceiving the British by pretending to withdraw or bluffing them by throwing up large clouds of dust. This was despite the fact that two-way radios were not available until 1942 (and often fell apart due to the vibration of the tanks), the effective range of the 47mm gun was only 600m and the ammunition supply in tanks was limited; this meant that they were forced to sprint forward at their top speed of 13kph (!) to reduce the range to 400m. The arrival of the FIAT-Ansaldo mobile 75mm assault gun improved the tactical ability and effectiveness of the Ariete Division and the newly arrived Littorio Division to some extent, until the arrival of new medium tanks on the British side reversed the position. (25: 153)

Finally, the ordinary Italian soldier. Logistically, the Italian Army was unable to supply sufficient ammunition, fuel, vehicles, weapons and food to its fighting men. Their rations were far below the level of the Germans and British in both quality and quantity. The field kitchens were supposed to be fuelled by wood, which was scarcely ever available in North Africa. Only those units that were able to manufacture or capture an oil-fired field kitchen could prepare hot food; the rest were forced to eat their meals cold. Other 'secondary employment conditions' on the battlefield were also poor. Field hospitals were ineffective throughout the war, postal service to the home front was haphazard, and the period between leaves was 37 months.* Clothing and footwear were of inferior quality, and there was a constant shortage of all kinds of small items such as buttons, knives, pens, razor blades – things that can make life at the front more tolerable. All in all, conditions were such as to undermine the morale of any unit in the long run. The Italian High Command paid little or no attention to this aspect of military organization, despite the fact that the problems were regularly pointed out by the Germans. The accumulation of 60 tons of neglected military mail in Bologna in July 1940 was dismissed as of no importance – merely evidence of a pathological Italian need for daily news from family and friends, which one would normally not be interested in. (25: 157)

5.5 Evaluation of the British Army

Strategic dimension

As in early 1941, the British Army had to completely revise its strategy. In 1941 it had to deal with the German occupation of the Balkans and Greece, while in 1942 the advance of Japan put Britain's possessions in the Far East in acute danger. This meant that British troops were rapidly transferred there from the North African theatre.

Tactical dimensions

The first phase of the campaign in January and February showed that the British had spread their relatively limited resources over far too large an area. Only two divisions, the 4th Indian and 1st Armoured, could be deployed, but instead of concentrating the two divisions in one place, their various brigades were dispersed across the breadth and depth of the front. This was certainly a consequence of the British view that brigades, and not divisions, let alone two of them, were the largest organizational unit that could be commanded in a coordinated way. The British simply lacked experience in operating larger units.

* The Germans had a deployment period of twelve months or less.

This first phase was also characterized by Auchinleck's major involvement. In the period from 25 January to 1 February he was constantly at Ritchie's side, and not without reason: from distant London, on almost a daily basis, Churchill pointed out to Auchinleck how important the continuation of *Acrobat* was, while giving his commander-in-chief unasked-for advice of all kinds. (3: 59)

In the run-up to Operation *Theseus* in May and June, British organization was characterized by the establishment of the 'boxes' at Gazala. In an attempt to tackle Rommel, the British developed the concept of a linear static front in the form of boxes containing infantry, artillery and (infantry) Matilda and Valentine tanks, combined with a mobile tank reserve. Given their experiences with mobile warfare and their success in the defence of Tobruk, this was a logical concept, although again tanks and infantry were separated. The idea was that the static defence line would stop the Germans, and any breakthrough would be absorbed by the tank units positioned behind it. In addition, the Germans' attention would be split over the various reinforced positions.

However, this meant that the strength of the infantry divisions was divided across the boxes, and the British were well aware of the danger that if their tank units were not successful, the boxes could fall one by one like ripe fruit into the hands of the Germans. The infantry units in the boxes would no longer be able to move because their vehicles had been transferred to the rear. In other words, they would be forced to stay where they were. In practice, this was exactly the 'worst case' scenario which unfolded: Rommel made a southward flanking movement, and the British mobile tank reserves, deployed one by one, were destroyed by the German tanks and anti-tank guns. The boxes could not support each other due to the lack of transport and tanks, so they were taken out in sequence.

The already divided British organizational structure also lost effectiveness because of the way in which the various tank reserves were deployed: their great losses of tanks forced the British to continuously send reinforcements to the front and to regroup units, which caused considerable organizational dislocation and had a negative effect on the morale of the crews, already low after their defeats and lack of sleep. It would probably have been wiser, for example, to send the 1st Armoured Brigade into battle as a whole, instead of deploying it regiment by regiment as reinforcements for the 4th Armoured Brigade. (3: 99–100)

British C3I structure

Auchinleck tried to maintain tight control over the course of events throughout this entire period. However, this did not work out well because – quite apart from the 'fog of war' – communication in the hierarchy was slow in terms of both control and feedback. In addition, command and communication centres of all kinds were regularly overrun. Communication and coordination between the different units became increasingly difficult, making combined operations almost impossible to execute after the fighting began. Infantry divisions, tank divisions and the units in the boxes each fought their own war; almost nowhere were the efforts of all combined. Moreover, Churchill played a prominent role, from a distance, in decision-making. He repeatedly demanded that attacks be carried out and that British units should not retreat, while Auchinleck received messages from the battlefield that emphasized the real need to withdraw. This sometimes led to a paralysis in decision-making at key points in the battle. (14: 231) The result was that the British high command was sharply divided over the strategy to be followed. In line with British tradition, lower in the hierarchy, the orders of Auchinleck or Ritchie were tested against the actual situation on the ground and were often regarded not so much as orders as a basis for further discussion, which obscured their original intention. (11: 143) At the operational level, radio traffic often became impossible shortly after an attack had begun, resulting in a complete loss of coordination between the tanks and other tank units. They switched to hand signals, and in extreme cases – sometimes even in less pressing situations – commanders could be seen walking between their tanks to give instructions to the crews. This applied also to the concentration of the tanks. Ritchie certainly tried to deploy his tank units in a concentrated manner at the right time and at the place, as for instance on 12 and 13 June. But at the level of the Armoured Brigades, the various regiments were deployed one by one, thus diluting their striking power. This had everything to do with the attitude of many squadron and tank commanders,* who, in the best cavalry tradition, preferred individual duels to operating in larger groups. (3: 141)

Rommel later commented critically on Ritchie's tactics:

> Because Ritchie had deployed his tanks in a fragmented manner, he gave us the opportunity to tackle the British units one by one. The splitting of the British tank force was incomprehensible, as there was no strategic or operational advantage to be gained from sacrificing the 7th Armoured Division in this way …The British should have concentrated on committing all their tank units at the same time. They should no more have been tempted to divide their forces in the period before the actual attack than by the diversionary manoeuvre on the Gazala Line. The complete motorization and mechanization of their units allowed rapid deployment anywhere on the battlefield where an attack threatened. Desert warfare has often been compared to naval warfare, and rightly so. It is also not wise to seek a confrontation at sea with half the fleet in port. (36: 97–8)

These tactics resulted in harrowing scenes on the battlefield. Despite two years of combat experience, attacks in the cavalry tradition were still carried out frontally and by small units. It was not unusual for the squadron commander's tank to hoist a black banner (in naval and cavalry tradition the signal to attack). Disabling this tank was the logical first goal of the Germans, after which the commander's coordination of the fighting inevitably fell away. Something similar happened to Major (later Sir John) Hackett,** as commander of a squadron of the 8th Hussars. After his tank was destroyed, he had no choice but to stand on the afterdeck of another tank and give its commander instructions as to which opponents should be targeted. (14: 236–7)

These tactics (and perhaps their inability to learn) also made the British easy victims of the well-known German 'sword and shield' tactic. An example of this came in the attack on 6 June by the 22nd Armoured Brigade and a regiment of Matildas on the Ariete Division and the two Panzer Divisions. The Ariete Division retreated, pursued by the British, who then ran into a line of 88mm Flak and other anti-tank guns. (14: 259–60) On 13 June, the Germans again successfully applied the tactic. When the tanks of the 4th Armoured Brigade were attacked by German units, the tanks of the 22nd Armoured

* The problems probably lay even lower in the organization, namely at the level of the squadron commanders rather than the brigade commanders: during Operation *Theseus*, the brigade commander, with one exception, came from the Royal Tank Regiment, and only one commander was a real 'cavalry' man. (3: 142)

** Sir John Hackett distinguished himself later in the war, including during Operation *Market Garden*, and later became Commander-in-Chief of the British Army and senior NATO commander. After retirement he began a career as Principal of King's College, London and wrote the novel *The Third World War*.

Brigade were lured into the attack and surprised by a screen of anti-tank guns. Squadron after squadron was deployed in an uncoordinated manner and wiped out. Coordination eventually collapsed completely because the British headquarters had to withdraw hastily for fear of being overrun. (29: 151)

War reporter Alan Moorehead was also critical of British organization and tactics. This is what he wrote about one action, probably the 21 July attack:

> With the infantry the tanks went in …and this was another of those heart-breaking mistakes and misunderstandings that kept cropping up in the midst of British attacks …It was a brand new battalion of tanks from England. The crews had trained and trained thoroughly but they were new to the desert. Only three weeks before, they had come ashore in Suez with their Valentines. One wonders if it is a good thing to send troops into action immediately after they arrive in the desert. [In preparation for the attack, the engineers had cleared a path through the minefield.] So in they went at dawn, these fresh-faced boys from England and they were full of confidence and courage for this, their first action. Someone gave them the wrong direction … They missed the track entirely and ran instead on the mines and there the German gunners caught them in a crossfire. Of the eighty odd tanks, only a score came back. Two years of training, months of building, a voyage half around the world – everything went wrong in a minute. Because they were given the wrong direction.

Despite the carnage, British morale was unbroken. A crew member of one of the surviving tanks told Moorehead of his fears and experiences immediately after the battle. After his story, 'he added quite sincerely and simply, "We would like to have another crack at them, Sir."' (21: 29)

This is exactly what Air Chief Marshal Tedder, Commander-in-Chief of the RAF in the Middle East, meant when he said that that in 1941 and 1942 the British Army suffered from an 'excess of bravery and a shortage of brains'. (28: 111)

Rommel had this to say about the British deployment at Got el Ualab, for example: 'This brigade was a living example of the strengths and weaknesses of the British soldier. Exceptional courage and perseverance were combined with unprecedented rigidity in the areas of speed and flexibility.' (36: 109)

There was yet another problem at a higher level in the hierarchy: the large number of personnel changes over the period of eighteen months.

Overview of command structure per offensive

Operation	C-in-C	Eighth Army	Corps Commanders
First encounters	Wavell		
Brevity & *Battleaxe*	Auchinleck	Beresford – Peirse	Gott
Crusader	Auchinleck	Cunningham*	Norrie
Theseus	Auchinleck	Ritchie	Godwin-Austen Ritchie Norrie Gott
El Alamein	Alexander	Montgomery	Harrods Leese Lumpden

* Until 26 November 1941

Commanders and units thus had to operate in constantly changing combinations. Moreover, the lack of an unambiguous doctrine on the British side meant that a very wide range of often personal views and ideas took precedence. The result was that none of those involved knew where they stood at a given time in a given situation, in terms of both command and execution.

Only with the arrival of Montgomery did clarity emerge in this area, as we will see in the next chapter.

British troops

Operation *Theseus* once again witnessed acts of great personal courage on the British side, often in compensation for weaknesses in the field of tactics and command. However, this resulted in enormous losses of tanks and men. It also seems that after this period the British began to have serious problems finding enough men for their tanks. Although an almost inexhaustible number of tanks were available, every tank knocked out by the Germans inevitably led also to losses among its crew. This, combined with limited training and education, meant that in all likelihood the level of English tank crews continued to decline and that too few experienced officers remained to look after new batches of recruits. Moreover, due to the unpredictability of the fighting, there were also significant losses among the higher ranks, so that there were fewer and fewer officers with experience in waging tank warfare in the desert. (3: 190)

Deployment of troops

It is often difficult to keep track of which British units were deployed where during the different phases of the conflict. This is because the British were constantly moving entire divisions to new trouble spots. At the beginning of 1941 this was to the Balkans and Greece in the wake of the German advance; at the beginning of 1942 it was to the Far East in response to the threat from Japan. In between, small, little-known campaigns were carried out against the Italians in East Africa. The following table attempts to provide an overview of the various troop movements.

Troop movements in 1941 and 1942

	1941			
	Q1	Q2	Q3	Q4
1st Armoured Division	Training in GB	Training in GB	Training in GB	En route to the front
7th Armoured Division	Egypt	At the front	At the front	At the front
4th Indian Division	East Africa	At the front	At the front	At the front
2nd NZ Division	Greece/Crete	Greece/Crete	At the front	At the front
1st SA Division	East Africa	East Africa	At the front	At the front

	1942			
	Q1	Q2	Q3	Q4
1st Armoured Division	At the front	At the front	At the front	At the front
7th Armoured Division	Egypt	At the front	At the front	At the front
10th Armoured Division		Egypt	At the front	At the front
70th Armoured Division		Tobruk	At the front	At the front
4th Indian Division	At the front	At the front	At the front	At the front
5th Indian Division		At the front Tobruk	At the front	At the front
2nd NZ Division			At the front	At the front
1st SA Division		At the front	At the front	At the front
2nd SA Division		Tobruk	At the front	At the front

The 22nd Armoured Brigade of 1st Armoured Division arrived in North Africa as early as July 1941 and was involved in Crusader.

These movements meant there was little continuity in the deployment of units, making it difficult to pass on knowledge and experience; moreover, new troops unfamiliar with mobile desert warfare were constantly arriving. It is difficult to determine whether and how the necessary training took place. The complaints of Auchinleck and many others show that basic training was apparently inadequate and that additional training was unsatisfactory, too.

Recovery system

The British built up their own recovery system and at this stage of the conflict were able to tow damaged tanks off the battlefield during battle. Each brigade had its own recovery unit and mobile workshops. Large tank transporters with their low-loaders* took tanks from the battlefield to mobile workshops, and crews could normally expect them back within three days. If the repairs took longer, the tanks were towed to a tank 'hospital' or to Tobruk station, from where they were transported by train to the Nile Delta, where every possible repair could be carried out. There was thus a continuous stream of damaged tanks from the front to the rear areas, and a stream of repaired and new tanks returning to the front. (29: 140)

* In fact, they were not classic low-loaders, but trailers with high clearance.

Chapter 6

El Alamein: the Collision of Two Worlds

6.1 The arrival of Montgomery

While Rommel, convinced that for the time being a stalemate had been reached, toured the front to thank his troops and hand out decorations, Churchill increased the pressure from London on Auchinleck to attack. He refused and opted instead to strengthen his units, which now enjoyed short supply lines and were in excellent defensive positions. Auchinleck's refusal, however, led to his replacement by General Sir Harold Alexander, Commander-in-Chief Middle East, while the Eighth Army became acquainted with a new commander in the person of Lieutenant General Bernard Montgomery. The latter's appointment would mark a turning point, not only for the Eighth Army but for all British forces. Montgomery took a realistic view of the strengths and weaknesses of the British Army. He was also charismatic and could be charming. In the first weeks of his appointment he visited his soldiers everywhere at the front and talked to them in order to get a good picture of the actual condition of the Eighth Army. He also sent selected officers to the various units to prevent their commanders from concealing any weaknesses. These visits confirmed his ideas, and he saw the need to fundamentally change the army's organization and tactical doctrine. Instead of waging war according to German rules, with their emphasis on mobility, personal initiative and combination of arms, he intended to play the game that the British were good at: a linear, relatively static front with superiority in manpower and weapons which would hold the Germans and could function as the basis for an offensive.

Based on this and other factors, he formulated the following principles for the Eighth Army:

- Command was centralized. Orders were now orders and no longer just starting points for discussion. Montgomery used a directive style of leadership that left no room for personal interpretation at lower levels of command.
- Personal initiative was not tolerated because experience showed that it led to chaos and a waste of resources.
- Plans for offensives were made by Montgomery himself and not by staff officers. These plans were more than a framework; they were drawn up in detail and had to be adhered to in detail. Everything had to be focused on converting the mobile battlefield into a linear static front, the type of First World War trench warfare that the British, given their limitations, were strongest at, and which was effective given the experiences at Tobruk.
- A static, linear line of defence was preferable to mobile warfare.
- The troops had to await and absorb enemy actions from well defended positions, with well placed anti-tank guns and well camouflaged tanks. This had to be done under strict central direction and coordination; personal initiative was prohibited.

- Montgomery emphasized the importance of training, having found that the Eighth Army's level was far below par.
- He strengthened the position of artillery within the organization, considering it the most effective weapon system at his disposal.
- He did not want to see any more cavalry-style charges; these had proved ineffective against German units.

This was all strongly reminiscent of the way the First World War was fought by the British. A greater contrast with the German way of war is hardly conceivable.

Montgomery also believed totally in himself and in his troops and missed no opportunity to express this belief. He regarded the Eighth Army as 'his' army, which he could dispose of as he saw fit, and the diplomatic, flexible Alexander shielded him from military or political intrigues in Cairo or London which could thwart his plans.

Soul mates …in a way

Perhaps without realizing it, Rommel and Montgomery had much in common. Both displayed considerable flair and had a good grasp of public relations, Rommel in his British Perspex motorcycle goggles, Montgomery in his Australian hat adorned with regimental pins. They both rejected luxurious headquarters in the rear in favour of staying at the front with their men. However, there were also major differences: while Rommel remained chivalrous and diplomatic towards his opponent at all times, Montgomery described the most important task of his men as follows: 'Kill Germans wherever you find them.' Montgomery would never, like Rommel, show himself at the front once battle was joined or display personal courage. He preferred to leave that to others and, after the start of the fighting, would withdraw to his trailer, a variation on the British 'chateau generalship' of the First World War. (17: 188)

Montgomery's reforms were a breath of fresh air for the British Army, which had been subjected to constantly changing organizational concepts and doctrines in recent years, as we have seen. He also finally initiated a training programme for the infantry units. Elimination of machine-gun nests and small defensive positions was taught at platoon level, and subsequent training took place at company, then battalion level. Newly arrived units were combined with more seasoned ones to achieve an optimal exchange of knowledge and experience. Unnecessary activities such as guard duty and marching were abolished, in order that all time be devoted to training and acclimatization to desert conditions. Over time, training increasingly emphasized night-time actions and cooperation with tanks. Coordination between infantry and artillery was practised, the latter providing a barrage for the infantry to advance behind in the coming offensive. Orientation by compass was also prioritized. (23: 82–3) All in all, the training was similar to that which the Germans had operated as standard for years.

Montgomery also realized that training alone was insufficient to overcome the animosity between the various branches, and he aimed to forge them into a single whole. This animosity had deepened in recent times into distrust and sometimes open hostility, especially between infantry and tank units. It reflected British society, the infantry divisions representing the workers, and the tank divisions, the upper classes. The infantry accused the tank crews of failing to cooperate with them and abandoning them at times of crisis.

The tank crews, in turn, accused the infantry of distracting them from their real role as truly mobile units and making them less effective and more vulnerable. The fact that after the Italian campaign in 1940 none of this supposed effectiveness in a mobile role had proved itself, and that they had always come off worse in combat with German units, was conveniently overlooked. (21: 87; 3: 141) Before El Alamein, no one had bothered to explain to the infantry that tanks regularly had to take on fuel and ammunition and therefore sometimes had to leave the battlefield. Nor had the feelings and fears of the infantry been made clear to the tank crews. Neither arm understood the needs of the other, and no one had ever discussed or explained it to them.

The artillery complained (rightly) that they were never given the opportunity to support the other arms with concentrated fire, and that their strength was dispersed among the different units. The engineering units complained that they were only called on after damage had already been done, which meant they were constantly put into a difficult position. Another sore point was that tank crews regularly took a car to go shopping in Cairo. They were therefore always well supplied, which led to ill feeling between them and others. The more people complained, the easier it was to blame others for their own failures. This was bad for morale, and Montgomery worked to put an end to it. (23: 90)

The role of the tank reconsidered

There were two types of tank crew, each with its own origin: the cavalrymen and the men of the Royal Tank Regiments (RTR). As representatives of the upper classes, the cavalrymen with their Cruisers generally looked down on the men of the Royal Tank Regiments with their Infantry tanks. There were also differences in tactics. The cavalrymen, who had only recently exchanged their horses for tanks, still had a strong preference for the '*arme blanche*' (close-quarters combat), approaching the enemy as nearly as possible and fighting individual duels. This led to the well-known but not very successful charges carried out by British tanks. Montgomery analyzed recent tank battles and concluded that many of the failures were due to the attitude of the tank crews. The days of the charge had to be over, and tank regiments were no longer allowed to go into battle in small units and without infantry or other support. Montgomery decided to manage the tank units tightly; only he would determine where and when they were to be deployed. In the meantime, the tank crews and their commanders had to adapt to their new role, train in cooperation with the infantry and absorb the new tactics. It should come as no surprise that it was among these units that Montgomery encountered the greatest resistance to his reforms. (23: 88–9)

Montgomery did his best to help officers and men overcome their prejudices and to create a 'corporate identity', so that everyone should feel part of the Eighth Army rather than just his own arm or regiment (23: 47). To make the organization 'mean and lean', he reduced the large bureaucratic General Headquarters in Cairo to a small, workable unit. The General Headquarters, which had grown enormously in recent years, was largely staffed by officers who had never been to the front. These 'Cairo Canaries' had successfully continued to live their pre-war lives, with short working hours, long lunches and siestas, all a mark of their assumed social status. The departure of these men, to the front or back home, had not only an immediate effect on social life in Cairo, but also a positive one on the *esprit de corps* of the Eighth Army. (23: 47) Montgomery's entourage would be limited in the future to veterans from the previous phases of the war in North Africa.

> 'It's a general called Montgomery', said McMaster (a non-commissioned officer of one of the Armoured Brigades, to Lieutenant Colonel Peniakoff, commander of the Polish units). 'A short, wiry fellow, with a bee in his bonnet about PT. The first thing he did when he took over was to order half an hour's physical training for Army Headquarters Staff every morning before breakfast. Tubby brigadiers came out in their vests and ran. They heaved and they panted, shaking their fat paunches, for everyone to see, and when they couldn't make the grade they got the sack. Sacked them right and left, he did, all the fat bastards.' McMaster chuckled ferociously. 'A few days ago he visited the regiment. Talked to the officers, then to the NCOs. He told us everything: what his plan was for the battle, what he wanted the regiment to do, what he wanted me to do. And we will do it, Sir. What a man!' (21: 132)

In this way, Montgomery showed that he took his officers and men seriously and was doing his best to prepare them for the coming battle. He also knew how to deal with the troops from the Antipodes.

> He was evidently struck by the nonchalant 'down under' way in which the New Zealanders, like the Australians, reacted to the sight of top brass, for he remarked casually to General Freiberg: 'Your men are not very keen on saluting, I see.'
>
> 'Oh, just give 'em a wave, Sir', said the unabashed Freiberg. 'You will find they'll wave back.'
>
> When Monty drove off again, he waved. And the soldiers he passed politely returned his greetings in their informal way. (14: 309)

Montgomery realized better than anyone that restoring the confidence of the men was one of the keys to success. (*Photo IHC*)

Who was this General Montgomery? Born in 1887, the son of a bishop, he was educated at St Paul's School and enlisted in the Royal Warwickshire Regiment after Sandhurst, having failed to achieve a high enough score in the Indian Army entrance tests. He would have preferred the Indian Army because the pay was higher, and he was a cadet with little money. He had almost been expelled from Sandhurst for violent behaviour, which was also evident during his first posting in India, when he and his companions demolished the Bombay Yacht Club one evening. Montgomery was particularly to blame for this because, unlike his fellows, he had been sober (he would abstain from alcohol for the rest of his life). He restored his reputation in the First World War, when he was seriously wounded leading his Company and served so well in subsequent staff positions that by the end of the war he had risen to lieutenant colonel and command of a battalion. In 1939 he was commander of the 3rd Division, fought with it the May campaign of 1940 and managed to evacuate it skilfully via Dunkirk. He subsequently commanded V and then XII Corps in England. After the fatal accident suffered by General Gott, Cunningham's intended

Command structure of the Eighth Army

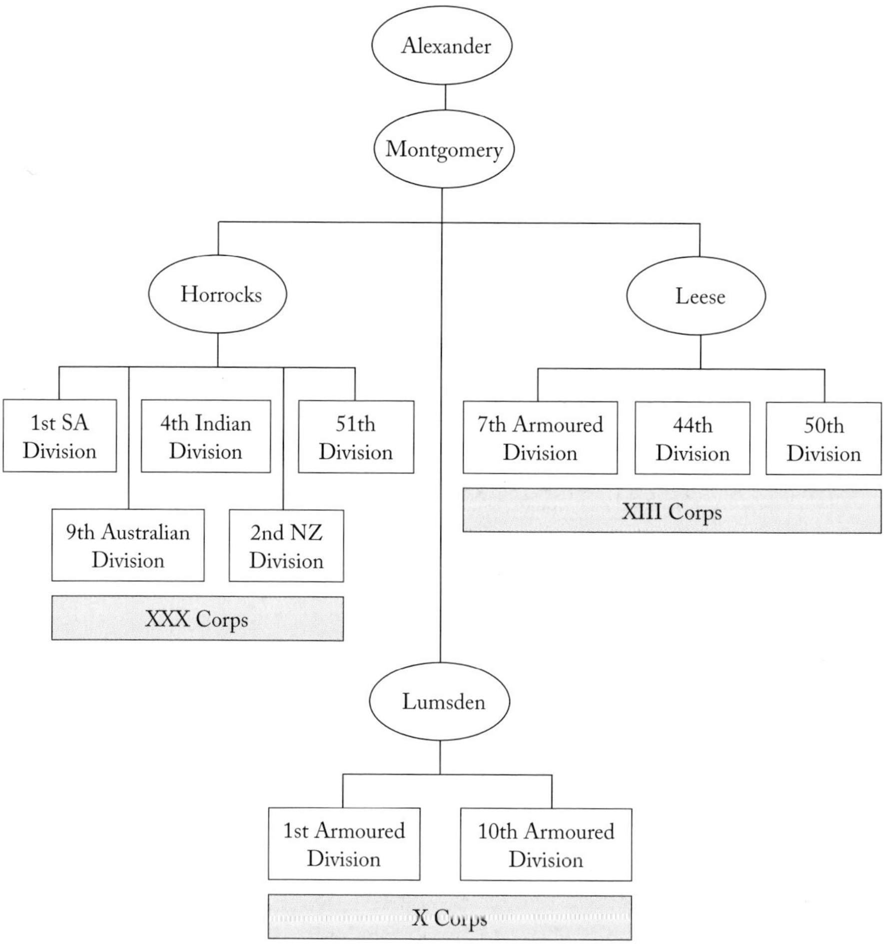

successor as commander of the Eighth Army, Montgomery was chosen to take command and arrived in North Africa in August 1942.

However, Montgomery's appointment and the new elan he brought with him were not the only changes from a few months earlier. The possibilities for German offensive action were now limited by geographical factors. While previously there had always been an opportunity for wide outflanking manoeuvres, Rommel now faced on a 60km front physical barriers in the form of the Mediterranean Sea to the north and the Qattara Depression to the south. The latter consisted of a series of undulating dunes and hills about 200m high, terrain through which troops could not possibly travel.

To take advantage of this opportunity, Montgomery modified Auchinleck's original plan. That plan had called for a collection of 'boxes' of brigade strength, built around artillery positions. The surplus infantry would be stationed in the Nile Delta as a strategic reserve. Mobile tank units would have to fight the German tank units around these 'boxes' between El Alamein and the Nile Delta. If the German units did manage to break through, the British headquarters, protected by a strategic reserve, could be evacuated to Palestine and continue the fight from there. The plan resembled Gazala's box system in many respects, and Montgomery immediately realized that it was wiser to deploy the surplus infantry in a static defence line, supported by minefields that were difficult to penetrate. (3: 137) In doing so, he built on the strengths of the British Army: defending a static line from which, after an artillery bombardment, a classic infantry attack could be launched, with tank units in a supporting role. Should the British succeed in building such a solid front, Rommel in turn would have no choice but to launch an attack at one point in the line in an attempt to break through.

6.2 The situation of the Axis troops

Rommel, fearing a new attack by the numerically superior British, urged his men, including the staff and support units, not to withdraw. A breakthrough by the British could lead to the destruction of the Germans' C3I capability, along the lines of German offensive doctrine. He had already suffered a serious blow in that area with the loss of the 621st Nachrichten Abteilung under Seebohm. If a breakthrough were to succeed, it would not be difficult for the British to clear the various pockets of resistance one by one and achieve a complete victory. Rommel assumed that a major British attack would not take place before early September, and he quickly began to receive the necessary reinforcements. The following were delivered by air:

- 5,400 troops in July to replace losses from existing units
- two regiments of the 164th Leichte Division (we have already seen the first units in action on 5 July, and in the following weeks 1,000 troops per day followed)
- 1st Fallschirmjäger Brigade, an elite Luftwaffe unit under General Ramcke

However, none of these troops had their own transport or heavy weapons. The 164th for a short time only had bicycles, but they were a welcome addition to the thin defensive line. The Italians also sent two new divisions, the Bologna Infantry Division led by General Gioda and an excellent paratrooper unit, the Folgore Division, trained by German officers.

After the experiences of the past month, Rommel displayed considerable cynicism about the combat value of these Italian units, with the exception of the Folgore Division, which provided a good example of the professionalism that Italian units could achieve when well trained and well led. But he realized that when push came to shove, only German soldiers and German officers could turn the tide.

The units that Rommel ultimately had at his disposal were:

- The DAK under von Bismarck consisting of:
  - The 15th and 21st Panzer Divisions
  - The 90th Leichte Light Division
  - The 164th Infantry Division
- The Italian X Corps (infantry) under Gioda consisting of:
  - Brescia Division
  - Pavia Division
- The XX Mobile Corps under Baldassare consisting of:
  - Division Ariete
  - Littorio Division
  - Trieste Division
  - Folgore paratroop division
- The XXI Corps (infantry) under Navarrini consisting of:
  - Trento Division
  - Bologna Division

In addition, there were several artillery regiments, anti-tank units, *Aufklärungsabteilungen*, etc. However, as we will see, disease and malnutrition would take a heavy toll on the troops.

Artillery, ammunition and fuel also continued to arrive, thanks in part to the great efforts of the Luftwaffe. Ammunition dumps were built, fortifications dug and extensive minefields laid in case the British attacked first. The Panzerarmee Afrika was in fact preparing for a classic positional battle, the type of warfare that was far removed from their doctrine, training and approved style of fighting.

Despite their fresh supplies, the Axis forces were vastly outnumbered. At the start of Rommel's attack on Alam El Halfa in August, the Panzerarmee had 203 tanks at its disposal, half of which were PzKpfw IV F2s, while the British had a total of 767 tanks and hundreds of new 6-pounder anti-tank guns. (17: 189) In addition, the climate and food shortages began to place an increasingly heavy burden on the troops: a total of 9,418 men were reported sick in August, and the Panzerarmee was still 16,000 below its nominal strength. Furthermore, there was a shortage of 210 tanks, 175 armoured personnel carriers and 1,500 other vehicles. (17: 189) The fuel supply situation remained critical: the tanks had only one full tank each, giving them a range of 150–175km over relatively flat terrain. Despite Italian promises, further fuel deliveries failed to materialize in August: a six-ship convoy was destroyed after Enigma messages were intercepted.

Command structure of the Panzerarmee Afrika

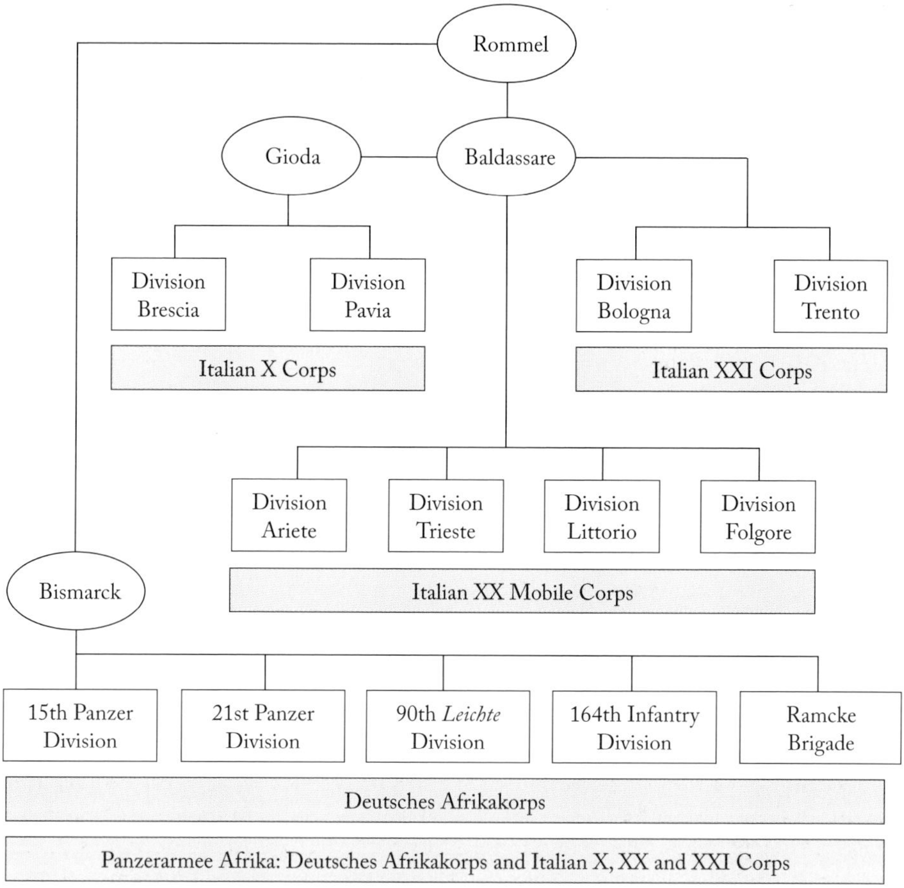

Rommel and Gause (with goggles) planning new actions in Rommel's staff car. (*Photo BTM*)

Intelligence

The battle in the field of intercepting information became increasingly one-sided in this phase of the conflict. The Germans were still convinced that the Enigma code could not be cracked. This meant that all kinds of top secret communications between Rommel and the OKW were on British desks within a few hours. In other words, every plan of attack was an open book to Montgomery, from the medical report drawn up by Professor Horster on Rommel's physical condition to the sailing times of the various convoys. Montgomery was thus able to take the necessary countermeasures in time and send reinforcements to the most threatened parts of the front. Ultra interceptions mainly played a role in the preparatory phase; once battle was joined, the British had to fall back on listening to radio traffic. The Y Service, which intercepted German messages in the field, played an important role at this tactical and operational level. Many Jewish refugees from Germany, who could understand dialects and jargon of all kinds, worked for this service. In the past, Rommel had been able to rely on Captain Seebohm's 621st Nachrichten Abteilung for tactical and operational intelligence, but after July this option was removed. The study of material captured from this Abteilung led to all kinds of radio procedures being tightened on the British side. The papers also showed that the Germans had gained a good idea of the strength of the British armed forces by deciphering messages from the military attaché at the American Embassy in Cairo, Colonel Fellers (they had access to the American diplomatic code). This leak was then quickly plugged. (11: 149; 17: 189)

Having outlined the starting position of both sides, we will now examine the fighting around El Alamein. This fell into two phases:

- A first phase in which Rommel tried to break through the British defence lines at Alam el Halfa
- A second phase in which Montgomery would try to break through the lines of the Axis powers in Operation *Lightfoot*: the historic battle of El Alamein

6.3 The first offensive at El Alamein: the Battle of the Alam el Halfa Ridge

Rommel wanted to attack the British positions at El Alamein as quickly as possible because he knew that Montgomery would receive such a large number of reinforcements that an offensive after September would have little chance of success. He set the date for his offensive as 30 August. The once physically strong German commander had now become a shadow of his former self, suffering from low blood pressure, chronic gastric and intestinal problems, inflamed eyes, a nasal infection and a swollen liver. On 20 August, his doctor, Professor Horster, recommended either a period of recuperation in Germany or some temporary treatment in Africa. Rommel wanted a Panzer general as his replacement and asked for Guderian. However, Guderian had fallen out of favour with Hitler, so Rommel decided to postpone the offensive. In the meantime, Berndt arranged for a good cook and fresh food, and kept Goebbels informed through his personal channels. This did not alter the fact that Rommel was physically ill and needed time to recover, but the hope of a quick victory in the coming offensive and the opportunity to enjoy a well-deserved rest for some time afterwards kept him going. Rommel's plan was as follows:

- The northern sector of the British defence line was too strong to break. This part of the front would be attacked as a diversionary manoeuvre by the 164th Leicht Division and the Fallschirmjäger Brigade Ramcke, together with some Italian divisions
- Rommel's mobile forces would gather in the south at the Qattara Depression to force a breakthrough and attack the British from the rear

The Qattara Depression was so inaccessible that it was not possible to carry out a wide southward movement as the Germans had done at Gazala. The position of the German forces at the Qattara Depression was as follows: the 90th Leichte in the north, in the centre the Italian XX Mobile Corps with the Ariete and Littorio Divisions, in the south the two Armoured Divisions of the DAK and in the extreme south the various *Aufklärungsabteilungen*. This combined force would first have to fight through extensive minefields and then veer north-east towards the Alam el Halfa Ridge with the aim of cutting off the British from their supplies by attacking them from the rear. This force would then advance east, towards the Nile Delta.

The DAK could count on approximately 200 tanks, half of which were IV F2s; their direct British opponents, the 8th and 22nd Armoured Brigade, each had 210 at their disposal, mainly new Grant tanks. Whether or not the offensive could be continued depended on fuel supply which, as we have seen, had been effectively disrupted by the British. Rommel therefore hesitated until the last moment as to whether or not to launch the offensive, despite Kesselring's guarantees that he would fly in fuel if necessary. If fuel remained in short supply, only a limited offensive would be possible. While Rommel was weighing everything up, his tank units, after travelling for two nights, gathered at the southern tip of the Qattara Depression. Unnoticed by the British, the shift in the balance of power to the south had succeeded. For the rest, thanks to Ultra, the British were aware of the intentions of the coming offensive and had thoroughly prepared to face it.

Churchill visited the front in North Africa in the period before the offensive. He was impressed by Montgomery and his preparations.

> I was taken to the key point Southeast of the Ruweisat Ridge. Here, amid the hard, rolling curves and creases of the desert lay the mass of our armour, concealed and dispersed yet tactically concentrated ...Every crevice of the desert was packed with camouflaged concealed batteries. Three or four hundred guns would fire at the German armour before we hurtled in our own. (14: 314)

The attack itself began on 30 August at 10.00 pm. The main thrust quickly became bogged down in unmapped minefields, within which British infantry were entrenched, supported by heavy machine guns and artillery. Many of the German vehicles fell victim to mines and attack from the air. Von Bismarck was killed by a mortar shell in the first hours of the attack, and Nehring was seriously injured when his command vehicle was hit by a British fighter-bomber. When the tank divisions finally managed to break through the minefields the next morning, they were ordered not to advance eastwards towards the open desert with the aim of attacking the British from the rear around the Alam el

Halfa Ridge, but rather to advance north and concentrate their strength on the Alam el Halfa Ridge itself. This change of plan played into Montgomery's hands: he had turned the Ridge into a death trap for the German units. Based on the new orders, the DAK first advanced east under cover of a sandstorm and then turned north. There, at the foot of the Alam el Halfa Ridge, they became stuck in soft sand late in the afternoon of 31 August, right under the noses of the 22nd Armoured Brigade.

Major General Roberts saw them coming:

> On they come, a most impressive array …It is fascinating to watch them, as one might watch a snake curl up ready to strike. But there is something unusual too; some of the leading tanks are Mk IVs, and Mk IVs have in the past always had short-barrelled 75mm guns used for close support works and firing HE only, consequently they are not usually in the front. But these Mk IVs have a very long gun on them; in fact it looks the devil of a gun. This must be the long barrelled stepped up 75mm the 'Intelligence' people have talked about.* (21: 133)

Over the next hour, the sandstorm subsided and British tanks and artillery were able to open fire on the virtually immobile and unprotected German units. The new DAK commander, General von Värst, could tell Rommel nothing other than that he could no longer make a detour to the east due to lack of fuel. On the night of 31 August/1 September, British bombers took over the attack, and the new day showed a battlefield full of burning German tanks and vehicles. The air raids, artillery bombardments and lack of fuel made it impossible for the Germans to improve their position. By 2 September it was clear that the attack had failed, and a demoralized Rommel ordered the units to conduct an organized retreat. Kesselring commented on this decision by Rommel: if the attack had continued, the German units could have surrounded the British, who had already been outflanked. British fuel dumps would undoubtedly have been captured, and the attack could have been continued to the north and east. Now the same units had used the last of their fuel to fight their way back. Hitler, Ramcke and others also questioned Rommel's decision. Kesselring blamed it on his physical state: the old Rommel might have indeed continued the attack. In the end, all the Germans had taken were British minefields, which they made part of their own defence line. The losses on the German side were high: 3,000 dead and wounded, 50 tanks, 50 pieces of (anti-tank) artillery and 400 trucks. The British suffered 1,700 dead and wounded and lost almost 70 tanks and 20 anti-tank guns.** However, the British could afford such losses, while they represented a major setback for Rommel. In addition, Montgomery achieved a first, psychologically very important, victory over Rommel; his efforts of the past period were beginning to bear fruit, and it strengthened his authority among officers and men.

Rommel withdrew to his headquarters and awaited the arrival of his replacement, General Stumme, who arrived on 19 September and, after an extensive briefing by Rommel, started to repair the damaged relations between Germans and Italians. Rommel had left specific orders for Stumme regarding the construction of the defensive line. Since

* These IV F2s had already been at the front for more than a year. It is striking that Roberts had not been informed about them.

** Other sources give 536 dead, 400 lorries and 38 tanks on the German side, or 68 tanks, 67 planes and significantly more deaths.

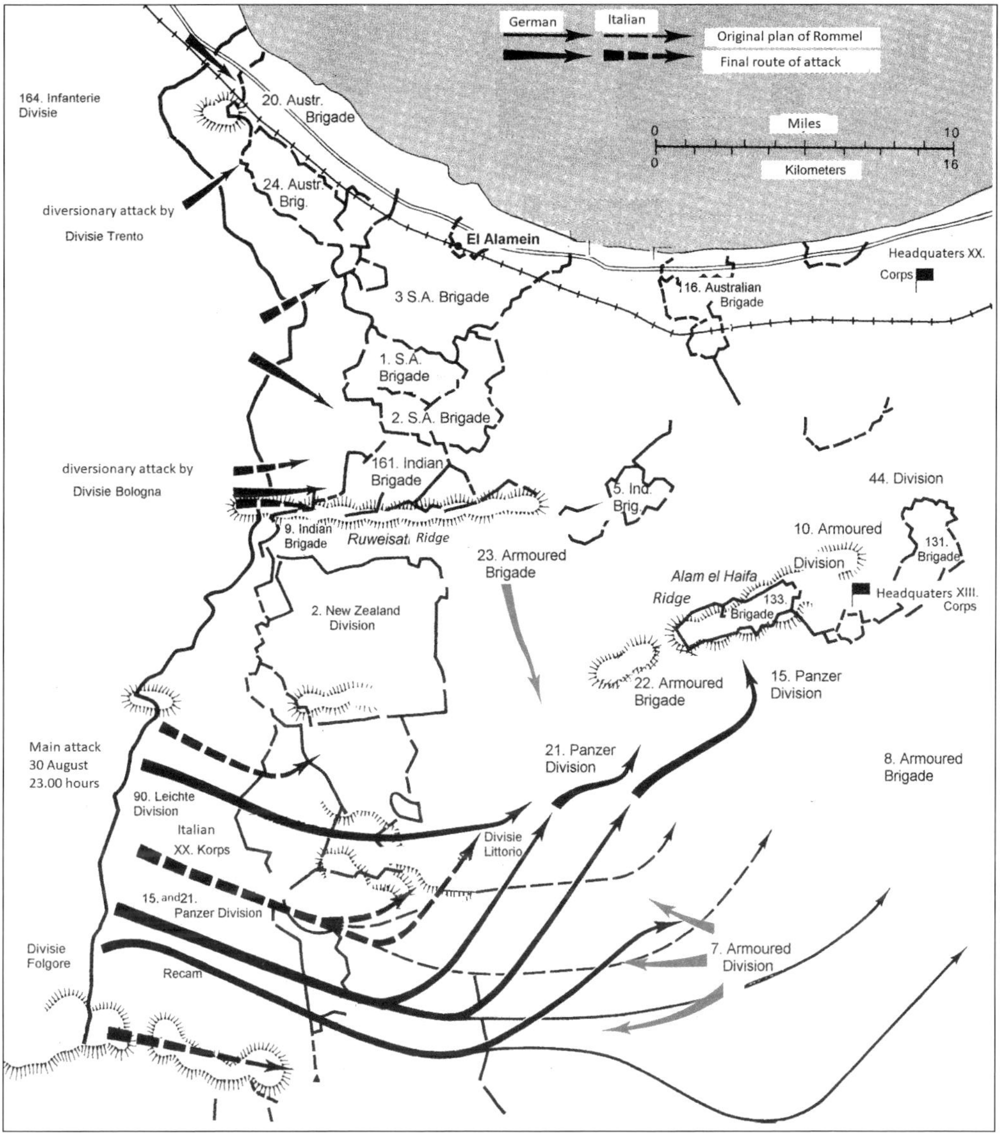

The Battle of Alam el Halfa Ridge.

outflanking movements were impossible, Montgomery would have to attack frontally, and this necessitated a defensive line in depth.

A number of factors would determine the position of the Axis troops in the near future:

- British air superiority
- The shortage of transport: none of the newly arrived units had their own transport, making the mobile warfare of the recent past an impossibility. On the other hand, the British units had more and more vehicles at their disposal, which shifted the balance of mobility to their side
- The shortage of fuel meant that available quantities had to be handled with extreme care

Construction of German fortifications: the 'Devil's gardens'
Rommel had explicit ideas about the construction of the German defence line. This had to be an uninterrupted line of square minefields sown with thousands of mines and booby traps. In the rear, these minefields would be guarded by battle posts manned by one company from each infantry battalion. About 2,000m behind the minefields would be the main body of the infantry battalion; behind it, the heavier field and anti-tank guns would be positioned, and behind that, the tank units as a mobile reserve. A total of 445,000 mines, of which 3 per cent were the anti-personnel type, were incorporated into this defence line. The idea was that any British advance would be halted by the minefields. Behind the static defence line, the Italian infantry divisions were combined with or flanked by German units. Behind them, the 15th Panzer Division and the Littorio Division in the north and the 21st Panzer Division with the Ariete Division in the south formed the mobile reserve. Should the British break through, they could be attacked from the north and south by this mobile tank reserve. (17: 195)

Rommel left for Germany on 23 September, visiting Mussolini in Rome on the way. In Berlin, on 30 September, in the presence of Keitel and Berndt, the latter dressed for the occasion in party uniform, Hitler presented him with a field marshal's baton, and he was then guest of honour at a party meeting in the Sportpalast the same evening. Rommel took the opportunity to ask Hitler for weapons of all kinds, such as new tank types, the Nebelwerfer 42 rocket-launcher and smoke generators. He blamed the failure of the last offensive on the Italians, whose careless attitude to security, he alleged, had revealed to the British his plans for the attack on the Alam el Halfa Ridge and the convoy routes. This accusation was, as we have seen, unfounded. The British had promoted the idea of an Italian 'betrayal' by allowing the Germans to capture forged documents showing the role that the Italians were said to have played. In reality, it was not the Italians but the decoding of Enigma messages that allowed the British to view Rommel's plans. Before leaving for his home in Wiener Neustadt with vague promises about the supply of new materiel to counterbalance the growing combat power of the British, Rommel also complained about the shortcomings of Italian equipment, the poor level of training of their officers and their flight when faced by Australian and New Zealand units attacking with bayonets.

6.4 The final confrontation: El Alamein

Now the final confrontation was approaching. At this stage of the conflict the forces were more out of balance than at any other time to date. In theory, both sides could deploy four infantry and four tank divisions. On the Axis side, half consisted of Italian units with, as we have seen, limited combat effectiveness. The exception to this was the Folgore Division and to a certain extent the two tank divisions, the Ariete and Littorio. The German units were 17,000 men below their nominal strength: 37,000 instead of 54,000. Of these 17,000 missing men, 10,000 were sick, not least as a result of the poor food supply; in the weeks before the major British offensive no fresh vegetables or meat were available. This led, for example, to the operational strength of the 15th Panzer Division falling from 9,178 to 3,294 (!) men, as was apparent in the following incident:

> Lieutenant Buchholz was sitting with a number of comrades in their fortified gun emplacement enjoying the setting sun when the peace was rudely disturbed by a New Zealand soldier who began to leisurely slip through the barbed wire. Indignant about this vandalism, Buchholz urged him to make himself scarce as quickly as possible. However, he turned out to be part of a reconnaissance unit, which promptly opened fire. In the ensuing firefight a number of Flak gunners were killed and three New Zealanders were taken prisoner. 'They were big guys, these three, with chests like beer barrels, who looked around the reinforcements smiling and said kindly, "Proper Children's Crusade you are running here, aren't you?"' Buchholz looked around and felt a stab through his body. 'The man was right, the young soldiers looked like a church choir, exhausted by dysentery, pale and bloodless like children who had grown up in a cellar.' (14: 314)

Buchholz and his men were not the only ones to meet their opponents before the battle: in the same period, a well-hidden unit of the 8th MG Battalion captured an Australian general who was walking absent-mindedly through the lines. According to the troops who caught him, he was a nice fellow who looked rather like a teacher. They passed the news on to headquarters, and within half an hour Rommel landed in his Fieseler Storch. The men listened with interest to the general, who said he was particularly pleased to have met Rommel in person and extensively praised the German general's skill and the quality of the German Army. 'But', he said, 'it is impossible for the German people to win against more than sixty countries, no matter how good you may be.'

The message could not have been more clear.

Rommel ultimately had 211 German tanks and 320 Italian ones at his disposal, although the value of the latter was questionable. The supply situation had become increasingly

The battle increasingly took on the character of trench warfare. The photo shows a soldier of the Ramcke brigade at an advance post. Within reach are weapons for close-range fighting: hand grenades and a pistol to fire flares and illuminate the terrain between the lines.

dire. The Axis troops needed 300 tons of fuel per day for routine movements, while during combat this could rise to 600 tons per day. This meant that every week a ship with approximately 2,000 tons of fuel had to successfully complete the crossing. The aim was to collect 6,000 tons, enough for ten days of fighting, by the end of October. This ambition was literally dashed by an attack on an Italian convoy on 20 October, which saw the loss of the valuable tanker *Panuco* with 1,650 tons of fuel. It was certainly not the first time that the British had successfully intercepted a convoy, but in this crucial period they were helped inadvertently by Rommel, who continuously requested detailed information via Enigma about convoys' precise composition, sailing times and routes. Thanks to Ultra, the British knew where and when to expect them. Ultra also intercepted messages planning new fuel convoys for the later period of 22–27 October. Consequently, at the end of October the Axis troops only had enough fuel for three days of fighting, and of this, 600 tons were in Benghazi, almost 1,000km from the front. It should therefore come as no surprise that Montgomery's offensive was launched during this vulnerable period.

Montgomery, in turn, had 195,000 men and 1,029 tanks at his disposal, including more than 250 new Shermans. These tanks were built in America to British specifications, well armoured and armed with a 75mm gun, a 7.5mm machine gun in the hull and a 12.5mm machine gun mounted on the turret. Their maximum speed was approximately 35kph. The most remarkable feature of this tank was its 460 HP Chrysler engine, which was made up of five truck engines. In 1941, American factories produced 14,000 Shermans, a number that would rise to 21,000 by 1943.

Montgomery's logistics route was approximately 60km long and excellently protected, and new supplies reached him every day. In addition, the British had total air superiority, with 500 fighter planes and 200 bombers which could strike at will.

The latest weapon: the Sherman tank, developed to British specifications and the backbone of Allied tank units in the years to come. (*Photo IHC*)

The balance of power prior to El Alamein

	Germans/Italians	British
Men	37,000 Germans 45,000 Italians	195,000*
Total	82,000**	195,000
Tanks	85 PzKpfw III L/42 85 PzKpfw III L/60 11 PzKpfw IV L/24 30 PzKpfw IV F 2 L/43	170 Grants 252 Shermans 216 Crusaders*** 119 Stuarts 194 Valentines
Subtotal	211 German tanks 320 Italian tanks	
Total tanks	531	1,029

The British also had an impressive number of anti-tank guns and other artillery at their disposal: 500 2-pounder and 753 of the new 6-pounder anti-tank guns, in addition to 832 25-pounder howitzers, all provided with substantial amounts of ammunition. The Germans had 78 88mm Flak guns, some of them well dug in and protected.

In the run-up to the British offensive, christened *Lightfoot*, Montgomery showed himself to be as great a master of deception as his opponent: under the code name Bertram, everything was done to give the Germans the impression that a future offensive would be aimed at the southern part of the front. German aerial reconnaissance showed large stock dumps being built up in the south, mainly of ammunition. A long pipeline was started which, it appeared, would certainly not be completed before mid-November. Apparently little was happening in the north, although there were large numbers of trucks there, but the majority of the tanks were still stationed in the south. In reality, tanks were being moved from the south to the north at night and parked under dummy trucks, their caterpillar tracks carefully erased and replaced with tyre tracks. Radio traffic, provided by the staff of the 8th Armoured Division, also increased in the run-up to the offensive in the south, giving the impression that large tank formations were preparing for battle. The tank units in the north, in turn, maintained total radio silence. British preparations were thus completely hidden from the eyes and ears of the Axis.

In addition, Montgomery introduced another innovation: all units and the men involved were informed of the main lines of the coming offensive. This began with meetings for all senior officers on 19 and 20 October at the Amriyah cinema in Alexandria. Through the various levels in the hierarchy, all troops were ultimately informed in detail about their goals and how they were to be achieved. Non-commissioned officers gathered their men around them and sketched in the sand what was going happen and what role they would play. At the same time, all leave was cancelled. In this way everyone became involved in the plans, and a feeling of unity and ambition developed throughout the Eighth Army.

* Based on nominal strength, but no indication that this differed from reality.
** Based on the nominal strength, but in practice much lower due to the many cases of sickness on the German side.
*** Some of them with the new 6-pounder gun.

At 9.15 pm on 23 October, *Lightfoot* was launched, much earlier than the Germans and Italians had expected. The main lines of the offensive were as follows. The infantry divisions of XXX Corps were to fight their way through the minefields in the northern part of the front. The gap thus created would allow X Corps to advance with its tanks to engage the tanks of the Axis. XIII Corps with its tank and infantry units would undertake the necessary diversionary manoeuvres which were to hold the 21st Panzer Division and the Ariete Division in the south. The second mission of XIII Corps was then to force its way through the minefields in the second phase of the offensive. This would allow the 7th Armoured Division to advance, so that the German units would be surrounded in a pincer movement, from the south by the 7th Armoured Division and from the north by the tank units of X Corps.

Montgomery's original plan was to confront Rommel's tank units. However, the training level of the crews of the new Shermans – the tanks that were a match for the PzKpfw III and IV – turned out to be too low to go into such a confrontation with a reasonable chance of success. On this basis, Montgomery decided to concentrate on the systematic destruction of the German infantry. To protect these units, Rommel would have to deploy his tanks against well-entrenched British anti-tank guns and dug-in tanks. In this way, Rommel's fighting power would be weakened, while the British could replenish their losses from their almost inexhaustible supplies. In other words, this was to be a battle of materiel, which Rommel was bound to lose in the end. Montgomery estimated that the breaking point would be reached in ten to twelve days. This strategy was completely in line with his view that he should dictate the conditions of battle, instead of letting Rommel do so.

The attack itself was extremely methodical in design and execution. It began with a classic half-hour artillery bombardment delivered by 882 guns along the entire front. They fired 600 shells each over the next five and a half hours, with a ten-minute rest every hour to allow the barrels to cool, an average of 2.5 shells per minute. While diversionary manoeuvres were being carried out in the south, in the north the barrage began to creep up on the Axis positions according to a precise timetable, meanwhile detonating the mines of Rommel's 'Devil's gardens'. Just behind this barrage, the first infantry units followed, supported by Valentine tanks. These units were specially trained to stay on course and were supported by navigation officers with rangefinders and compasses. Engineers with mine detectors ensured that the last mines were cleared, while commando units marked the attack routes with white ribbon, and in some places anti-aircraft guns fired incessant tracer ammunition to indicate the boundaries between the different attack sectors. At certain points the artillery barrage stopped, indicating that strongholds had to be built at those points according to previously drawn up plans. Enemy gun positions were simultaneously eliminated one by one by concentrated fire from multiple batteries, using equally precise planning. In this way it was possible to create two corridors through the minefields on the first night. During the 24th and 25th, infantry and engineer units managed to capture a number of German minefields and were slowly but surely fighting their way forward. However, no definitive breakthrough was achieved.

When *Lightfoot* started, Rommel was still with his family in Wiener Neustadt. After the first news arrived, Hitler immediately contacted him, especially since it was unclear what had happened to Stumme. After the start of the attack Stumme had driven to the front, but then no one heard from him again. It later turned out that he had succumbed to a heart attack. In the following days, Rommel flew to the front via a number of stops, arriving on the evening of 25 October. After acquainting himself with the progress of the fighting, he took a gamble and ordered the 21st Panzer Division and related artillery units to move from the south to the northern part of the front. The consequence of this was that these units would never be able to return, due to the shortage of fuel, if the British chose to launch an attack on the southern part of the line. On 27 October, the German units launched an attack on the British, who had meanwhile entrenched themselves on a ridge. The attack fizzled out under heavy artillery fire and air strikes, and the German units were pinned down on flat ground that offered little protection. Retreating and waiting for the British tank units beyond the range of the artillery would have been the obvious thing to do, if the shortage of fuel had not made this impossible. The sinking of two further Italian tankers meant that there would be no more fuel in the near future.

During the 28th, Rommel ordered even more German units to advance from the south to the north, leaving the defence of the southern part of the front to Italian and a very limited number of German units. The British, for their part, were building up a force in the hole they had punched in the northern minefields. At 9.00 pm that day, the second phase of *Lightfoot* began.

This started with an attack by the 9th Australian Division through the minefields nearer the coast. This division encountered a battalion of the 125th Panzer Grenadiere Regiment which, supported by a screen of anti-tank guns, was able to repel the attack. This setback forced Montgomery to revise his strategy: after five days of fighting and 10,000 dead and wounded, he had not come much closer to his goal. There was a lull in the fighting, during which Rommel also tried to find a way out: he realized that on this front the British would be able to deploy an overwhelming superiority in men and materiel and destroy his forces unit by unit. The final blow came on the morning of the 29th: the last tanker on its way, the *Luisiana*, was sunk off the port of Tobruk. There was now no alternative for the Panzerarmee Afrika other than to withdraw to the Fuka Line, an easily defensible area further to the west. In the afternoon of the same day, Rommel ordered all supporting units to fall back even further west to the Mersa Matruh Line. He did not discuss this strategic decision of the highest order with either his Italian allies or the OKH or OKW. A veiled retreat now began.

On the 30th a single ship succeeded in reaching Tobruk with 600 tons of fuel, and that same day, Kesselring reported that various Luftwaffe transport units were being transferred from the Eastern Front to the Mediterranean to supply the *Panzerarmee Afrika* with fuel and ammunition; further attacks by the 9th Australian Division were also repulsed. Meanwhile, General Krause, the commander of the artillery units, inspected the Fuka Line and reported that it was excellent for defensive activities. Planning began for the retreat of the combat units and the setting up of the first fortifications there. Fallschirmjäger Brigade Ramcke, the only non-motorized German unit, was cautiously informed of the impending retreat. Ironically, more and more fuel was now reaching the Panzerarmee, so that it eventually had 1,200 tons at its disposal. The same applied to ammunition, but during the retreat, 12,000 tons of ammunition would have to be blown up, much to Kesselring's dismay, due to a lack of trucks to transport it.

In the meantime, Montgomery had continued to build up his strength behind the front, and on the night of 1/2 November the offensive entered a new stage. Behind an artillery barrage delivered by 200 guns, and supported by fighter-bombers, British units started to advance through the previously partially cleared minefields in the north of the

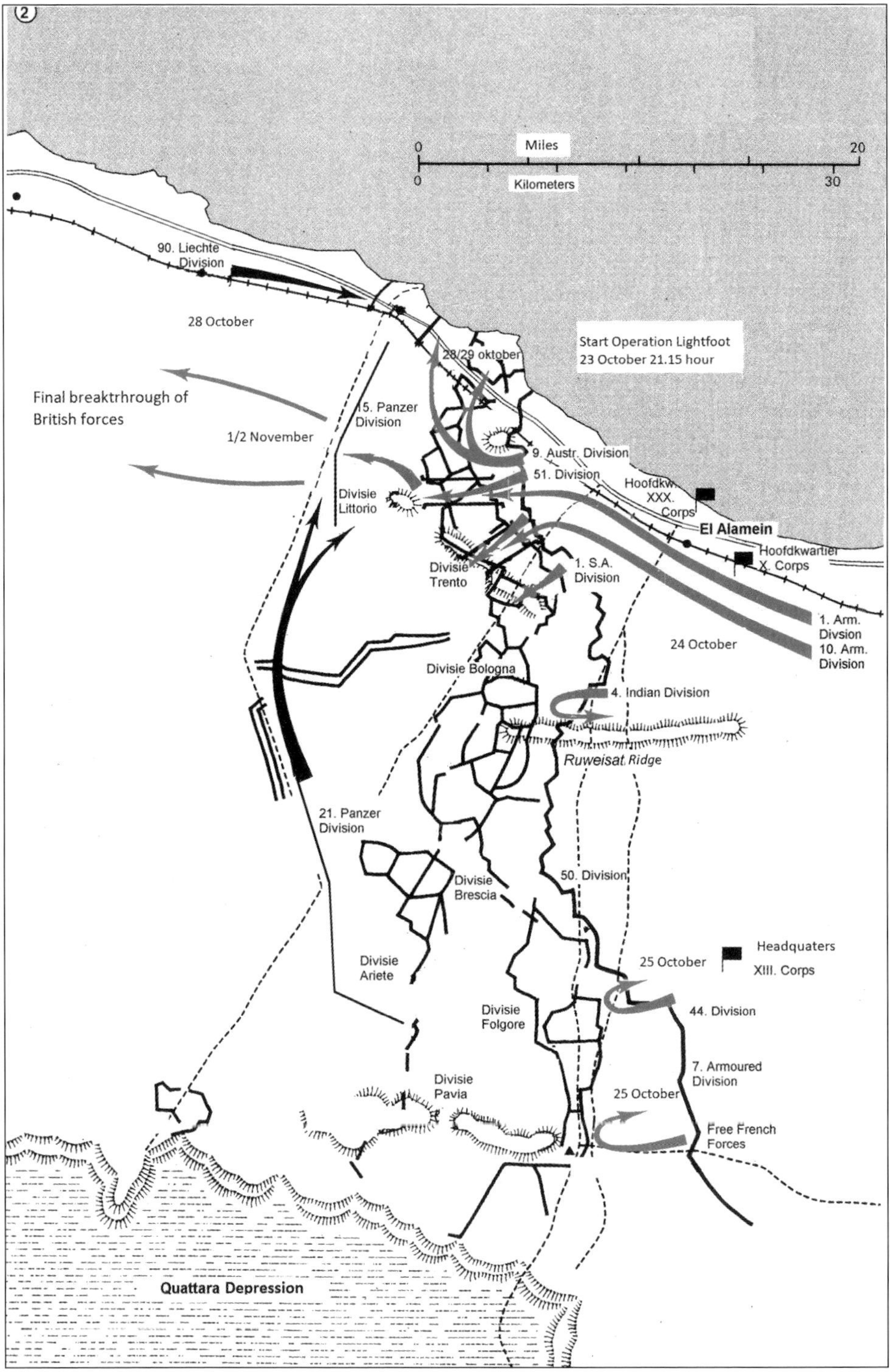

The Battle at El Alamein.

defence line. A gap 1,000m wide opened up in this line, and no matter how many tanks were destroyed, new ones continued to roll west. In addition, dozens of armoured cars had managed to break through during the night and made the area behind the front line unsafe for the Germans. At 11.00 am the defensive line finally gave way and a mass of 400 tanks rolled through the gap, followed by another 400 in a second wave.

Fierce fighting took place throughout the day. Many of the British tanks turned out to be new Shermans, with long-range guns and armour that seemed to withstand even the Flak 88 guns. The British tank force advanced west and then turned north-east, threatening to encircle a large number of German units. To counter this, Rommel ordered the Ariete Division and the last German artillery units to advance north. With thirty-five operational tanks still in a thin defensive line, Rommel ordered a retreat to the Fuka Line at the end of the afternoon. The plan was for the Italian X and XXI (infantry) Corps to begin their fall back to the west during the night, shielded the next day by tank units in the form of the Italian XX Corps in the south, the DAK in the centre and the 90th Leichte Division in the north. Neither Berlin nor Rome was informed of these plans, to prevent them from being countermanded.

A major problem was how to manage the retreat, especially since a number of Italian units had started to withdraw in unstructured disorganized manner on their own initiative: the Littorio Division no longer seemed to be under the control of its officers, and a broad stream of vehicles from this division were racing west. The same seemed to apply to the Trieste Division. While the front appeared to calm down, the flow of vehicles on the coastal route to the west increased by the hour.

News of this retreat reached Rome and Berlin during the morning of 3 November. Hitler exploded in anger and demanded in a telegram to Rommel that he should stand his ground: in Hitler's words, the *Panzerarmee Afrika* had to choose between death and victory. Rommel was torn between his loyalty to Hitler and to his men. In the meantime, von Thoma, von Bismarck's successor, came in with increasingly disturbing reports. While the two tank divisions still had thirty-five tanks at the beginning of the morning, by the afternoon this had fallen to only twenty-four. With Hitler's forceful telegram in their minds, Rommel and von Thoma came to a compromise: in general line they would try to hold out at all costs, but within this overall intention a limited withdrawal would be permissible. During the afternoon a radio message was sent to Hitler summing up the state of affairs: 50 per cent casualties in the infantry, engineer and anti-tank units, 40 per cent in the artillery units, just twenty-four tanks still operational, the Littorio and Trieste Divisions had virtually disintegrated. Furthermore, Berndt was dispatched to Hitler's headquarters to explain the position of Rommel's forces and to ask for the order to hold out at all costs to be rescinded. In the meantime, Rommel passed his order on to all units, and a difficult night followed, during which he struggled with the decision he had made despite the pressure from Hitler.

Kesselring was flown in on the morning of 4 November to provide moral support to Rommel, and he fully endorsed Hitler's orders, which had so often come in handy in the Soviet Union. However, when he learned that only twenty-four tanks were operational, he suggested that the orders should be interpreted primarily as a request, and that Rommel should act on his own judgment. Kesselring suggested contacting Hitler again by radio, explaining the situation and asking permission to retreat. While this message was being sent, the Trento and Bologna divisions were in danger of being routed. Italian officers were ordered to urge their troops forward again, and the Italian X Corps received a similar warning. Von Thoma had meanwhile come up with his own decision: having dismissed the order to hold out as 'insane', he had driven with a tank to the epicentre of the fighting and surrendered. Until the end of the afternoon, Rommel held fast to Hitler's orders, but by then, the Ariete Division had fought itself to death and XX Corps had completely disintegrated. This was enough for Rommel: at the end of the afternoon he ordered the retreat. Hitler did eventually sanction the earlier proposal to withdraw at 9.00 pm, but news of this only reached Rommel the next day.

And so, on 4 November, the difficult retreat of 70,000 men over almost 2,000km began. The British ultimately lost 2,400 men during *Lightfoot*, with 3,000 missing and 9,000 wounded; the Germans lost 1,100 men dead, 3,900 wounded and 7,900 missing; the Italians lost 1,200 dead, 1,600 wounded and 20,000 missing.

6.5 Evaluation of the German Army

Strategic dimensions

The supply situation of the Afrika Korps and ultimately the Panzerarmee had suffered from a major bottleneck during the past year and a half. Rommel received neither the divisions nor all the materiel he requested. He had to accept that the army leadership did not see his front as important enough to make sufficient divisions available, but he complained constantly, partly for tactical reasons, about the quantity of supplies he received for the forces he had. As we have seen before, the Italians and their navy were not to blame for this: a very significant part of the supplies shipped succeeded in reaching North Africa. We have seen earlier that whenever Rommel successfully advanced eastwards, the supply lines between Italy and North Africa were put under pressure by the British. But until El Alamein, the German units had somehow always been able to maintain their fighting power despite these problems. Nor had their combat effectiveness been broken by the sickness which constantly undermined the deployability of the units.

It was only at El Alamein that the supply situation began to become so dire that it seriously hampered Rommel's room for manoeuvre. Logistics became the strategic factor par excellence at this stage; the arrival of a single ship could determine the outcome on the battlefield. And the situation would only worsen for the Germans in the months that followed, as we shall see in the next chapter.

Logistics in North Africa depended on a number of important factors which hindered the proper supply of units.

Firstly, there was no food to be found locally, and everything had to be shipped via Italy. Even water had to be transported often hundreds of kilometres from its source to the troops at the front. In other words, for basic necessities, the Germans were dependent on long supply lines, which put pressure on the available logistical capacity in the form of lorries.

Secondly, the distances were enormous. The distance from Tripoli to Benghazi was the same as that from Brest Litovsk to Moscow, 900km. However, Benghazi was only a stopover on a journey of over 1,800km between Tripoli and Alexandria. None of the parties involved had any experience in covering such distances, and there was only one road, the Via Balbia, which became a favourite target for enemy fighter-bombers. There were desert tracks that could be used at certain times of year, but these caused a great deal of wear and tear to vehicles.

Luftwaffe transport units carried out a lot of logistical work and often suffered great losses. The large, but slow and vulnerable Me 323s were used as a last resort for transport across the Mediterranean. (*Photo IHC*)

In order to keep things running, workshops had to have a very diverse stock of spare parts available, given the diversity of equipment in use. Tanks also required a great deal of maintenance; engines and other essential parts did not last long in the desert.

In conclusion, Rommel ignored a number of important factors in the field of logistics, namely:

- The combined capacity of the ports in North Africa in fact determined the number troops to be deployed
- The unloading capacity of individual ports meant that the size of convoys had to be limited, which made escorting them expensive in terms of naval units and fuel
- Transport over land required a large number of trucks and other vehicles that far exceeded the capacity of the *Wehrmacht*
- The battle in the Mediterranean over convoy routes was of much less importance than was assumed, since the Italians, except perhaps in the period November–December 1941, proved capable of delivering the agreed quantity of supplies
- In line with this, the decision not to conquer Malta at the end of 1942 had a much smaller effect on logistics than the limited capacity of the port of Tobruk, which was also within range of RAF bombers operating from Egypt

In addition, the long supply lines proved to be particularly vulnerable to enemy action, as was demonstrated during *Crusader*. When combined, these factors meant that in any given scenario, logistical reality could never measure up to military ambitions. Realistically, Rommel could only operate satisfactorily as a *Sperrverband* (the name Hitler gave to his

The transport fleet suffered terribly under the conditions in North Africa. On the right is a completely worn-out truck. (*Photo S. Klein*)

North African force) within 450km of the port of Tripoli. It is in fact astonishing that the DAK and later the Panzergruppe or Panzerarmee were somehow able to provide for their needs in such a way to pose a constant and serious threat to the British in North Africa.

These facts later dawned on Rommel, who wrote:

> An absolute prerequisite for an army to survive a battle is a sufficient supply of weapons, fuel and ammunition. In fact, the battle is decided by logistics even before it has begun. The bravest soldier can do nothing without weapons, weapons cannot do anything without ammunition, and neither weapons nor ammunition are of any value in manoeuvre warfare unless there are vehicles with sufficient fuel to move them around. Maintenance and repair facilities must be comparable in quantity and quality to those available to the enemy. (36: 314)

Tactical dimensions

The Germans adapted their tactics for eliminating anti-tank guns to the new situation of a linear front. The location of the often statically positioned British anti-tank guns was first mapped out by reconnaissance units, and then attacked by aircraft, infantry and artillery. Only when the guns had been largely silenced and the landmines cleared, did the tanks appear on the battlefield to clean up pockets of resistance and force a breakthrough. Large-scale tank battles were avoided as much as possible unless there was a clear superiority in numbers.

Psychological warfare

The Germans also used psychological warfare in this phase to create chaos. At El Alamein, a small number of armoured cars and tanks attacked the British lines at night, firing with everything they had, using their searchlights and, literally and figuratively, kicking up a lot of dust. As a result, the entire line was put on high alert, only for the real attack to take place elsewhere. (3: 190)

6.6 Evaluation of the British Army

Montgomery's arrival led to a number of fundamental changes in the British Eighth Army. He had a keen eye for the strengths and weaknesses of the organization, knew what he wanted and succeeded in making radical reforms of all sorts.

In addition to the more general observation that none of the commanders up until then had succeeded in 'making the machine work', he recognized the following fundamental weaknesses:

- Lack of discipline at the top
- The inability of the high command to impose its will on lower echelons in the hierarchy, and the watering down of orders from top to bottom, causing men to lose control of events
- Inertia within the C3I structure
- Low level of training
- An overly defensive attitude
- Inability to concentrate forces at the right time and in the right place
- Outdated tank doctrine (3: 140)

Based on this initial analysis, he implemented a large number of reforms. He realized better than anyone that he should not play the game according to Rommel's rules, since the British Army was not capable of doing so. In his eyes, the British were eminently suited to operating from a static defence line and should not be tempted into manoeuvre operations, the type of warfare the Germans specialized in.

From this perspective, he placed most emphasis on the infantry and artillery, the latter being the most effective arm. Tanks were only to be deployed in a supporting role and certainly not given a free hand as they had been up to that point: in Montgomery's eyes, the cavalry mentality of the tank units had to be suppressed at all costs, since this had led to such disastrous consequences in the past.

The Battle of Alam el Halfa Ridge was an early example of how tanks would be used in the future: when the German armoured retreated, the heavier British tanks were not allowed to pursue; only the fast M3 Stuarts were allowed to carry out flanking attacks. As we have seen, the Germans were also extremely skilled at making a coordinated and damage-free withdrawal. Not everyone was so cautious, however.

> Just before the minefields, a last opportunity offered to cause a bit more aggravation, and somewhat hastily McGinniley drove up a small eminence. While he was still focusing his binoculars, he saw the muzzle flashes of three guns simultaneously, felt a crash and an impact, and fell down in the fighting compartment. Blood ran down

> his face and uniform, and his gunner bent over him. 'You have been wounded.' 'You don't say', said McGinniley angrily. (14: 318)

The plan that Montgomery had in mind was to slowly but surely destroy the German units with a strategy of attrition, by deploying superior manpower and equipment. His vision was orthodox, born out of necessity and in line with the experience and methods of the First World War, and it turned out to work in practice. Rommel was the first to acknowledge this:

> I had tried to break through this immobile, static mode of warfare in which the British excelled and in which their infantry and tank crews were trained, in order to fight on the open plains near Alexandria. There I could have made the most of our superiority in the desert war, but I failed. (36: 124)

The chain of command was also tightened: everyone knew what was expected of him and how much room for manoeuvre he had. The plans for the offensive were not a guideline or a framework to be filled in at one's own discretion, but had to be followed in detail.

Montgomery also introduced a system of feedback, partly outside the hierarchy, which enabled him to gain a good picture of each unit's current combat power. Furthermore, it was he, not his staff, who drew up the plans for the upcoming offensive and worked them out in detail. The units involved were given strict instructions based on these plans, which could not be deviated from. The offensive itself was orthodox in design and was carried out methodically and systematically.

Men and leadership

Montgomery launched an extensive training programme to improve the training level of the men, first in small groups, then in larger units. The training was practical in nature, linked to what was expected of men in the upcoming offensive.

Montgomery practised a directive style of leadership. There was room for discussion in advance, but once he had made a decision he did not tolerate deviation from the plan or personal interpretation of it. During the preparation of the offensive, all the men were briefed by Montgomery on the elements that were important to them, and there was not expected to be any divergence from these.

Perhaps the most importantly of all, Montgomery managed to pull the morale of the Eighth Army out of its downward spiral and to give the men renewed confidence to take on Rommel. That this confidence was justified was evident from the results of the first encounter at the Alam el Halfa Ridge. It was also apparent that Montgomery was able to use his negative character traits to good effect. Sir John Hackett wrote:

> His great talent for leadership was shown in the way he managed to exploit even the negative sides of his character to positive ends: his egotism, his ambition, his ruthlessness, which at times bordered on spitefulness, were all used when necessary to get people thoroughly worked up and then steer their fury and energy into the right channels …he would never allow himself to think that a mistake could have been made in his circle for which he was not himself responsible. (14: 309)

Montgomery later explained his views on leadership as follows:

> One of the first responsibilities of a Commander-in-Chief is to create what I have called 'atmosphere' as a state of mind in which his staff, his subordinate commanders and his troops will live and work and fight. His arms must know what he wants; they must know the very fundamentals of his policy; and they must be given firm guidance and a clear lead. Inspiration and guidance must come from above and permeate the whole force. If this happens, all concerned will go ahead on the lines laid down, the force will acquire balance and cohesion, and the results will be evident in battle ... In addition to 'atmosphere' there are two basic requirements for generalship. The first is to create the fighting machine and forge the weapons to his own liking. This involves a profound knowledge of the conduct of war, and of training.
>
> The second is to create an organization at headquarters which will enable the weapon to be wielded properly. The fighting machine must be set into motion, at the appropriate time, so that it can develop its maximum power rapidly. The troops must be launched into battle in a way which promises the best prospects of success – and the troops must know this. The 'stage management' of the battle must be first class. (*The Memoirs of Field Marshal Montgomery* pp. 20–21)

His experiences in the First World War had taught Montgomery how vulnerable soldiers could feel, hence his emphasis on creating trust among his men:

> But in those days I came to realize the importance of the soldier knowing that behind him were commanders, in their several grades, who cared for him. The general who looks after his men and cares for their lives, and wins battles with a minimum of losses, will have their confidence. All soldiers follow a successful general. (*Memoirs* p.23)

Montgomery also found communication to be of great importance:

> Sometimes I spoke to large numbers from the bonnet of a jeep, sometimes I spoke to just a few men by the roadside or in a gun pit. I would also address them less directly by means of written messages at important phases in the campaign or before a battle. These talks and messages fostered the will to win and helped to weld the whole force into a fighting team which was certain of victory. (*Memoirs* p. 23)

El Alamein showed that Montgomery had excellent control over all these aspects of generalship. And in a broader context, El Alamein was a showcase for the kind of warfare the Allies would employ successfully for the rest of the war: deploying a superior force of men and materiel in an essentially orthodox way of warfare, with an important role for detailed plans and little room for individual initiative. But we are not there yet; in the next chapter we will reflect on the long road back for Rommel and his troops.

Chapter 7

The Way Back

7.1 To the Mersa el Brega Line and beyond

On 4 November the great retreat of the Axis troops began. In the following weeks, they fought their way in a disciplined manner back to Tripoli, which would eventually fall on 23 January. Despite shortages of everything and constant air attack, and faced by superior numbers, the Panzerarmee always managed to evade its pursuers. Rommel had already shown after *Crusader* that he was a master at covering a retreat, while his opponents always had to remain alert to possible counter-attacks. Montgomery tried several times to encircle his retreating enemy, but without success.

The balance sheet after El Alamein showed that the Italian X Corps, half of the Trento Division and the Bologna Division of the Italian XXI Corps had been left without transport at El Alamein. The other half of the Trento Division and the XX Corps were more or less wiped out by 4 November. The DAK itself still consisted of approximately one regiment, the 90th Leichte Division had been reduced to one and a half battalions and one third of the 164th Leichte Division had survived the battle. Rommel could also deploy a dozen tanks. With these units and hastily formed Kampfgruppen, the British attacks

On the lookout: German tanks, including a PzKpfw IV F2, and motorcyclists scan the horizon for enemy units. The non-motorized units were able to seek the protection of the few remaining tanks.

were repelled. The only bright spot was the unexpected arrival of General Ramcke with 800 men from his Fallschirmjäger Brigade on 7 November. These non-motorized units had withdrawn on foot, attacked a British convoy during the night, captured trucks and then raced west through the mass of British troops.

The supply situation was desperate. About 150km to the west, beyond the traffic-congested Sollum and Halfaya Passes, there were 7,000 tons of ammunition in Tobruk, while 900km further west, in Benghazi, there were 5,000 tons of fuel – supplies that were of no use to Rommel at a time when the mass retreat hugely exacerbated the need for fuel, and offensive actions were rendered impossible due to the lack of it. On 8 November, twenty-four new tanks would also be landed in Benghazi. The only bright spot was the weather: heavy storms prevented both sides from moving quickly, slowing the pace of the fighting. On 7 November, the British made a first attempt to enclose the Axis troops in a southward flanking movement. However, they had already retreated further west, and the British found only disabled equipment. Meanwhile, a 40km-long traffic jam had formed at the passes of Sollum and El Halfaya. Protected by the 90th Leichte Division, and with good traffic management, the supply units of the *Panzerarmee Afrika*, many of them in trucks towed by others, would succeed in getting through the passes in the coming days, eventually followed by the combat units. Once the passes had been negotiated, and the units had reached relative safety, it was possible to restore some order to the chaos of the supply and administrative units.

While the 90th Leichte Division and other units were engaged in rearguard actions, mines were laid and road infrastructure was destroyed behind them under the leadership of the newly arrived Major General Bülowius, the new commander of the Panzerarmee engineers. Bülowius succeeded in giving the pursuing troops a nightmare job. Buildings were undermined, real minefields alternated with fake ones, airfields were rendered unusable for weeks and booby-traps meant that British troops could not touch anything without risking their lives. On 8 November, Berndt rejoined Rommel, bringing Hitler's request to set up a defence line 'somewhere in North Africa'. Hitler would also ensure that Rommel had access to the latest version of the Flak 88 gun with a higher muzzle velocity, as well as the first twelve Tiger tanks. All these commitments were only of relative use, however, for on the same day it emerged that an Anglo-American invasion force of 100,000 men led by General Alexander had landed in Algiers and Morocco: Operation *Torch* had begun, and Rommel was now in danger of being crushed between two armies.

Startled by the opening of a second front in North Africa, Berndt rushed back to Hitler at Rommel's request with a plan to evacuate all German units from North Africa, a proposal that was rejected by Hitler. This was not entirely unexpected: Hitler was forced to take into account the political dimensions of the conflict, for giving up North Africa would lead to the collapse of the Berlin-Rome Axis. Moreover, it might threaten Mussolini's own position, which could destabilize Italy and perhaps even persuade the country to change sides. Berndt was once again promised that the Panzerarmee would be rebuilt to its former strength, and told that an evacuation was out of the question.

Meanwhile, the remaining Axis forces withdrew further west, travelling through the Halfaya Pass and leaving Tobruk to the British. Coordinating the withdrawal of the non- or poorly motorized Italian units continued to pose a problem, especially considering that the British were fully motorized. However, given his previous experience with Rommel,

Montgomery was extremely cautious about advancing too hastily. Rommel fuelled this caution by constantly harassing the leading elements of the British to slow their advance.

The fuel situation remained dire for the Axis. On some days no more than forty tons arrived instead of the required four hundred. Despite pleas to the Luftwaffe to bring in only fuel, to the surprise of everyone, 1,100 reinforcements were airlifted in on November 11. The troops had insufficient weapons and lacked transport. The coordination of the various ships – in addition to tankers, naval vessels such as destroyers also transported fuel to North Africa – became increasingly chaotic. Thanks to Ultra, the British had accurate information on all ship movements and were able to effectively cut off supplies. The result was that vehicles were sometimes forced to stand still for days. The only help for the Axis was the weather: due to the persistent rainfall, the ground had become boggy and the vehicles of the pursuing British had become stuck in their hundreds, as evidenced, for example, by aerial reconnaissance of the Msus region on 17 November. Thanks to the fuel flown in by the Luftwaffe, it was somehow always possible to get everything moving in time, and the Panzerarmee was able to escape from the Benghazi region before the British could get free of the desert. The feared southward flanking movement did not occur, and the Germans were able to evacuate Cyrenaica without any problems.

A few days later, the fuel crisis reached a temporary nadir at Agedabia. The Axis troops were out of reach of transport planes from Italy; there were 500 tons in Tripoli and ten tons in Buerat, but even the latter was 250 miles to the west. However, a small miracle now occurred. Oil drums from one of the ships torpedoed by the British, the *Hans Arp*, were washed up on the beach along the entire route from Agedabia to Mersa el Brega; all Panzerarmee vehicles could now be refuelled, and on 23 November the last units reached the Mersa el Brega Line. A journey of more than 1,200km had thus ended almost without

Italian units digging trenches at the Mersa el Brega Line. The severe shortage of motorized units forced Rommel to resort to classical methods of defence.

losses: of the original 90,000 German troops, including Luftwaffe and other units, 72,000 men (!) reached this line – no small achievement.

The Mersa el Brega Line was defended by two units of the Young Fascists, the Pistoia and Spezia Divisions, under the command of Marshal Bastico. Hitler and Mussolini had decided that Rommel's retreat should end here. The line ran from the coast through a 15km-long salt flat, with rugged and impenetrable terrain to the south. Rommel, however, did not consider the line suitable, since it seemed to him that it could be bypassed with a deep southward flanking movement to launch an attack from the rear. He had neither the tanks nor the fuel, artillery and anti-tank guns to wage a mobile battle with an opponent advancing southward. Moreover, the supply route to Buerat, the nearest port, consisted of a straight road of 425km over flat land: all fuel, ammunition, food and materials had to be transported via this road, and any vehicles on it could easily fall prey to air strikes.

On 24 November, Kesselring and Rommel discussed the situation with Bastico and Cavallero. Rommel stated that for a realistic defence of the Mersa el Brega Line he would need fifty PzKpfw IV F2s, fifty 75mm Pak guns, eighty 105mm artillery pieces, transport vehicles and 4,000 tons of supplies. At that point he only had thirty-five tanks and fifty-seven anti-tank guns at his disposal, while the British could deploy 420 tanks and 300 armoured cars against him. The meeting ended in an argument, with Rommel being accused of defeatism.

A response from on high was inevitable, and on 26 November Rommel received orders from Mussolini to attack the advancing British units. Rommel ignored this and discussed with Navarrini the possibility of a retreat more than 300km west of Tripolitania. However, he knew that he could not continue to avoid Mussolini, which is why he and Berndt left for a meeting with Hitler on 28 November without informing the army leadership. The purpose of the meeting was not only to prepare Hitler for the coming retreat, but also to persuade him to give up his military ambitions in North Africa in the long term. The facts presented by Rommel about the current situation were accepted by Hitler, but his proposal to give up North Africa was angrily rejected by the Führer. North Africa was not to be surrendered, and Hitler promised Rommel all the support he needed. In addition, Rommel should not withdraw any further but take up defensive positions on the Mersa el Brega Line.

Together with Göring, who would back him up, Rommel travelled to Rome in a special state train to discuss the state of affairs with Mussolini. The trip to Rome also offered Berndt the opportunity to influence Göring into fully supporting Rommel's plan to build a defence line at Gabes. However, this was to no avail, Kesselring rejected the plan, and during two discussions with the Italians in Rome it was agreed that all shipping capacity would be deployed to Tunisia in the coming period. Mussolini did allow Rommel to withdraw to the Buerat Line, 300km east of Tripoli, but only if the British actually attacked the Mersa el Brega Line. Bitter and demoralized, Rommel flew back to North Africa on 2 December; his troops had been thrown back on their own resources and could no longer count on any support in the coming period.

Meanwhile, the British, having regrouped, had finally reached the Mersa el Brega Line on 23 November. As they prepared to attack, Rommel had gathered enough fuel to withdraw. The Italian infantry units were the first to receive the order to retreat on the night of 6 December. Despite all agreements about secrecy, they left with lights on and horns blowing loudly, but without being noticed by the British. Somehow, in the following days, the Axis forces managed to scrape together enough fuel to gradually withdraw all other units. When the British artillery opened the offensive on 11 December, they were shelling empty positions from which the last German infantry units had already withdrawn. The only remaining German forces were armoured units, which gradually fell back to a new defensive position, the Buerat Line, during 12 December. When the British finally attacked en masse, they encountered nothing but empty territory, expertly undermined by Bülowius' units.

Rommel had once again outsmarted his opponent, but he knew this game could not last much longer. Due to a lack of tanks, anti-tank guns, armoured personnel carriers and, above all, fuel, he was no longer able to wage the type of mobile warfare at which he and his units excelled. He knew he had to leave the open terrain of Libya and retreat to Tunisia, where the ground conditions offered him better opportunities to continue the fight. In the days that followed, the Panzerarmee managed to get through the eye of the needle again. Encircled by 1,500 British vehicles and constantly attacked by fighter-bombers, the Panzerarmee conducted a fighting withdrawal. They could no longer expect fuel, since the three most recent tankers had been torpedoed in the preceding days. On 15 December the situation became so desperate that the remaining tanks of the 21st Panzer Division transferred their fuel to the 15th Panzer Division, so that at least one unit could remain operational during the night while awaiting any new deliveries.

Rommel inspected the Buerat Line on 17 December. The line was surrounded by tens of thousands of mines, mainly the anti-personnel type that had little effect against tanks. It also had the disadvantage that it could be circumvented by a southward flanking movement. More mountainous terrain, such as the Mareth Line on the border of Libya and Tunisia, was better suited to the Panzerarmee, whose units were increasingly armed only with rifles and machine guns. The Buerat Line served, however, to protect Tripoli and secure the supply routes, although as the port was constantly bombarded and almost no

Rommel was, as always, constantly with his units. Here he is standing in his Horch staff car talking to men in a captured American M3 armoured personnel carrier. The vehicle still has its original olive-green colour, but the German war cross has been painted on the sides and the turret.

ships docked there, its strategic value, in contrast to its political importance, had declined. The Buerat Line could be held, Rommel told Bastico, if there was enough fuel for the tanks. Rommel still had sixty tanks available, with twelve in reserve at Buerat and ten without fuel in Tripoli. Many of the latter were PzKpfw IV F2s.

Rommel warned Bastico that without sufficient fuel and ammunition he would be forced to fall back further west, with the aim of combining the fighting forces in Libya and Tunisia. These comments provoked a furious response from Mussolini, who demanded that the Buerat Line be defended to the last and, referring to the Italian infantry units left without transport at El Alamein, that under no circumstances should Italian units be left behind 'like the first group'. This response further disheartened Rommel, and he seriously considered the possibility of surrender. He accused Mussolini of giving him impossible orders and demanded that Kesselring ship supplies for his units to Tunisia. Harsh words were exchanged between Rommel, Rome and Berlin. Surprisingly, the Italian commanders agreed with Rommel: Navarrini and General Bitossi, the commander of the Littorio Division, regularly pleaded with Rommel to withdraw the 45,000 non-motorized troops further to the west. Rommel demanded that Bastico give him a free hand to carry out Mussolini's orders. When Bastico forwarded this demand to Cavallero, the latter remarked that Rommel had so far only used such freedom to withdraw. Cavallero was also the first to suggest to Kesselring the possibility of recalling Rommel to Germany and replacing him with an Italian general. He also raised this with Mussolini, who liked the idea.

Meanwhile, Montgomery was also experiencing serious supply problems which meant that only a limited number of British units could operate at the front. To Kesselring's annoyance, Rommel did nothing about these units, a failure which Kesselring saw as evidence of indecision on the part of Rommel.

Rommel, Kesselring, Bastico and Cavallero sat round the table again on 31 December. As reported by Bastico, Mussolini's new instruction was that the Buerat Line could be abandoned, provided there was no other option. Rommel was allowed to fall back to the next line, the Tarhuna-Holms Line, on condition that he held the front at Tripoli for six weeks. That was how long it would take to make the port of Tripoli unusable.

The fall back to the Tarhuna-Holms Line took place on 16 January, after the Panzerarmee had been able to celebrate a quiet Christmas and New Year. Once again, the infantry units were the first to withdraw to the west, followed by the tanks. But Rommel also knew that it was futile to hold the Tarhuna-Holms Line at all costs, and on 23 January, just over a week before the surrender of the Sixth Army at Stalingrad, German units began to withdraw from Tripoli; the last phase of the conflict in North Africa had begun. On 26 January, a dejected Rommel drove across the border into Tunisia and set up his headquarters in Ben Gardena. The new defence line, the Mareth Line, was made up of a series of old French forts in Tunisia. The 21st Panzer Division had already moved there in mid-January to reinforce existing German units. The only bright spot that Rommel saw was the possibility of now deploying his experienced units against the inexperienced Allied formations.

7.2 Tunisia

As we have seen, the Americans and British landed in French North Africa with 100,000 men on 8 November. After overcoming minimal resistance from the Vichy forces, an

The landscape of Tunisia is clearly different from that of Libya and Egypt, as can be seen in this photo. A SdKfz 251, which belongs to the 10th Panzer Division, as can be seen from the sign on the front, drives in front of a captured American M3 half-track.

armistice was concluded on 10 November. However, the Germans had responded quickly to the impending danger and on 9 November had occupied El Aouina airfield outside Tunis. In the following days, more German units were flown in to cover the rear of the units in Tripolitania. In mid-November, about 5,000 men from the 5th Fallschirmjäger Regiment had landed, led by Lieutenant Colonel Koch. Since North Africa was still under the rule of Vichy France, permission had to be obtained from Marshal Pétain to enlarge this force. In the meantime, the Allies advanced only slowly, so that after Pétain's final approval was given at the end of November, the German force could be increased to 15,000 men. These units were supported by 130 tanks, including the previously promised Tiger I, and a Luftwaffe unit. They protected the ports and prevented any further advance by American units in the following period. The British First Army made another attempt to take Tunis and Bizerta during November and December, but this was repulsed.

On the arrival of German units in Tunisia, the command structure became slightly confusing. The first commander was Nehring, who was wounded on 31 August 1942 when commander of the DAK, and was now *General der Panzertruppe*. He set up a temporary headquarters, the Stab Nehring, operational between 14 November and 9 December, to organize the newly arrived units. Nehring was replaced by von Arnim on the latter date, probably because he, like Rommel, believed that it was pointless to defend Tunisia.

After the arrival of the Panzerarmee Afrika under Rommel in Tunisia on 23 February, a reorganization became necessary, given the size of the force. The new formation was called '*Heeresgruppe Afrika*' and consisted of two large units, namely the *Panzerarmee Afrika*/First Italian Army led by the Italian General Messe, and the *Panzerarmeeoberkommando* 5 (Pz-AOK 5) under Colonel General von Arnim. From 23 February to 9 March Rommel was commander-in-chief of the Heeresgruppe Afrika, and from his departure for Germany until the final surrender on 13 May, von Arnim was in command.

After reaching the Mareth Line in Tunisia, Rommel took stock of the new situation. He expected that the Eighth Army would not advance further west in the coming period because Montgomery would need time to re-supply and regroup his troops. He therefore turned his attention to the First Army. Although these units had been pushed

A new generation of tanks: the PzKpfw VI Tiger
There had been interest in heavy tanks in Germany for a long time; as early as 1937 this had resulted in the VK 3001 project, aimed at designing a heavy tank to force breakthroughs. The experiences in combat with the French Char Bs and British Matildas in 1940 had further stimulated German interest, and the development of a heavy tank with a speed of 40kph was officially launched later that year as Project VK 3601. Daimler Benz, MAN, Henschel and Porsche were the companies requested to put forward the first designs. In May 1941 the decision was made to equip this tank with a version of the famous 88mm Flak gun, which had proved itself in North Africa to be the only answer to heavy tanks such as the Matildas. The weight of the tank could be up to 45 tons. Encounters with Soviet T-34s and KV-1s in the following months reaffirmed the need for a tank design that could match such adversaries. Henschel and Porsche ultimately emerged as the two possible manufacturers, while Daimler Benz and MAN focused on project VK 3002, the tank that was to be an answer to the Soviet T-34. Both companies were invited to show their two prototypes at the Rastenburg testing ground on Hitler's next birthday, 20 April 1942. Ultimately, the Henschel prototype was chosen for production under the name PzKpfw VI Tiger H, later renamed Tiger E. Production began in August 1942, and a total of 1,350 were made during the war. (35: 103)

back in limited counter-attacks by von Arnim in January, they continued to pose a threat. Rommel planned an attack along two axes: *Frühlingswind* under von Arnim with his Pz-AOK 5 towards the Kasserine Pass, and *Morgenluft* under Rommel towards Tebessa. The differences of opinion and temperament between von Arnim and Rommel did not bode well, and although the attack started on 14 February, it did not go to plan due to poor coordination and differing ambitions. Rommel wanted to take advantage of all the opportunities that presented themselves and advance as quickly and deeply as possible, while von Arnim chiefly looked to improve his position. Initially, however, everything went well: von Arnim, like Rommel, advanced quickly, and on 18 February the Kasserine Pass was captured, the American units suffering heavy losses at the hands of the veterans of the DAK.* Commander-in-Chief Alexander realized that a German breakthrough had to be prevented at all costs and sent significant reinforcements to the front in the following days. Von Arnim's northward attack then failed to materialize, and a definitive German breakthrough was prevented. On 22 February, Rommel decided to halt any further attacks. In terms of numbers, the encounter was undoubtedly a victory for the Axis, with 10,000 casualties among the Allies as against 2,000 on the Axis side. However, the Axis troops could no longer expect reinforcements, while the Allies were gaining strength every day. Rommel was impressed by the commitment of the American soldiers and the quality and

* The Americans were shocked by their losses at Kasserine, where the Germans achieved an absolute combat effectiveness of 5.00 and, given the balance of forces and the fact that the Americans were in a defensive position, a relative combat effectiveness that was much higher. The Americans realized how much it would still take to achieve a combat effectiveness comparable to that of the Germans. But, as Rommel noted in 1944 after D-Day, the Americans, unlike the British, learned quickly.

Sherman tanks rush to Kasserine to reinforce the American units. The Battle of Kasserine sent shockwaves through the Americans, who realized that they would have to pull out all the stops in the coming years to take on the excellently trained and superbly led German troops.

degree of standardization of the American equipment: this would cast its shadow over the battle for the next two years.

Rommel's attention now turned back to the Mareth Line and Montgomery's Eighth Army. On 6 and 7 March, Rommel attacked the British at Medinine, but this attack was repulsed by more than 500 British anti-tank guns. Fifty German tanks were lost in these battles, more than a third of the total number they possessed in North Africa. It would be Rommel's last appearance in the theatre; two days later, he flew to Germany after handing over command to von Arnim.

Montgomery in turn planned an assault on two axes: a frontal attack on the Mareth Line and a 300km-deep southward flank attack. The frontal attack quickly stalled, after which Montgomery decided to reinforce the units advancing south. The Axis troops, fearing an encirclement, withdrew westward to Wadi Akarit, but were given no rest there and attacked again on the night of 6/7 April. The end was now fast approaching. By mid-April the Axis forces had been pushed back into a small area around Tunis and Bizerta. Against the thirteen Axis divisions, mostly operating below their nominal strength, were ranged nineteen Allied divisions; and against the 130 tanks and 500 artillery pieces of the Axis, the Allies could field 1,200 tanks and 1,500 guns. The Germans were simply unable to cope with this superior force, and on 12 May at noon, von Arnim surrendered on behalf of the Heeresgruppe Afrika and the DAK. The last messages from the DAK were sent at midnight by General Cramer, commander of the DAK:

> Ammunition blown up. Weapons and equipment destroyed. The Afrika Korps fought to the end in accordance with its orders. The Afrika Korps will rise again. *Heia Safari*!*

* Literally 'Hooray Safari', the title of a military song popular with German soldiers.

General Alexander, the Supreme Allied Commander, was in turn able to send the following telegram to Churchill:

> Sir, it is my duty to report that the campaign in Tunisia has ended. All enemy resistance has ended. We are masters of the African shore.

Thus ended the North African campaign, after more than two years; a campaign that is still fascinating to study because of the personalities, the dynamics and the drama of the operations involved; a campaign that will always yield different perspectives, as Rommel put it in 1943:

> The last word in the struggle on the African front has not yet been spoken. Therefore, nothing definitive can be said. A military analysis of the events on this secondary theatre of war on the African continent is also not possible today. That remains a matter for the future. (9: Foreword)

True indeed.

Epilogue

Now that the dust of the previous chapters has settled, it may be interesting to examine the two armies one last time, in order to analyse the similarities and differences between them. We will look at:

- vision and doctrine
- structure
- communication
- people, teams, training
- leadership
- morale/social cohesion

Vision and doctrine

In broad terms, the characteristics of the German and British Armies in terms of their vision and doctrine are shown in the table below.

German Army	British Army
Clear coherent vision of the organization	Vision fragmented by the regimental system, no corporate identity
Vision based on European, large-scale wars	Vision based on colonial 'small wars' and 'low intensity conflicts'
Clear doctrine in the form of *Auftragstaktik* tactics	Doctrine (if any) fragmented, unclear
Adjustment of vision and doctrine based on fundamental analysis of experiences in the First World War	Only very limited analysis of experiences in the First World War, leading to discussion but not to a clear doctrine
Mission-oriented	Order-oriented
Tactical doctrine in the form of a variation on *Hutiertaktik*, with emphasis on creating chaos and destroying the enemy's C3I capacity A mobile non-linear battlefield	No clear tactical doctrine (see also under doctrine regarding tanks) apart from being aimed at maintaining control A static linear battlefield
Central element is cooperation between the different weapon systems (*Verbunden Waffen/Einheitsprinzip*)	Cooperation under pressure, due to the regimental system

Despite its flaws, it must be said that the British system had served the British Empire very well. With its relatively small land army, Britain had been able to conquer and hold a significant portion of the world. The British excelled at 'small wars' and 'low intensity' conflicts conducted at a great distance from the mother country. However, these methods were no answer to the German way of war, as became obvious in May 1940 and again in North Africa in 1941 and 1942.

In the course of the conflict in North Africa, the British Army's need for one clear mission and vision became increasingly clear; they simply could not afford to take on the Germans with multiple different ones. Given that their units came from all over the British Empire, and sometimes had nothing more in common than a language and an administrative-political system, it was a considerable challenge to forge them into a single entity. A number of fundamental problems that resulted from this were not addressed by the British commanders-in-chief, perhaps because their background meant they did not see it as a weakness.

Montgomery eventually put an end to the relative freedom that all had enjoyed to 'do their own thing'. He succeeded in forging a kind of corporate identity, that is to say *his* ideas about how an organization should be run were incorporated into the Eighth Army. His way of management was largely based on principles that the Germans had abandoned several decades ago: a directive order-oriented style of leadership, and a preference for a static, linear front, with massive deployment of artillery and men, ideas that evoked memories of the First World War. As Montgomery noted, British units were not capable of much else, since they lacked a shared, modern doctrine that capitalized on the opportunities offered by mechanization; moreover, troops, officers and NCOs were poorly trained, and the decision-making structure was slow and cumbersome. As the war progressed, too, the need for a fundamental review of the mission and vision of the British Army receded, because the Allies' overwhelming superiority in men and equipment made this unnecessary. Higher losses were simply accepted as inevitable.

Montgomery did formulate some important principles, but then had no time to elaborate on them or was not entitled to do so. In the years after the Second World War, the British Army became part of NATO and adopted NATO doctrine. It was not until 1985 that a document specifically devoted to British military doctrine was published: *Design for Military Operations – the British Military Doctrine (BMD).*

Surprisingly, the three principles of the new British Army command philosophy recall the Gemans' *Führung und Gefecht der Verbundenen Waffen* from the 1920s:

1. The importance of making timely decisions
2. The importance of understanding the intention of the commander both generally and specifically
3. Clear responsibility to fulfil that intention based on:
   - Clear understanding of common doctrine
   - Mutual trust between commanders
   - Obedience to orders
   - Initiative to act within any freedom of action given, or purposefully in the absence of further orders (16: 4/6)

Nowadays, the American 'Mission Command' doctrine is very popular; it is in a way a somewhat diluted version of *Auftragstaktik*, in which all kinds of important preconditions are ignored.

In addition to their activities within NATO, the British continued to engage in 'small wars' and 'low intensity conflicts' with great success. Examples of this were the guerrilla wars in Malaya (against communist insurgents) and Kenya (against the Mau Mau): in both conflicts the British Army succeeded in putting down guerrilla movements. This type of post-colonial war suited them perfectly.

The role of the tank

It is also necessary to consider the tank, the decisive weapon of armies in the Second World War.

German Army	British Army
Clear role for tanks in combination with other weapon systems	Still searching for a role for tanks. Two possible roles: • Infantry support (Infantry tank family) • Independently operating units (Cruiser tank family)
Main battle tanks complementary to each other (PzKpfw III and IV)	Main battle tanks not complementary due to different roles
Tanks deployed in a concentrated manner at the *Schwerpunkt*	Tanks deployed (often frontally) in small units
Tanks combined with infantry and anti-tank units	Tanks deployed either with infantry (Infantry tanks) or independently without infantry and anti-tank units
Recovery units active during and after battle	Recovery units only available later in the war during and after battle
Tank and other units spend the night on the battlefield	Tank units spend the night in a laager located at a distance from the battlefield

In the German view, tanks, infantry and anti-tank units formed a single organizational unit that should operate as a single entity on the battlefield. In the course of the conflict in North Africa, recovery and supply units increasingly became part of this mobile fighting force. This ensured that deployability, mobility and effectiveness of tanks on the battlefield could always remain very high. The main tank types complemented each other, as did the anti-tank guns and the 88mm Flak guns. These combined units (Kampfgruppen) operating in a fluid manner were particularly difficult to tackle.

The British, on the other hand, were still pondering the role of the tank on the modern battlefield. In the British view, tanks could be deployed in an independent role or in support of the infantry. The first role was based on pre-war views that the tank could operate as an independent weapon, not linked to the infantry. This was reinforced by the attitude of the cavalry, which believed that this mobile role was its privilege. The cavalry mentality of tank units meant that time and again they were not deployed in a concentrated manner; rather, squadron and tank commanders each sought out individual combat. They were no match for Germans operating as a single unit, and evident weaknesses in the design of the various tank types also played a role.

This cavalry mentality remained firmly anchored until El Alamein, particularly within the lower echelons of the tank units, who tended to engage their German opponents in individual duels as '*arme blanche*' (close-quarters) in the cavalry tradition. Despite attempts by corps and division commanders to deploy tank units in a concentrated manner, this mentality meant that striking power was diffused across a large number of smaller units. As a result, the effectiveness of the British Armoured Brigades was never as great as that of the German units. Auchinleck, Montgomery and Rommel agreed that a ratio of 3:1 between British and German units was required to give both sides an equal chance. It was Montgomery who put an end to the cavalry-style modus operandi and forced the tank units to cooperate with the infantry under strict centralized control.

The so-called Infantry tanks were employed to support infantry units. These clumsy but heavily armoured tanks initially posed a problem for the Germans, which was solved by the deployment of 88mm Flak guns and a change in tactics. This type was replaced by other, faster tanks in the course of the conflict, and as the war progressed, the old distinction between Infantry tanks and tanks in an independent role began to disappear. However, these separate roles persisted to some extent until the end of the Second World War, as units with Shermans were sometimes deployed in one role and sometimes in the other (the origin of the term 'battle tanks').

In addition to these points, the effectiveness and mobility of British armoured units was undermined by the absence of sufficient recovery vehicles to tow broken-down tanks away from the battlefield. Salvage capacity increased in the course of 1942, however, and communication between tanks and between tanks and headquarters was also improved considerably by the installation of two-way radios in all tanks.

Organization

The main differences between the German and British Armies in the field of structure are shown in the table below.

German Army	British Army
A clear, unambiguous vision of the structure through a clear overall vision	Constant searching for a structure to meet the changing demands of the battlefield
Clear, central role of the *Reichswehr/ Wehrmacht* (clear 'corporate identity') and General Staff	Unclear, constantly discussed role of the British Army and CGIS
Structure aimed at interchangeability of units (modular system)	Regimental system creating barriers between units
Ability to operate in larger groups due to focus on cooperation	Initially forced to work with relatively small units due to regimental system
Decentralization of responsibilities and powers	Centralization of responsibilities and powers
General Staff as a knowledge and intellectual centre	Lack of a knowledge and intellectual centre
Staff Officer Corps as an important binding and guiding element in the field of doctrine, etc.	Each regiment with its own officer tradition/doctrine
Adaptation of doctrine to evolving practice through rotation system of staff officers	Unclear system per regiment
A quality system embedded in the organization through experience reports	No systematic evaluation, unclear what was done with any evaluation carried out

The German structure was built on an overarching mission and vision, and North Africa was a showcase for the way the German Army operated. No significant changes were made in it during the course of the conflict.

The British, on the other hand, had to engage in a learning process that would last several years. Problems continued to arise in the following areas: cooperation within larger units, a slow C3I structure, differences of opinion on how orders should be interpreted at lower levels in the organization, the differing traditions of the various regiments, contrasting views on doctrine and a romantic view of warfare in some units. There was a strict separation between the various arms, sometimes leading to a degree of animosity between regiments. As a result, cooperation between regiments often proved difficult, especially when operating in large formations or those with a diverse composition. It was also significant that there was no system of evaluation and no intellectual centre such as the German General Staff, to accumulate experiences and translate them authoritatively into adjustments to doctrine, methods and techniques. As a result, such matters were dealt with on an ad hoc basis. The British Army owed much in this area to Montgomery, who formulated a clear doctrine based on his assessment of its capabilities at that time and who managed to enforce it. In addition, he clearly demarcated where responsibility and authority lay in the structure and tolerated no deviation from this.

Communication

The characteristics of the German and British Armies in the field of communication are shown in broad outline in the table below.

German Army	British Army
Communication equipment as an integral part of the organization	Communication equipment initially a low priority, later growing in importance
Good C3I capacity	Lack of a good C3I structure

In the German Army, good C3I capability was one of the essential criteria for rapidly advancing and independently operating units. Much attention was therefore paid from the start to communication equipment, which had to enable optimum coordination between the echelons of the various units. In North Africa, there were specific requirements for batteries and antennas, which led to adjustments, for example in the form of large tubular frames on vehicles. The C3I structure remained intact until the end, ensuring that communication back and forth was guaranteed at all times and that the organization could be managed effectively.

Communications equipment had never been high on the agenda of the British armed forces, and this had disastrous effects on the British C3I capability. The rather opaque command structure, the personal interpretation of orders by the various commanders and the sometimes slow and distant manner in which commanders responded: all these contributed to the British high command often being overwhelmed by events, sometimes causing the entire C3I structure to collapse. The situation improved during the conflict in North Africa, but the commanders of the various echelons still had to spend a great deal of time on personal contact, which often led to slow reaction from the British side. This also meant that feedback on actions was slow and often overtaken by fresh events.

Direction and coordination during fluid combat situations continued to be difficult, and people were often unable to respond quickly and effectively. This partly explains the poor performance of the British Army on the battlefield in North Africa. Montgomery's reforms also involved a simplification of C3I structure, which went some way to repairing this weakness in the organization. Rapidly changing situations had to be managed, and his detailed plans were an important mechanism in maintaining control and coordination over the units.

Men, teams and training

Here, too, we can conclude that German ideas worked in practice as they did in theory. Units transferred from Europe immediately demonstrated a very high level of combat effectiveness. The biggest problems for the Germans in North Africa were the endemic diseases such as dysentery, and the food supply. Disease caused the combat power of almost all units to be constantly below their nominal strength; food supplies were poor and in some periods drastically so. In this area the Germans were unable to match the performance of the British, who were familiar with tropical diseases and gave their men more balanced rations.

The British, as in the First World War, constantly complained about the low level of training of the men. It is unclear what caused this, since the duration of their training did not differ from that of German units. Perhaps the lack of clear job specifications and the decentralization of training to the different regiments were to blame. Reports show that divisions often arrived at the front relatively unprepared and needed a lot of time to acclimatize.

German Army	British Army
Clear vision of job specifications and the training programme	Job specifications and training programme in the hands of individual regiments, no coherence
Recruitment by *Wehrkreis*	Recruitment by region
High level and high intensity training	Relatively low level and low intensity training
Application of assessment and other psychological tests	No attention to psychological dimensions
Team building/performance and creating social cohesion (*Kampfgemeinschaft*) a central element	Team building mainly through identification with tradition and history of each regiment
Evaluations continuously leading to adjustments in the training programme	Unclear what was ultimately done with evaluations (if any)
Units/men given a high degree of individual responsibility with clear objectives and considerable freedom to come up with their own solutions	Units/men under central direction and coordination, based on detailed plans
Horizontal communication of great importance	Vertical communication of great importance

German Army	British Army
Non-commissioned officers considered of great importance and given their own responsibilities	Non-commissioned officers considered of much less importance, only given secondary responsibilities
Combination of *Feldheer* and *Ersatzheer*, among other things, to align theory and practice	Unclear system
Ersatzbataillone to acclimatize new troops to the front	Unclear whether acclimatization was given any attention
Little rotation of divisions between fronts	Much rotation of divisions between fronts

Apparently little was done in the British Army to pass on the battle experiences of men to their own or other units, so new British troops often became unwitting victims of tactics that the Germans had been using for years.

In addition, divisions often rotated between the different fronts, so there was little build-up of knowledge and experience of the area and the enemy. Divisions also came from various parts of the British Empire, with different backgrounds, ways of thinking and working, so that here too there was no great degree of uniformity. Montgomery was the first to tackle this fundamental weak point in the organization. He attached great importance to good training and ensured that the British Eighth Army was properly equipped for the first time to take on Rommel.

Leadership

The broad characteristics of the German and British Armies in terms of leadership style are shown in the tble below.

German Army	British Army
Clear vision of leadership style based on *Auftragstaktik* and other guiding documents	Style mainly determined by history and tradition; personal views of (higher) officers often decisive
Central themes were fast, unambiguous and agile thinking and acting, a high degree of independence, emphasis on a sense of responsibility and the awareness that unexpected developments were possible	Ultimately, a strongly hierarchical command structure with little emphasis on independent action, partly caused by low-level officers
High admission requirements, personal qualities of great importance	Unclear admission requirements, social position of considerable importance
Reduction of German Army after First World War led to high level of selected officers	Not applicable
Continuous focus on improving performance	Little focus on improving quality
High demands on non-commissioned officers, seen as an important management layer, partly responsible for creating social cohesion	Non-commissioned officers played an undervalued role in the hierarchy

German Army	British Army
Officers responsible for creating social cohesion; mutual respect and trust in relationships central elements	No explicit responsibilities in the field of social cohesion, regimental tradition the most important binding element
Clear criteria for evaluation and promotion	Unclear what criteria were used
Importance of good personal relationships in the vertical hierarchy	Unclear what importance was attached to personal relationships within vertical hierarchy
Mission orientation required equality and trust between officers and men	Clear distinction between officers and non-commissioned officers/men

The German command concept of *Auftragstaktik* placed decision-making power low in the organization. This was matched by a leadership style that assumed that the various units could actually act independently within a greater framework. North Africa demonstrated this leadership style and showed the German Army to be an extremely flexible organization.

On the British side, it was unclear what the preferred style of leadership was before Montgomery arrived. The views of the different regiments on this topic, but also those of the different nationalities, often determined the leadership style of each unit. Class distinctions within regiments, but also between, for example, the aristocratic cavalry and the 'ordinary' infantry, will undoubtedly have played a role in the way in which leadership was implemented. Within the officer corps, at least at the top, it appears that much was left to individual interpretation. Due to the lack of a common doctrine, these different interpretations often led to a lack of coherence in combat. Discussions on this subject were short-circuited by Montgomery, and he set the tone with a directive and hierarchical style of leadership, a style that was best suited to the situation of the Eighth Army.

Shared values/social cohesion

In broad terms, the characteristics of the German and British Armies in terms of shared values/social cohesion are shown in the table below.

German Army	British Army
Creating social cohesion is a key element of education and training and therefore an important binding element	Social cohesion based on class and regiment

Concerning morale, nothing more can be said than that the men of both armies consistently showed a very high level of commitment. Despite all of the above disadvantages, it remains a fact that the British were somehow able to resist an opponent who was superior in almost all areas. It was down to the quality of the individual soldier, not of the British officer corps or high command, that Rommel was not ultimately able to push through to the Nile Delta. However, the British soldiers paid a high price for the weaknesses of their organization, which should have been known about for years, but which had never been given serious attention.

Conclusions

Having given an overview of theory and practice, we now come to some final conclusions.

First of all, we must conclude that both organizations were built up to a greater (the German Army) or lesser (the British Army) extent on a clear mission and vision: the Germans on the mission of fighting a continental war, the British on the mission of defending their interests throughout the world. The British Army had certainly been very successful in this in the years before the Second World War, but in the confrontation with the Germans this earlier success proved fatal. Against a German Army balanced in breadth and depth, the British Army had no chance when the two sides were of equal strength. We have seen how, on the one hand, the mission of the German Army had been translated into all aspects of the organization, while on the other hand, the British Army was a diverse collection of people, ideas and opinions. The German Army had been able to refine its existing command concept – dating from the nineteenth century – over the course of twenty years, while the British Army had to construct a clear concept from a very diverse number of ideas in a very short period of time. Outdated ideas, structures and systems meant that the British Army never actually took this step. Montgomery, the most important British commander-in-chief, fell back on concepts that had proved their worth in the First World War. It is questionable whether the concepts applied in the Second World War were ever properly evaluated later: the Allies' superiority in men and materiel obscured, as it were, the real performance of the British (and partly the American) Army. Something similar also happened after the First World War: the British did not feel called upon to evaluate their performance, because they were the victors.

The question remains why the Germans, with their superior command concept, were driven out of North Africa and ultimately lost the war. There are many reasons for this, but among the most striking is the superiority of men and material on the Allied side.

Colonel David H. Hackford described his experiences with a German prisoner of war:

> I remember a German lieutenant captured at Salerno who I was guarding in 1946 in a prisoner-of-war camp. He was a real tough-looking Kraut and I was a young punk, a pimply-faced kid. He could speak perfect English, and I was riding him.
>
> I said, 'Well, if you are so tough, if you're all supermen, how come you're here captured and I am guarding you?'
>
> And he looked at me and said, 'Well, it's like this. I was on this hill as a battery commander with six 88-millimeter anti-tank guns, and the Americans kept sending tanks down the road. We kept knocking them out. Every time they sent a tank we knocked it out. Finally we ran out of ammunition and the Americans didn't run out of tanks. And that's it in a nutshell.' (8: 294)

Perhaps this is too simplistic, but the fact is that the image of the German Army in movies and popular literature does not do justice to the achievements of the German Army in the Second World War. Their successes were not based on superiority in men or resources, but on a clear and balanced command concept that still appeals today and was in no way inferior to current insights and views in the field of management and organization.

Appendix

Absolute and Relative Battlefield Performance

The Historical Evaluation and Research Organization (HERO) has built up a database of more than one hundred battles from the First and Second World Wars, supplemented with data from the Korean War and the wars in the Middle East. This database is used to map the combat effectiveness of the various armies. T. N. Dupuy, in his book *A Genius for War: The German Army and the General Staff*, gives a detailed list of the battles in this database. On the basis of this data, he calculated the battlefield performance of the combatants involved.

The distinction between absolute and relative battlefield performance is important. The first follows from the calculation of the losses on each side with equal strength; the second takes into account a number of circumstances and links them to a factor. These are the circumstances and factors concerned, in which operating from a defensive posture is the central theme:

- Hurried defence, a factor of 1.2 advantage
- Prepared defence, a factor 1.5 advantage
- Reinforced defence, a factor of 1.6 advantage

All kinds of combinations are of course possible. For instance, fighting initially from a prepared defence line, followed by hurried defence during a possible retreat. These are further elaborated below. It is striking that the Germans are always in a minority but always display higher absolute and relative battlefield performance.

A. Overview of German versus Allied units in World War I (10 encounters)

	Allied forces	German forces
Battle strength of the units involved	6,896,000	5,090,000
Number of casualties	2,349,000	1,866,000
Losses with equal combat strength	3,241,620	1,866,000
Absolute battlefield performance per man	1.0	1.73
Relative battlefield performance per man	1.0	1.44

The various encounters involved a total of 6,896,000 men on the Allied side and 5,090,000 on the German side: a difference factor of 1.36. If there had been as many Germans as Allies, the losses on the Allied side would have been correspondingly higher. The number of losses compared to each other yields the absolute battlefield performance: 1.73.This means that on the Allied side there were 1.73 victims per fallen German. The relative battlefield performance is a factor 1.2 lower because the Germans fought partly from defensive positions and thus had a relative advantage.

B. Overview of German versus Allied units in World War II (78 encounters)

	Allied forces	German forces
Battle strength of the units involved	1,783,237	940,198
Number of casualties	47,743	48,585
Losses with equal combat strength	89,838	48,585
Absolute battlefield performance per man	1.0	1.84
Relative battlefield performance per man	1.0	1.53

The various battles involved a total of 1,783,237 men on the Allied side and 940,198 men on the German side: a difference factor of 1.8. If there had been as many Germans as Allies, the losses on Allied side would have been correspondingly higher (factor 1.8). The number of losses compared to each other yields the absolute battlefield performance: 1.84. This means that on the Allied side there were 1.84 victims per fallen German. The relative battlefield performance is a factor 1.2 lower because the Germans fought partly from defensive positions and thus had a relative advantage. Incidentally, this does not take into account the air superiority and the predominance in materiel on the Allied side. It is unclear what factor should be attributed to this, but it is clear that it should be at least a factor of 1.5, therefore the relative battlefield performance should be 2.25.

C. Kursk: Obeyan sector 5–11 July 1943

	Soviet forces	German forces
Battle strength of the units involved	98,000	62,000
Number of casualties	22,000	13,60013.600
Losses with equal combat strength	34,750	13,600
Absolute battlefield performance per man	1.0	2.55
Relative battlefield performance per man	1.0	4.08

The Soviets started the fighting at Kursk with 98,000 men versus 62,000 on the German side: a difference factor of 1.58. If there had been as many Germans as Soviets, the losses on the Soviet side would have been correspondingly higher (factor 1.58). The number of losses compared to each other yields the absolute battlefield performance: 2.55. This means that on the Soviet side, there were 2.55 killed per fallen German. The relative battlefield performance is a factor of 1.6 higher because the Soviets were in entrenched positions and thus had a relative advantage – relative battlefield performance 4.08.

D. Eastern Front 1944

	Soviet forces	German forces
Battle strength of the units involved	6,100,000	3,500,000
Number of casualties	5,000,000	1,100,000
Losses with equal combat strength	8,714,000	1,100,000
Absolute battlefield performance per man	1.0	7.90
Relative battlefield performance per man	1.0	6.07

The Soviets started 1944 with 6,100,000 men versus 3,500,000 on the German side: a difference factor of 1.74. The Soviets, unlike the Germans, were able to maintain their strength during the course of the year through the influx of new units. As a result, the German strength fell to around 2,500,000 men. If there had been as many Germans as Soviets, the losses on the Soviet side would have been correspondingly higher (factor 1.74). The number of losses compared to each other yields the absolute battlefield performance: 7.90. This means that on the Soviet side 7.90 were killed per fallen German. The relative battlefield performance is a factor 1.3 lower because the Germans had the opportunity to build reinforcements and therefore had a relative advantage. This does not take into account the fact that during the course of the year the combat strength on the German side fell from 3,500,000 to 2,500,000. If the average is taken as 3,000,000 men, the ratios are 2.03, 9.22 and 7.09 respectively.

E. El Alamein

	Allied forces	German/Italian forces
Battle strength of the units involved	195,000	82,000
Number of casualties	2,400	1,100/1,200
Losses with equal combat strength	5,520	1,100/1,200
Absolute battlefield performance per man	1.0	2.4
Relative battlefield performance per man	1.0	1.6

The British started fighting at El Alamein with 195,000 men versus 82,000 on the German/Italian side: a difference factor of 2.3. If there had been as many Germans and Italians as British, the losses on the British side would have been correspondingly higher (factor 2.3). The number of losses compared with each other provides the absolute battlefield performance: 2.4. This means that on the British side 2.4 men were killed for every fallen German or Italian. The relative battlefield performance is 1.5 times lower because the Germans and Italians were in defensive positions and thus had a comparative advantage. Incidentally, the Axis forces were made up of German and Italian units. The latter had clearly a lower battlefield performance than the Germans. In other words, if only German units had participated in the fighting, the battlefield performance would have been higher.

Bibliography

1. Alger, J. I. (1982), *The Quest for Victory*, Westport: Greenwood Press.
2. *Command Magazine* (1988), 'Hitler's armies, the evolution and structure of German armed forces, 1933–1945', New York: Combined Books, Inc.
3. Carver, Field Marshal Lord (1986), *Dilemmas of the Desert War*, London: B.T. Batsford Ltd.
4. Creveld, M. van (1974), *Fighting Power*, Westport: Greenwood Press.
5. Creveld, M. van (1977), *Supplying War: Logistics from Wallenstein to Patton*, Cambridge: Cambridge University Press.
6. Creveld, M. van (1986), 'On Learning from the Wehrmacht and Other Things', *Military Review*, January.
7. Dunigan, J. F. (ed) (1978), *The Russian Front: Germany's War in the East 1941–1945,* London: Arms and Armour Press.
8. Dupuy, T. N. (1977), *A Genius for War: The German Army and the General staff*, London: Macdonald and Jane's.
9. Esebeck, H. G. von (1943), *Helden der Wüste*, Berlin: Verlag der Heimbücherei.
10. Franz, P. (1984), 'Operational Concepts', *Military Review*, July.
11. Forty, G. (1977), *The Armies of Rommel*, London: Arms and Armour Press.
12. Griffith. R. (1992), *Forward into Battle*, Navato (Ca): Presidio Press.
13. Guderian, H. (1952/2000), *Panzer Leader*, London: Penguin Group.
14. Heckman W. (transl. from German by S. Saego) (1981), *Rommel's War*, Garden City (NY): Doubleday and Co, Inc.
15. Held, W. and Obermaier, E. (1992), *The Luftwaffe in the North African Campaign 1941–1943*, West Chester (PA): Schiffer Military History.
16. Holden Reid, B. (2000), *A Doctrinal Perspective, 1988–1998*, London: Strategic and Combat Studies Institute.
17. Irving, D. (1977), *Rommel: The Trial of the Fox*, London: Wordsworth Editions.
18. Jentz, T. J. (1998), *Tank Combat in North Africa*, Atgien (PA): Schiffer Military History.
19. Kurowski, F. (1985), *Der Afrikafeldzug*, Holzminden: Volker Hennig Verlagsbuchhandlung.
20. Laffin, J. (1965), *Jackboot: The Story of the German Soldier*, New York: Cassell.
21. Lewin, R. (ed) (1984), *The War on Land 1939–1945*, London: Random House.
22. Lewis, S. J. (1988), 'Reflections on German Military Reform', *Military Review*, August.
23. Lucas, J. (1982), *War in the Desert*, London: Arms and Armour Press.
24. Luftwaffen-Kriegsberichter-Kompagnie (1943), *Balkenkreuz* über *Wüstensand*, Oldenburg: Gerhard Stalling Verlag.
25. MacGregor Knox, A. (2000), *Hitler's Italian Allies*, Cambridge: Cambridge University Press.
26. Mackenzie, J. J. G. and Holden Reid, B. (eds) (1989), *The British Army and the Operational Level of War*, London: Tri-Service Press Ltd.
27. Messenger, C. (1976), *The Art of Blitzkrieg*, Shepperton (Surrey): Ian Allen Ltd.
28. Millett, A. R. and Murray, W. (eds) (1988), *Military Effectiveness, Volume III: The Second World War*, Boston: Mershon Centre, The Ohio State University.

29. Moorehead, A. (1965), *The Desert War*, London: Hamish Hamilton Ltd.
30. Murray, W. (1990), 'Force strategy, Blitzkrieg strategy and the economic difficulties: Nazi grand strategy in the 1930s'.
31. Murray, W. (1992), *German Military Effectiveness*, New York: The Nautical & Aviation Publishing Company of America.
32. Murray, W. and Millet, A. R. (eds) (1996), *Military Innovation in the Interwar Period*, Cambridge: Cambridge University Press.
33. Oeting, D. W. (1993), *Auftragstaktik,* Frankfurt am Main/Bonn: Report Verlag GmbH.
34. Ogilvie, R. (1995), *Krijgen is een kunst*, Amsterdam: Addison Wesley Publishing Co Inc.
35. Perrett, B. (1986/1997), *Knights of the Black Cross*, London: Wordsworth Editions Ltd.
36. Pimlott, J. (ed) (1994), *Rommel in His Own Words*, London: Greenhill Books.
37. Playfair, I. S. O. (1956/1974), *The History of the Second World War; The Mediterranean and Middle East II*, London: HMSO.
38. Posen, B. R. (1984), *The Sources of Military Doctrine: France, Britain and Germany between the two world wars*, New York: Cornell studies in security affairs.
39. Richey, S. W. (1984), 'The Philosophical Basis of the Air Land Battle', *Military Review*, May.
40. Rosinski, H. and Craig, G. A. (ed) (1966), *The German Army*, London: Pall Mall Press.
41. Samuels, M. (1992), *Doctrine and Dogma; German and British Infantry Tactics in the First World War*, New York: Greenwood Press.
42. Starren, H. (1998), *Grootmeester in Management*, Amsterdam: Teleac/NOT.
43. Strachan, H. (1997), *The Politics of the British Army*, Oxford: Clarendon Press.
44. Strawson, J. (1969), *The Battle for North Africa*, New York, Bonanza Books.
45. Toppe, A. (1991), *Desert Warfare: German Experiences in World War II*, Fort Leavenworth (Kansas): Combat Studies Institute, U.S. Army Command and General Staff College.
46. Warner, P. (1981), *Auchinlec: The Lonely Soldier*, London: Buchan and Enright Ltd.
47. Watson, B. A. (1995), *Desert Battle*, Westport: Praeger Publishers.
48. Wilt, A. F. (1990), *War from the Top: German and British Military Decision Making During World War II,* London: Tauris & Co.

Index